164

cocktails and
snacks

cocktails

and

snacks

**ROBERT
AND
ANNE LONDON**

GRAMERCY PUBLISHING COMPANY • NEW YORK

LIBRARY OF CONGRESS CATALOG CARD NUMBER: 65—25782

Art Director for Homemakers Research Institute
BEN ROSEN

Illustrators
JOHN BOLT, JR.   VIRGINIA WELTY
KENNETH SAGARA

Copy Editor
FRIEDA ROSS GORDON

Acknowledgments

For much technical information and the beautiful and valuable photographs which illustrate many of the recipes in this book, we gratefully acknowledge the generous co-operation of Ac'cent International, American Dairy Association, American Institute of Baking, Angostura Bitters, Artichoke Industries, The Best Foods Co., The Borden Co., California Dried Fruit Research Institute, California Foods Research Institute, H. J. Heinz Co., Kraft Foods Co., Libby, McNeill & Libby, National Cranberry Association, National Dairy Council, National Fisheries Institute, National Livestock and Meat Board, Poultry and Egg National Board, The Quaker Oats Co., Sunkist Growers, The Taylor Wine Co. Inc., Vita Herring, Western Growers Association, Wheat Flour Institute, The Wine Growers of California.

REVISED EDITION

This edition published by Gramercy Publishing Company,
a division of Crown Publishers, Inc.,
by arrangement with Wallace B. Black.
  b c d e f g h

preface

THIS is a bartender's guide and a cookbook for people who get fun and pleasure out of life by entertaining—who take their bars, pantries, and kitchens seriously but still want to be fresh and happy with their friends when the party hour arrives.

It is for the clever hostess who wants to have something a "little different" for her guests—who would like to be assured that her service will be attractive and in good taste and still not necessitate spending too much money for food and drink.

It is for the host or hostess who wants "quick and easy" snack ideas when the crowd pops in unexpectedly or stays late. The hundreds of snack recipes included here provide for any form of service. Hot or cold canapés, hors d'oeuvres or sandwiches may be ready when the guests arrive so they can help themselves, or your guests may help in the making of hot hors d'oeuvres in such a way that this becomes an integral part of the fun of the party.

Once the guest list is decided upon, the snacks and drinks and the most convenient form of service should then be planned. If the drinks are correctly prepared and the snacks carefully planned and simply served, you are almost automatically assured of a successful party.

For the average party you may want just the standard cocktails, correctly made; all of them are included here. In addition you will find hundreds of other drinks from which to choose, as well as cooling punch bowls for summer parties and non-alcoholic drinks for your friends who abstain from alcohol for one reason or another.

This book is complete in every respect and it has been designed to make things as easy as possible for the host or hostess. While hundreds of recipes for cocktails (and other beverages) and for snacks are included here, the emphasis has been placed on the simple, yet tasty and attractive types.

contents

contents
(continued)

cocktails and other mixed drinks

COCKTAILS are for the most part an American invention. They were first introduced into Europe during World War I, following the influx of American soldiers. Europeans were accustomed to drinking various forms of special wines which were generally known under trademarked names such as Amer Picon, Byrrh, Dubonnet, Cinzano Vermouth, and the like. These special wines are either red or white with the addition of combinations of aromatic herbs and were served at cocktail time before meals. The French word for such a drink is "apéritif." Many of these apéritif wines are used extensively in the recipes for our cocktails. On the pages that follow you will find all the cocktails that have stood the test of time and experience, on the part of both the professional bartender and the home host who mixes his own.

The variety of mixtures and the imposing list of names are sometimes frightening to a newcomer who turns the pages looking for an interesting drink. Cocktails are in the last analysis just little drinks made up from various people's ideas of what tastes good and sounds good. A relatively small number are constantly served by the bartenders of America and each individual host will usually "hit" upon his or her favorites or use an "old-timer" as the basis for a new individualized cocktail. Whatever the name, remember that most cocktails represent just slight modifications in the proportion of ingredients or the substitution of one ingredient for another. And above all, don't hesitate to use your own ingenuity in creating new drinks to please yourself and your friends. Although it is usually done by a professional bartender, nevertheless that is the way most cocktails originate. If a combination sounds good, it is tried. If it is good and catches on, it is given a fancy name and remains on the "bestseller" lists—carried from one part of the nation and the world to other parts.

Frequently a cocktail is created to honor a visiting celebrity and is named after that person. Many such drinks have stood the test of time and have remained favorites for years. All of those favorites are included here together with many newcomers of recent years.

The recipes in this book are classified according to the basic ingredient, i.e., the liquor, cordial, wine, etc. which predominates in the generally accepted version of the drink. That should help when you are looking for drinks made with gin, whisky, or any particular basic liquor. It is sometimes difficult to determine an exact classification for a drink; therefore if any problems are encountered in finding a particular drink, the index will be the final guide. It has been made as complete as possible to facilitate easy reference.

useful information

EQUIPPING YOUR BAR

In the average home, cocktails are usually mixed in the kitchen and brought to the room where they are served with various accompaniments. Whether they are prepared in the kitchen or at a home bar, a certain minimum of functional tools are required. All those listed below will be required for the kitchen or home bar. All the basic drinks are easy to prepare with this equipment. You could, of course, extend this list with a multitude of gadgets that could include all sorts of trick pouring devices, an electric blender, and so forth, but they just take up room. In the last analysis, a professional bartender uses only a few essential tools and that should be kept in mind when equipping your own bar.

You don't have to have a fabulously stocked liquor cabinet or wine cellar to give parties or serve drinks to unexpected callers. Here are the fundamental bottles for your bar: a bottle each of sherry, rye, Scotch, gin, vermouth, and bitters. The medium dry sherry will take care of the light drinkers. Rye or Scotch and bitters take care of the Manhattans. Gin and vermouth make the Martinis. All of them double for highballs and many of the other drinks offered in these hundreds of recipes.

BAR ACCESSORIES

1 metal mixing cup.

1 mixing glass which may be inverted in the metal mixing cup for a shaker.

1 long bar spoon to use for stirring.

1 cocktail strainer—rounded and perforated, or flat with flexible spring around the edge.

1 hard-wood muddler—a round-based wooden stick used for mashing various ingredients.

1 measuring spoon.

1 small measuring cup with a lip. Get the kind chemists use. Its graduated markings will make it easy to measure.

1 glass or plastic stirring rod. This is better than a metal spoon with carbonated water mixtures.

2 squeezers—regular type for lemons and oranges; pincer type for limes and lemon sections.

1 small sharp-bladed knife—stainless steel—for cutting lemon peels, etc.

1 bottle opener.

1 corkscrew. Get the lever type or double-action French corkscrew.

1 ice pick and/or a mechanical ice shaver.

1 canvas bag and mallet for crushing ice or a mechanical crusher.

1 vacuum ice bucket—to eliminate frequent trips to the kitchen.

GLASSWARE

Avoid novelty shapes and colored glass which disguise the good looks of a drink. Proper glasses should be selected because they do enhance the appearance of a drink just as correctly selected furniture makes for an attractive room. Cocktail glasses should preferably have stems because a drink is warmed by the hand, and a cocktail should remain cold. Old-Fashioneds are traditionally served in broad, almost straight, tumblers, usually measuring 6 ounces. Highballs are served in tumblers measuring 8 to 10 ounces. Collins and rickeys are served in 10 to 14 ounce glasses. Goblets can be used for wines, flips, and sours. Get the larger sizes of the highball glasses if you want to keep the number to a minimum and make them do for highballs, collins, and juleps. Liqueurs are traditionally served in tiny liqueur glasses, primarily because fine liqueur is expensive. If you want to dispense with the necessity of acquiring this extra set of glasses you need only remember that a little in a larger glass will taste just as good and in addition you will get the benefit of the aroma which is a goodly measure of the pleasure obtained from sipping a fine liqueur from a large glass. That's why fine old brandies are traditionally served in 18-ounce inhalers or "Napoleons." Connoisseurs like to pour a little into the bottom of the big glass, then swirl it around and enjoy the bouquet before slowly sipping it. It's a ceremony that most people don't bother with and if you'd like to go through the motions, the all-purpose tulip-shaped wine glass should be satisfactory. Your choices will, of course, be determined by budget and space limitations and the drinks you customarily serve. Selections may always be made so that various glasses may serve for several purposes. And remember that glasses as well as the shaker should be thoroughly chilled before using them.

1: Collins Glass, 2: Highball Glass, 3: Old-Fashioned Glass, 4: Sour or Delmonico Glass, 5: Whisky Glass, 6: Stemmed-Sour or Delmonico Glass, 7: Hot Whisky Glass, 8: Tom & Jerry, 9: Cocktail Glass, 10: California Cocktail Glass, 11: Champagne Cocktail Glass, 12: Cocktail or Wine Glass, 13: Brandy Inhaler (Napoleon), 14: Pipe Stem Sherry Glass

15: Pousse Café Glass, 16: Cordial or Liqueur Glass, 17: All-purpose Wine Glass, 18: Regular Hollow-stem Champagne Glass, 19: Saucer Hollow-stem Champagne Glass, 20: Plain Saucer Champagne Glass, 21: Pilsener Glass, 22: Pear-shaped Beer Goblet, 23: Standard Beer Goblet, 24: Balloon-shaped Beer Goblet, 25: Seidl, 26: Stein

MEASUREMENTS

Measuring terms differ in various localities. Most of the recipes which follow are for one cocktail. They are given in specific quantities. In this book the cocktails are based on the table of measurements given below. By using these measurements, it's easy to compute the requirements for greater quantities. To compute the number of drops required where they are called for in a recipe, use the following figures based on 3 drops per dash:

For 6 cocktails	⅕ teaspoon
For 10 cocktails	⅓ teaspoon
For 25 cocktails	¾ teaspoon
For 100 cocktails	3⅓ teaspoons

STANDARD MEASUREMENTS

Dash	3 drops
3 teaspoons	1 tablespoon (½ oz.)
1 pony	1 ounce
1 jigger	1½ ounces
1 large jigger	2 ounces
1 glass or wine glass	4 ounces
2 cups granulated sugar	1 pound
1 cup (milk or water)	8 ounces
1 pint	16 ounces
1 quart	2 pints or 32 ounces
⅕ gallon	25 ounces
1 gallon	4 quarts
Split	½ pint or 1 cup
A twist or curl of lemon	A thin slice of outer rind cut with curved knife

HOW TO FROST A GLASS

A "frosted" glass is suggested in a number of recipes. Properly done this will enhance the appearance and taste of the drink. The edge of the glass is first moistened by rubbing with a wedge of the suggested fruit, lemon, lime, or orange. The glass is then dipped into powdered or fine grain sugar to give the frosted appearance.

BAR SYRUP

Combine 4 cups sugar and 1 cup water in a saucepan and place over heat. Stir until sugar is dissolved. Reduce heat until mixture simmers. Simmer until liquid is clear. Bottle and keep either in the refrigerator or in an airtight container. If you wish to clarify syrup further, add 1 well-beaten egg white. Skim until perfectly clear.

COCKTAILS FOR A CROWD

When preparing cocktails for a large party, the arithmetic is as follows: A 3½ ounce glass will hold 3 ounces. Allow 1 ounce for melted ice if mixed thoroughly. If there are 25 people, this demands 50 ounces of the mixture. A Martini, therefore, would call for 32 ounces or 1 quart of gin and 16 ounces or 1 pint of vermouth, giving you 48 ounces of Martini mixture. The ice would bring it up to the correct amount.

In order to save time, the liquors may be mixed in advance for a crowd; however, if cocktails containing fruit juice are to be served, the final mixing should not be done until serving time. Sugar syrup may be prepared in advance. Fruit juices should be prepared at the last moment and added just before serving.

SUGAR AND SUGAR SYRUP FOR COCKTAILS

Many cocktails and other drinks require a sweetener of sugar in some form. For convenience it pays to prepare in advance simple bar syrup and store it in the refrigerator. It keeps almost indefinitely. If sugar is to be used in the cocktails, avoid powdered sugar because it contains some cornstarch. Use as fine a grain as possible of granulated sugar. The fine grain granulated sugar known as fruit or berry sugar serves the purpose very well. The recipes in this book specify "fine grain sugar" unless a powdered sugar is called for specifically for garnishing purposes, as with mint juleps when it is suggested that the decorative sprays of mint should be dusted with powdered sugar.

SHAKING OR STIRRING

Some cocktails are stirred while others are shaken. If shaking is called for, add the ice and shake vigorously. Strain and serve promptly. If a recipe calls for stirring, then stir it and do not shake. Specific instructions are given with each recipe. Usually cocktails containing wine as a principal ingredient are stirred, but there are exceptions to this rule, too. Never shake or stir a carbonated water vigorously because this releases the gas and leaves the drink flat in a very short time.

the bartender's dictionary

Abbott's Bitters: See Bitters.

Abricotine: A French apricot cordial.

Absinthe: A green, bitter liqueur made from wormwood and other aromatics which include anise, angelica root, and sweet flag root. Genuine absinthe has 70 per cent to 80 per cent alcohol. Wormwood is a toxic drug and excessive drinking of absinthe affects the digestive organs and nerve centers. It can cause delirium and idiocy. It is, therefore, illegal to make or sell absinthe as it was formerly made. Substitutes for it include Pernod, Oxygenée, and Herbsaint. These do not include wormwood, are similar in taste, but not as strong.

Advocaat: A thick creamy egg-yellow liqueur that is often referred to as "bottled Dutch eggnog" or "egg brandy" because it is made of sugar, egg yolks, and brandy. It is made in Holland.

Akvavit or **Aquavit:** A colorless Scandinavian liqueur with a caraway seed flavoring.

Amer Picon: A dark-brown aromatized French apéritif wine.

Anisette: A colorless liqueur with a sweetish, anise-seed flavor.

Angostura Bitters: See Bitters.

Apéritif: An alcoholic drink taken before meals to stimulate the appetite.

Applejack: A nickname for apple brandy.

Armagnac: See Brandy.

Aroma: Bouquet or perfume. The quality in a spirit or a wine which delights the sense of smell.

Arrack: A strong, Oriental alcoholic drink usually made from rice or molasses. In the Near East related names refer to an anise-flavored liqueur.

Bacardi: A brand of Cuban or Puerto Rican rum.

Barleycorn: Refers to any strong alcoholic liquor, especially whisky. The complete name, John Barleycorn, is a humorous personification.

Benedictine: A light greenish-yellow liqueur made from a secret formula, originally created by the Benedictine monks.

Bitters: A liquor, usually alcohol, containing an infusion of bark, herbs, roots, and other aromatic materials for use in cocktails and other beverages. Abbott's, Angostura, Fernet Branca, and Peychaud's are among the best known trademarked brands. The formulas are usually secret.

Bonded Warehouse: A warehouse in which alcoholic beverages are stored, under government supervision, and on which duties or taxes have not yet been paid.

Bottled in Bond: It refers to whisky at least four years old in the bonded warehouse before being tax paid, consequently while still under government supervision.

Bouquet: See Aroma.

Brandy: A liquor which is obtained from the distillation of wine or a fermented mash of fruit. Unless otherwise stated, the term brandy applies to the liquor obtained from the distillation of grape wine and its subsequent aging. The law requires that any brandies made from fruit other than grape must be referred to by the name of the fruit, as apple brandy, apricot brandy, cherry brandy, etc. Distinctions must be kept in mind between various fruit brandies and cordials. Some will have similar names but that is where the similarity ends. See entry under Cordials and Liqueurs. One of the most famous brandies is Cognac. To qualify as Cognac, the brandy must be distilled from grapes grown in a prescribed region around the city of Cognac in France. Second in fame is Armagnac which is produced in another region in France. Brandies should not be bottled at less than 80 proof (40 per cent alcohol). They are frequently allowed to age for many years. If a brandy is less than two years old, a statement showing the age must appear on the bottle. In extremely rare cases brandies have been allowed to age up to sixty years, but fine brandies are at their best after aging twenty-five to forty years. Brandy is aged in oak barrels which give it a little color. Caramel is added for additional coloring when it is bottled. Excellent brandies are made in the United States, most of them in California from wines which have proven themselves well qualified for the purpose.

Byrrh: A red, aromatized French apéritif wine.

Calisay: A Spanish liqueur probably flavored with barks and quinine.

Calvados: A pale, clear brown apple brandy. The French version of applejack, made principally in Normandy.

Cascarilla: A South American liqueur probably flavored with barks and spices with a brandy base.

Cassis: See Crème de Cassis.

Chartreuse: A widely imitated liqueur made from a secret formula in Spain and France by a French order of monks. It comes in two colors, yellow and green.

Cognac: See Brandy.

Initials on Cognac Labels: It has been the custom for many years to denote the various qualities of cognac by crowns, stars, vines, etc., and initials. While there is no uniform standard of quality used by all shippers the initials do mean or stand for the same words:

C. Cognac	P. Pale
E. Especially	S. Superior
F. Fine	V. Very
O. Old	X. Extra

Cointreau: A liqueur with a very sweet, pronounced orange taste made of brandy base.

Cordial Médoc: A French liqueur probably made of orange curaçao, cacao (cocoa), and Cognac.

Cordials or Liqueurs: The terms are interchangeable. In contrast to liquors such as whiskies and brandies, cordials are flavored by the addition of herbs, fruits, flowers, etc., to grain alcohol or other liquors (chiefly brandy) to attain a desired taste, aroma, and color, rather than by fermentation and subsequent distillation and aging. If the flavoring is fruit, there is a tendency to use the term cordial, rather than liqueur. The alcoholic content of cordials varies greatly. Most are sweet but there are some that have a dry aftertaste although they seem sweet while one is drinking them. Certain cordials are fairly standardized in the industry and very similar ones are produced by a number of manufacturers. Examples are fruit cordials like apricot, blackberry, and peach, or non-fruit cordials like menthe (white or green), triple sec or curaçao (orange base), kümmel (caraway), anisette (anise), and cacao (cocoa). Others have distinct flavors that are achieved only by the makers, apparently cannot be duplicated, and in some cases have become quite famous. Examples are Benedictine, Forbidden Fruit, Drambuie, Chartreuse, Cordon Rouge, Cordial Médoc, and Grand Marnier. New flavors and flavor combinations are developed and put on the market every year. Serve cordials at the end of meals. The sweetness may destroy the appetite if served before meals. Many liquor drinkers, particularly men, express a decided aversion to the sweeter ones and are likely to prefer those which have a dry aftertaste such as Drambuie, Benedictine, or Benedictine and brandy. Non-drinkers will usually like the sweeter fruit cordials such as cherry or peach.

Crème de Cacao: A chocolate-colored liqueur made from brandy, cocoa beans, spices, and vanilla.

Crème de Cassis: A deep-red liqueur made from black currants.

Crème de Menthe: A peppermint liqueur made from brandy and fresh mint. It comes colorless as well as green and red.

Crème de Moka: A liqueur made of brandy and coffee bean flavoring.

Crème de Noyaux: See Noyau.

Crème de Rose: A liqueur with a flavoring of rose petals.

Crème de Vanille: A liqueur flavored with vanilla beans.

Crème de Violette: A mauve-colored liqueur made from vanilla and cacao, perfumed with oil of violets.

Crème Yvette: A violet-colored liqueur with a sweet violet taste. It is similar to Crème de Violette.

Curacao: A liqueur named after the West Indian island, the home of the curaçao oranges, which are used in the making of this liqueur.

Drambuie: A clear, pale brown Scotch liqueur made of fine old Scotch whisky, flavored with honey, herbs, and spices.

Dubonnet: A French aromatized apéritif wine with a bitter sweet quinine taste.

Eau de Vie: French for spirits or brandy.

Eau de Vie de Marc: See Marc.

Elixir de Bacardi: A liqueur made of a rum base.

Fernet Branca: See Bitters.

Fiori Alpini: A pale golden-yellow Italian liqueur made of alpine flowers with the addition of herbs and spices.

Forbidden Fruit: An American liqueur made from brandy and citrus fruit.

Fraise: A French brandy made from strawberries.

Framboise: A French brandy made from raspberries.

Gin: The name is derived from the French word *genièvre* which means juniper. Gin may be regarded as simply a neutral spirit (a pure grade of alcohol) which has been flavored, and some gin is made that way. Most American and British gins are the type known as "London

Dry" and they are neutral spirits which have been redistilled over juniper berries and other aromatic materials such as angelica root, coriander, cardamon, and cassia bark and in that way have absorbed the flavors. Gins are never aged. Holland was the first country to produce gin and present-day Holland gin is a distinctive type, more aromatic and heavier in body than others. It is usually drunk straight with bitters and should not be used in cocktails. It would affect the final flavor of the mixed drink too strongly. Old Tom gin is somewhat similar to London Dry but has a sweetening added to it. When using Old Tom, allow for the sweetening by decreasing the amount of sugar or syrup called for in the recipe. Sloe gin which is made from sweetened dry gin flavored with sloes, a small blue-black, plumlike fruit, is not really a gin but a cordial.

Goldwasser: A liqueur made of brandy and various herbs and spices with tiny flecks of gold leaf floating in it.

Grand Marnier: A deep reddish-orange liqueur with a sweet orange flavor. It is made from a secret formula which features cognac and dried curaçao orange peel.

Grappa: A potent Italian brandy distilled from grape skins left over from winemaking.

Grenadine: A red syrup usually artificially flavored and colored. Originally it was made from pomegranates.

Herbsaint: See Absinthe.

Kahlua: A Mexican coffee liqueur made from brandy, coffee beans, and other ingredients.

Kirsch or Kirschwasser: A colorless brandy with a cherry and bitter almond flavor distilled from cherries and crushed cherry stones.

Kümmel: A liqueur flavored with caraway seed, anise, cumin, etc.

Liqueur d'Or: Another name for Goldwasser.

Liqueurs: See entry under Cordials.

Liqueur Jaune: Imitation of yellow Chartreuse.

Liqueur Verte: Imitation of green Chartreuse.

Mandarine: A liqueur made from brandy and mandarin oranges.

Maraschino: A strong, sweet cordial made from the fermented juice of the marasca, a small black and bitter wild cherry. The best grow in Dalmatia.

Marc: A French brandy that is made from skins, stems, etc. left over from winemaking. The complete name is "Eau de vie de Marc." It is similar to the Italian "Grappa."

Mazarine: An Argentine liqueur made of a secret formula.

Mead: An alcoholic liquor made of fermented honey, malt, yeast, spices, and water.

Mescal: Another name for Tequila, a Mexican alcoholic drink. See Pulque.

Metaxa: A popular Greek brandy.

Mirabelle: A liqueur made from small light-yellow plums that grow in France.

Monastique: A South American liqueur that resembles Benedictine.

Neat: Describes the drinking of whisky "straight," without a mixer or chaser.

Neutral Grain Spirits: They may be distilled from grains and other products such as potatoes, sugar, rice, sugar cane, etc. Most American distillers usually use fermented grain mashes and the distillation is carried out at a very high proof (over 190) which will result in a final product that is almost odorless, tasteless, and colorless. For mixing with a straight whisky, neutral spirits are cut with water and sometimes colored with a little caramel.

Noyau: A brandy-base liqueur flavored with a variety of fruits.

Old Tom Gin: See Gin.

Orange Bitters: Orange-colored bitters with a bittersweet, orange-peel flavor used in cocktails and other beverages.

Orgeat: A flavoring syrup, made from bitter almonds with a bitter-sweet almond-like taste, used in cocktails and other drinks.

Oxygenée: See Absinthe.

Parfait Amour: A French liqueur made of brandy, citrus fruits, and spices.

Passionola: A syrup made of passion fruit. It comes in 3 colors, green, red, and natural.

Perfume: See Aroma.

Pernod: See Absinthe.

Perry: A fermented drink (cider) made from pear juice. It also refers to sweet cider made from pears.

Peychaud's Bitters: See Bitters.

Pimm's No. 1 Cup: An English liqueur made from an old English formula.

Plum Brandy: See Mirabelle, Quetsch, Slivovitz.

Pousse Café: A deep-brown liqueur with a sweet vanilla and cocoa taste. It should not be confused with the rainbow-like mixture of liqueurs served under the same name.

Proof: A measurement of alcoholic strength. Each degree of proof equals half of 1 per cent alcohol. Therefore 100 proof whisky contains 50 per cent alcohol. Most blended whiskies are sold at 86 proof, containing therefore 43 per cent alcohol. Bonded straight whiskies are sold at 100 proof, containing therefore 50 per cent alcohol.

Prunelle: A yellow-brown liqueur made from plums with a sweet, fragrant plum flavor.

Pulque: A fermented drink, popular in Mexico, made from the juice of certain species of agave (the century plant). Tequila or Mescal, a colorless alcoholic liquor, is distilled from pulque.

Quetsch: A French brandy distilled from prune juice.

Quinquina: A red or dark-brown aromatized wine made from wine flavored with herbs and quinine.

Quinine Wines: Aromatized wines flavored with quinine, used in cocktails or as in France "straight" as apèritifs.

Rectify: Refers to any operation which changes the character of tax-paid spirits. Examples are: coloring, flavoring, redistilling, and sweetening.

Rock and Rye: A liqueur made from rye whisky, rock candy, and fruit juice.

Rum: A liquor obtained from the fermentation and subsequent distillation of any sugar cane product. It may be made from the fermented mash of juice crushed from the sugar cane plant, molasses, or other sugar cane by-products. In flavor rum may range from the almost characterless white rums to extremely strong flavored rums. The extreme variety in color, flavor, aroma, and bouquet results from differences in products used, methods of fermentation and distillation, and subsequent aging and coloring. Rum is made in most of the islands of the West Indies as well as on the Eastern seaboard of the United States (primarily New England and Philadelphia). The great range in the variety of rums may perhaps be best illustrated by saying that, whereas a tablespoonful of good Jamaica rum when added to a cup of strong coffee will give the coffee a strong rum flavor, a tablespoonful of strong coffee added to a cup of white rum gives the rum a predominantly coffee flavor. The heavy-bodied rums (Jamaica, Barbados, Demarara) should, therefore, be used in making full-flavored drinks and in cooking. The lighter and more delicate rums are used in certain cocktails like the Bacardi or the Daiquiri. Color has nothing to do with alcoholic content, which is specifically stated on the bottle. While there are no hard and fast rules, nevertheless one of the simplest ways of determining the type of rum to use is to keep in mind three major classifications: white label, gold label, and heavy rum.

White Label: Refers to light-bodied rum, light in color, with a delicate flavor and aroma. It usually has an alcoholic content of 86 proof. Use it in such drinks as Bacardi cocktails and Daiquiris.

Gold Label Rum: Refers to a darker-colored rum with a stronger flavor and stronger aroma. It has about the same alcoholic content as white label. Use it in cooking and in such drinks as Cuba Libre, Rum Collins, or Rum Manhattans.

Heavy Rum: Refers to rum that is very dark in color and with a pungent flavor and aroma. Alcoholic content may vary from 90 to 151 proof. Use it in such drinks as Planter's Punch, Rum Swizzles, and Rum Milk Punch.

Sake: A strong golden-colored Japanese rice wine.

Slivovitz: A light golden-brown plum brandy of Hungarian origin.

Sloe Gin: A liqueur made of gin and sloeberries. See Gin.

Southern Comfort: An American high-proof liqueur made from a secret formula.

Spirits: Any strong alcoholic liquor produced by distillation.

Stirrup Cup: The parting drink.

Strega: A golden-yellow Italian liqueur with a very sweet perfumed taste. It resembles Chartreuse.

Swedish Punch: A pale straw-colored liqueur with a sweet rummy taste. It is apparently made of rum and various flavorings.

Tequila: A Mexican alcoholic drink. See Pulque.

Triple Sec: A liqueur with a sweetish orange taste. It may be referred to as the "colorless curaçao." It is similar to Cointreau.

Van der Hum: A South African liqueur with a tangerine flavor.

Vermouth, French: The dry aromatic apéritif wine which has become an integral part of many cocktails. The alcohol content is 19 per cent.

Vermouth, Italian: The sweet aromatic apéritif wine which like the French vermouth is used in many cocktails. The alcohol content is 17 per cent.

Vieille Cure: A French liqueur made from a secret formula. It resembles Chartreuse.

Vodka: The national drink of Russia, now made in this country. As sold it contains 40 per cent to 60 per cent alcohol. It is illegal to sell it with less than 40 per cent alcohol. It is usually drunk straight.

Whisky: (Spelled "whisky" or "whiskey" with the former preferred.) Whether it is rye, bourbon, Scotch, Irish, or Canadian, whisky is a product obtained from the aging of the distillate of a fermented grain mash. The grain may be corn, rye, barley, wheat, or oats. Age may be anything from a few weeks to many years. Aging may take place in charred oak barrels as with American rye and bourbon, or in sherry casks as with Scotch or Irish. Some are bottled "straight" while others may be blended from several types of whisky with or without neutral grain spirits added.

> **Bourbon Whisky:** The name is derived from Bourbon County, Kentucky, where it was first produced. Like rye, it is generally made from several kinds of grains, but in bourbon the percentage of corn included in the mash usually runs between 65 per cent to 75 per cent. The law requires that it have at least 51 per cent corn in the mash.
>
> **Rye Whisky:** By law it must be made from a mash containing at least 51 per cent rye. About 66⅔ per cent rye is usually used. Much of the rye produced is used in blended whiskies.
>
> **Aging Whisky:** By law all bourbon and rye have to be aged in charred oak barrels. The more deeply the barrels are charred, the more flavor, aroma, and color in the final product. The longer the whisky ages in the barrels, the more effect the charring will have on the final product. This aging takes place in government bonded warehouses where liquor must remain at least two years to be legally classified as rye or bourbon. Most straight whiskies are aged four to eight years.
>
> **Blended Whisky:** There are two types. The first is a mixture of at least 20 per cent (by law) straight 100 proof whisky and neutral grain spirits. Most of the better known brands of this type contain 35 per cent to 40 per cent straight whisky. The law requires the maker to state the amount and approximate age of the whiskies in the blend. Blends which contain a minimum of 51 per cent rye or bourbon may use the title "Rye (or Bourbon)— A Blended Whisky." The second type consists of a number of blends of straight whiskies of varying ages that have been blended together to get certain characteristics. They contain no neutral spirits and as a result are higher in price. The proofs will range from 86 per cent to 90 per cent.

Sour Mash Whisky: Usually a type of bourbon whisky. Some of the "spent" mash from a straight whisky mash is included in a new mash. Fermentation is continued for a longer period to create a more lactic (sour) acid than in regular mash.

Scotch Whisky: (Always spelled "whisky.") The distinctive "smoky" flavor of Scotch is obtained by the drying of the barley malt, used in the fermented mash, on wire screens over peat fires. The distillation of this mash of the dried barley malt is aged in casks which were previously used for sherry wine. All Scotch whisky is a blend of several varieties of Highland barley malt whisky plus Lowland Scotch grain whisky which has also been aged in sherry casks. Each blender combines aged whiskies which he considers outstanding for certain qualities to arrive at a product that fills his requirements. The new blended product is then aged again in sherry casks for six months or more. The law requires that all Scotch whiskies exported to the United States must be at least four years old.

The taste range in Scotch whisky is very wide because of the variety in blends. One brand may be a very heavy-bodied, smoky type, and another very light-bodied lacking the extreme smoky flavor. Both may be excellent in quality. Personal preferences decide the choice.

Irish Whisky: (Always spelled "whiskey" on labels.) It is usually made from a fermented mixture of both malted and unmalted barley, rye, oats, and wheat. The green barley malt that is used is dried in solid-floor kilns so that the smoke from the peat fires does not flavor the product in the way that Scotch whisky is flavored. The product of several distillations is blended to produce a desired whisky in much the same way Scotch is blended.

Canadian Whisky: Canadian whiskies are lighter-bodied than American whiskies because they are proofed out at between 150 and 160 proof whereas American whiskies are usually distilled at 140 proof or lower. In addition flavor is attained as in Scotch or Irish whisky by the blending of a variety of Canadian whiskies to get a desired product. A rye and barley mash is generally used.

Woody: The smell and taste acquired by a liquor or a wine which has lain too long in cask.

brandy and cognac cocktails

APPLEJACK COCKTAIL

1½ ounces applejack
¾ ounce lemon juice

½ ounce grenadine or 1 teaspoon
fine grain sugar

Shake with cracked ice. Strain into cocktail glass.

APRICOT COCKTAIL #1

1½ ounces apricot brandy   Juice of 1 lemon

Shake with cracked ice. Strain into cocktail glass.

Apricot Cocktail #2: Use ½ ounce each of lemon and orange juice.

BOMBAY COCKTAIL

2 ounces brandy
¼ ounce sweet vermouth
¼ ounce dry vermouth

3 dashes curaçao
Dash of anisette

Shake with cracked ice. Strain into cocktail glass.

BRAIN DUSTER COCKTAIL

1 ounce brandy
¾ ounce Pernod or Herbsaint

3 dashes Angostura or Abbott's
bitters

Shake with cracked ice. Strain into cocktail glass.

BRANDY COCKTAIL #1

1½ ounces brandy
Dash of Angostura bitters

Dash of dry gin

Shake with cracked ice. Strain into cocktail glass.

BRANDY COCKTAIL #2

1½ ounces brandy
½ ounce curaçao

½ teaspoon bar syrup
2 dashes Angostura bitters

Stir well with cracked ice. Strain into cocktail glass. Add a twist of
lemon peel, if desired.

BRANDY VERMOUTH COCKTAIL

1½ ounces brandy   Dash of Angostura bitters
½ ounce sweet vermouth

Stir with cracked ice. Strain into cocktail glass.

BULL FROG COCKTAIL

Same as Hop Toad Cocktail.

B. V. D. COCKTAIL

1½ ounces applejack   ¾ ounce sweet vermouth

Shake with cracked ice. Strain into cocktail glass. Serve with twist of lemon peel.

CHERRY BLOSSOM COCKTAIL #1

1½ ounces cherry brandy   3 dashes lemon juice
1 ounce brandy   3 dashes grenadine
3 dashes curaçao

Shake with cracked ice. Strain into cocktail glass. Another version of this popular cocktail with sloe gin as the base ingredient is in the cordial cocktail section.

CHICAGO COCKTAIL

1½ ounces brandy   Dash of Angostura bitters
2 dashes curaçao

Shake with cracked ice. Strain into a large cocktail glass or champagne glass with frosted rim. Fill glass with chilled champagne.

DEPTH BOMB COCKTAIL

1½ ounces brandy   ¼ teaspoon grenadine
1 ounce applejack   ¼ teaspoon lemon juice

Shake with cracked ice. Strain into cocktail glass.

DEVIL COCKTAIL

1 ounce brandy   Pinch of red pepper
1 ounce green crème de menthe

Shake brandy and crème de menthe with cracked ice. Strain into cocktail glass. Top with red pepper.

EAST INDIA COCKTAIL

1½ ounces brandy   2 dashes Angostura bitters
 2 dashes maraschino liqueur 2 dashes orange curaçao

Shake with cracked ice. Strain into cocktail glass. Serve with cherry
or twist of lemon peel.

FLYING FORTRESS COCKTAIL

½ ounce Cointreau   ¾ ounce vodka
½ ounce anisette   1 ounce brandy

Shake with cracked ice. Strain into large cocktail glass.

HONEYMOON COCKTAIL

1½ ounces applejack   Juice of ½ lemon
 ½ ounce Benedictine   3 dashes curaçao

Shake with cracked ice. Strain into cocktail glass.

HOP TOAD COCKTAIL

1½ ounces apricot brandy   Juice of 1 lemon

Shake with cracked ice. Strain into cocktail glass.

JACK-IN-THE-BOX COCKTAIL

1½ ounces applejack   ½ ounce pineapple juice
 ½ ounce lemon juice   2 dashes Angostura bitters

Shake with cracked ice. Strain into cocktail glass.

JACK ROSE COCKTAIL

Juice of ½ lemon   1½ ounces applejack
½ ounce grenadine

Shake with cracked ice. Strain into cocktail glass.

JERSEY LIGHTNING COCKTAIL

 2 ounces applejack   Dash of Angostura bitters
½ teaspoon fine grain sugar

Shake with cracked ice. Strain into cocktail glass.

JOHNNIE APPLESEED COCKTAIL

1½ ounces applejack
½ ounce curaçao

2 dashes Angostura bitters

Shake with cracked ice. Strain into cocktail glass.

LIBERTY COCKTAIL

1 ounce applejack
½ ounce white label rum

½ teaspoon lemon juice
½ teaspoon fine grain sugar

Shake with cracked ice. Strain into cocktail glass.

MOTHER SHERMAN FRAPPE

2 ounces apricot brandy
¾ ounce orange juice

4 dashes orange bitters

Shake vigorously with shaved ice until glass frosts. Strain into large cocktail glass.

NETHERLAND COCKTAIL

1½ ounces brandy
½ ounce curaçao

Dash of orange bitters

Stir well in cracked ice. Strain into cocktail glass.

PANAMA COCKTAIL

1 ounce brandy
¾ ounce crème de cacao

¾ ounce sweet cream

Shake with cracked ice. Strain into cocktail glass.

PRAIRIE OYSTER

1 egg
Dash of Worcestershire sauce

1½ ounces brandy

Carefully break the egg into a 6-ounce glass. Add Worcestershire sauce and brandy. Blend lightly with the white of egg, keeping yolk intact.

ROYAL SMILE COCKTAIL

¾ ounce applejack
¾ ounce dry gin

Dash of grenadine or raspberry
syrup
Juice of ¼ lime

Shake with cracked ice. Strain into cocktail glass.

SARATOGA COCKTAIL

¾ ounce applejack   ¾ ounce dry gin
¾ ounce sweet vermouth   Dash of orange bitters

Shake with cracked ice. Strain into cocktail glass.

Variations: Any favorite brandy may be substituted for applejack. Orange juice may be substituted for orange bitters.

SIDECAR COCKTAIL #1

Juice of ½ lemon   1¾ ounces brandy
¾ ounce Cointreau

Shake with cracked ice. Strain into cocktail glass.

SIDECAR COCKTAIL #2

¾ ounce lemon juice   ¾ ounce Cointreau
¾ ounce cognac

Shake with cracked ice. Strain into cocktail glass.

STAR COCKTAIL #1

1¼ ounces applejack   2 dashes Angostura bitters
1¼ ounces dry vermouth

Stir with cracked ice. Strain into cocktail glass. Twist a piece of lemon peel over top.

STAR COCKTAIL #2

¾ ounce applejack   Dash of orange bitters
¾ ounce sweet vermouth

Shake with cracked ice. Strain into cocktail glass.

STINGER #1

2 ounces brandy   ¾ ounce white crème de menthe

Shake with cracked ice. Strain into cocktail glass.

STINGER #2

1⅓ ounces brandy   1⅓ ounces crème de menthe

Pour brandy into cocktail glass. Top with crème de menthe.

ZOOM COCKTAIL

2 ounces brandy   ½ ounce fresh cream
¼ ounce honey

Shake with cracked ice. Strain into cocktail glass.

cordial and liqueur cocktails

ABSINTHE COCKTAIL

1½ ounces Pernod or Herbsaint   2 dashes Angostura bitters
1½ ounces bar syrup

Shake with cracked ice. Strain into cocktail glass. Serve with twist of lemon peel.

Note: Pernod and Herbsaint are absinthe substitutes. Absinthe is illegal because it contains a drug, wormwood.

ABSINTHE FRAPPE

1½ ounces Pernod or Herbsaint   2 dashes Angostura bitters
½ ounce anisette

Shake with shaved ice until the glass frosts. Strain into large cocktail glass.

BENEDICTINE FRAPPE

Fill a cocktail glass with shaved ice. Pour in Benedictine. Serve with two short straws.

CHERRY BLOSSOM COCKTAIL #2

1½ ounces sloe gin   ¼ ounce lemon juice
½ ounce orange juice   ¼ ounce maraschino cherry juice

Shake with cracked ice. Strain into cocktail glass.

DOCTOR COCKTAIL

1½ ounces Swedish Punch   Juice of ½ lime
¾ ounce Jamaica rum

Shake with cracked ice. Strain into cocktail glass.

GOLDEN SLIPPER COCKTAIL

¾ ounce yellow Chartreuse   1 egg yolk
¾ ounce brandy

Shake with cracked ice. Strain into cocktail glass.

MAIDEN'S BLUSH COCKTAIL

1½ ounces Pernod or Herbsaint   1 teaspoon grenadine
¾ ounce dry gin

Stir well with cracked ice. Strain into cocktail glass. Serve with twist of lemon peel.

MAIDEN'S PRAYER COCKTAIL

1 ounce Cointreau   ¼ ounce lemon juice
1 ounce dry gin   ¼ ounce orange juice

Shake with cracked ice. Strain into cocktail glass.

MEMPHIS BELLE COCKTAIL

Put a cherry and half a peach in the bottom of a champagne glass. Fill with shaved ice. Add 2 ounces Southern Comfort. Serve with short straws and a small spoon.

PARISIAN COCKTAIL

¾ ounce dry vermouth   ¾ ounce dry gin
¾ ounce crème de cassis

Shake with cracked ice. Strain into cocktail glass.

RED LION COCKTAIL

1 ounce Grand Marnier   ½ ounce lemon juice
1 ounce dry gin   ½ ounce orange juice

Shake with cracked ice. Strain into cocktail glass. Serve with twist of lemon peel.

RHETT BUTLER COCKTAIL

1½ ounces Southern Comfort   1 teaspoon curaçao (optional)
Juice of ¼ lime   ½ teaspoon fine grain sugar
Juice of ¼ lemon

Shake with cracked ice. Strain into cocktail glass.

SCARLETT O'HARA COCKTAIL

2 ounces Southern Comfort   Juice of ¼ lime
¾ ounce cranberry juice

Stir in cracked ice. Strain into cocktail glass.

SLOE GIN COCKTAIL #1

2 ounces sloe gin   ¾ ounce dry vermouth

Stir well in cracked ice. Strain into cocktail glass.

SLOE GIN COCKTAIL #2

2 ounces sloe gin   2 dashes Angostura bitters
2 dashes orange bitters

Stir well in cracked ice. Strain into cocktail glass.

SUISSESSE #1

½ ounce anisette   1 egg white
1 ounce Pernod or Herbsaint

Shake well with cracked ice. Strain into large cocktail glass.

SUISSESSE #2

¼ ounce anisette   1½ ounces Pernod or Herbsaint

Shake with cracked ice. Strain into large cocktail glass. Fill with carbonated water.

VIRGIN'S COCKTAIL

¾ ounce Forbidden Fruit   ¾ ounce dry gin
¾ ounce white crème de menthe

Shake with cracked ice. Strain into cocktail glass.

WIDOW'S DREAM COCKTAIL

2 ounces Benedictine   Sweet cream
1 whole egg

Shake Benedictine and egg with cracked ice. Strain into a 6-ounce highball glass. Fill with sweet cream.

YOUNG JEFF COCKTAIL

1¼ ounces sweet vermouth   2 dashes grenadine
1¼ ounces sloe gin   3 dashes Angostura bitters

Shake with cracked ice. Strain into cocktail glass.

gin cocktails

ABBEY COCKTAIL

2 ounces dry gin
¾ ounce orange juice

Dash of sweet vermouth
2 dashes Angostura bitters

Shake with cracked ice. Strain into cocktail glass. Serve with cherry.

ADMIRAL COCKTAIL

2 ounces dry gin
½ ounce cherry liqueur

Juice of ½ lime

Stir with cracked ice. Strain into cocktail glass.

ALASKA COCKTAIL

2 ounces dry gin
¾ ounce yellow Chartreuse

Dash of orange bitters

Stir with cracked ice. Strain into cocktail glass.

ALEXANDER COCKTAIL #1

1½ ounces dry gin
¾ ounce crème de cacao

¾ ounce sweet cream

Shake well with cracked ice. Strain into cocktail glass.
Brandy or Rum Alexander: Substitute brandy or rum for gin.

ALEXANDER COCKTAIL #2

Use ⅓ each of dry gin, crème de cacao, and sweet cream.

ALEXANDER'S SISTER COCKTAIL

¾ ounce dry gin
¾ ounce crème de menthe

¾ ounce sweet cream

Shake with cracked ice. Strain into cocktail glass.

ANISETTE COCKTAIL #1

1 ounce dry gin
½ ounce anisette

½ ounce sweet cream
½ egg white

Shake well with cracked ice. Strain into large cocktail glass. Serve with grating of nutmeg on top.

APPETIZER COCKTAIL

1 ounce dry gin
1 ounce Dubonnet

Juice of ½ orange
3 dashes Angostura bitters

Stir with cracked ice. Strain into cocktail glass.

APRICOT GOLDEN DAWN

1 ounce orange juice
1 ounce dry gin

½ ounce apricot liqueur

Shake with cracked ice. Strain into cocktail glass.

AVIATION COCKTAIL

1½ ounces dry gin
½ ounce lemon juice

¼ ounce maraschino liqueur

Shake with cracked ice. Strain into cocktail glass.

BERMUDA ROSE COCKTAIL

1½ ounces dry gin
Dash of grenadine

Dash of apricot brandy
⅓ ounce lemon juice

Shake with cracked ice. Strain into cocktail glass.

BEST HOMEMADE COCKTAIL

1½ ounces dry gin

Juice of ½ orange

Shake with cracked ice. Strain into cocktail glass.

BIJOU COCKTAIL

¾ ounce dry gin
¾ ounce sweet vermouth

¾ ounce green Chartreuse
Dash of orange bitters

Stir well with cracked ice. Strain into cocktail glass. Serve with twist of lemon peel and a cherry.

BLACKOUT COCKTAIL

½ ounce blackberry brandy
2 ounces dry gin

Juice of ½ lime

Shake with cracked ice. Strain into cocktail glass.

BLUE MOON COCKTAIL #1

1½ ounces dry gin   ½ ounce lemon juice
½ ounce crème yvette

Stir well with cracked ice. Strain into cocktail glass.

BLUE MOON COCKTAIL #2

1½ ounces dry gin   1 egg white
½ ounce maraschino liqueur

Shake with cracked ice. Strain into large cocktail glass.

BRONX COCKTAIL (Standard)

1 ounce dry gin   ¾ ounce dry vermouth
¾ ounce sweet vermouth   ½ ounce orange juice

Shake with cracked ice. Strain into large cocktail glass.

BRONX COCKTAIL (Dry)

2 half slices of orange   1½ ounces dry gin
1 small stick of pineapple ¾ ounce dry vermouth

Place fruit in mixing glass. Muddle well. Add cracked ice, gin, and vermouth. Shake well. Strain into large cocktail glass. (If desired, fruit may be transferred into cocktail glass.)

CAFE DE PARIS COCKTAIL

1½ ounces dry gin   1 egg white
3 dashes anisette   1 teaspoon fresh cream

Shake well with cracked ice. Strain into large cocktail glass.

CASINO COCKTAIL

1½ ounces dry gin   4 dashes orange bitters
4 dashes maraschino liqueur 4 dashes lemon juice

Shake with cracked ice. Strain into cocktail glass. Serve with a cherry.

CLOVER CLUB COCKTAIL

2 ounces dry gin   1 egg white
4 dashes grenadine   Juice of ½ lime or lemon

Shake well with cracked ice. Strain into large cocktail glass.

CLOVER LEAF COCKTAIL

Same as Clover Club with sprig of mint on top.

COOPERSTOWN COCKTAIL

1 *ounce dry gin*
¾ *ounce dry vermouth*

¾ *ounce sweet vermouth*
2 *sprigs mint*

Shake with cracked ice. Strain into cocktail glass. Garnish with mint.

CORNELL COCKTAIL

1 *ounce dry gin*

1 *ounce dry vermouth*

Shake with cracked ice. Strain into cocktail glass.

DAMN-THE-WEATHER COCKTAIL

1 *ounce dry gin*
½ *ounce sweet vermouth*

½ *ounce orange juice*
3 *dashes curaçao*

Shake with cracked ice. Strain into cocktail glass.

DARBY COCKTAIL

1½ *ounces dry gin*
½ *ounce lime juice*

½ *ounce grapefruit juice*
1 *teaspoon fine grain sugar*

Shake with cracked ice. Strain into large cocktail glass. Top with a squirt of soda. Serve with a cherry.

EAGLE'S DREAM COCKTAIL

1½ *ounces dry gin*
¾ *ounce crème yvette*

Juice of ½ lemon
1 *egg white*

Shake well with cracked ice. Strain into large cocktail glass.

FALLEN ANGEL COCKTAIL

1½ *ounces dry gin*
Juice of ½ lemon or lime

2 *dashes crème de menthe*
Dash of Angostura bitters

Shake with cracked ice. Strain into cocktail glass. Serve with cherry.

FRENCH ROSE COCKTAIL

1 *ounce dry gin*
½ *ounce cherry brandy*

½ *ounce cherry liqueur*

Shake with cracked ice. Strain into cocktail glass.

GIBSON COCKTAIL (Dry)

1½ *ounces dry gin*

¾ *ounce dry vermouth*

Stir with cracked ice. Strain into cocktail glass. Twist lemon peel over top. Serve with pickled pearl onion.

GIBSON COCKTAIL (Sweet)

1½ ounces dry gin   1 ounce sweet vermouth

Stir with cracked ice. Strain into cocktail glass. Twist lemon peel over top. Serve with pickled pearl onion.

GIN COCKTAIL #1

1½ ounces dry gin   2 dashes Angostura bitters

Shake with cracked ice. Strain into cocktail glass.

GIN COCKTAIL #2

1½ ounces dry gin   Dash of orange bitters

Shake with cracked ice. Strain into cocktail glass. Twist lemon peel over top.

GIN 'N' BITTERS

1½ ounces dry gin   5 dashes Angostura bitters

Put bitters and an ice cube in an Old-Fashioned glass. Add gin. Serve with stirring rod.

HARVARD COCKTAIL

1½ ounces dry gin   Dash of Pernod
¾ ounce dry vermouth   2 dashes of grenadine

Shake with cracked ice. Strain into cocktail glass.

HAWAII COCKTAIL #1

1½ ounces dry gin   Dash of orange bitters
1 ounce pineapple juice   1 egg white

Shake with cracked ice. Strain into large cocktail glass.

HAWAII COCKTAIL #2

1½ ounces dry gin   3 dashes orange bitters
½ ounce pineapple juice

Shake with cracked ice. Strain into cocktail glass. Serve with cherry.

HONOLULU COCKTAIL

¾ ounce dry gin
¾ ounce Benedictine

¾ ounce maraschino liqueur

Shake with cracked ice. Strain into cocktail glass.

HULA HULA COCKTAIL

1½ ounces dry gin
¾ ounce orange juice

Dash of curaçao

Shake with cracked ice. Strain into cocktail glass.

IDEAL COCKTAIL

1 ounce dry gin
½ ounce dry vermouth
½ ounce grapefruit juice

1 teaspoon fine grain sugar
3 dashes Angostura bitters

Shake with cracked ice. Strain into cocktail glass. Serve with cherry.

KNOCKOUT COCKTAIL

¾ ounce Pernod or Herbsaint
¾ ounce dry vermouth

¾ ounce dry gin
1 teaspoon white crème de
menthe

Stir with cracked ice. Strain into cocktail glass. Serve with cherry.

LEAP YEAR COCKTAIL

1½ ounces dry gin
½ ounce sweet vermouth

½ ounce Grand Marnier
Dash of lemon juice

Stir with cracked ice. Strain into cocktail glass. Serve with twist of
lemon peel over top.

MAIDEN'S DELIGHT COCKTAIL

1½ ounces dry gin
4 dashes orange curaçao

4 dashes grenadine
Dash of lemon juice

Shake with cracked ice. Strain into cocktail glass.

MARTINI COCKTAIL (Sweet)

2 ounces dry gin

¾ ounce sweet vermouth

Stir well with cracked ice. Strain into cocktail glass. Serve with cherry.

MARTINI COCKTAIL (Medium)

1½ ounces dry gin
¾ ounce dry vermouth

¾ ounce sweet vermouth

Stir well with cracked ice. Strain into cocktail glass. Serve with olive.

MARTINI COCKTAIL (Dry)

2 ounces dry gin

¾ ounce dry vermouth

Stir well with cracked ice. Strain into cocktail glass. Serve with olive and a twist of lemon peel, if desired.

NAPOLEON COCKTAIL

2 ounces dry gin
2 dashes Dubonnet

2 dashes Fernet Branca
2 dashes curaçao

Shake with cracked ice. Strain into cocktail glass. Serve with twist of lemon peel.

ORANGE BLOSSOM COCKTAIL #1

2 ounces dry gin
¾ ounce orange juice

¼ teaspoon fine grain sugar

Stir well with cracked ice. Strain into cocktail glass with edge frosted by rubbing with piece of orange and dipping in powdered sugar.

ORANGE BLOSSOM COCKTAIL #2

Use ⅓ each of Old Tom gin, sweet vermouth, and orange juice.

PALISADES COCKTAIL

1½ ounces dry gin
¾ ounce apple cider

2 dashes Angostura bitters

Shake with cracked ice. Strain into cocktail glass.

PARADISE COCKTAIL

1½ ounces dry gin
¾ ounce apricot brandy

¼ ounce lemon juice

Shake with cracked ice. Strain into cocktail glass.

PEACH GOLDEN DAWN COCKTAIL

1 ounce orange juice
1 ounce dry gin

½ ounce peach liqueur

Shake with cracked ice. Strain into cocktail glass.

PINK LADY COCKTAIL #1

½ egg white
½ ounce grenadine
½ ounce lemon juice

¼ ounce applejack
1 ounce dry gin

Shake well with cracked ice. Strain into large cocktail glass. Decorate with a sprig of mint, if desired.

PINK LADY COCKTAIL #2

1 egg white
½ ounce applejack
2 dashes of grenadine or
raspberry syrup

Juice of ½ lime
1 ounce dry gin

Shake well with cracked ice. Strain into large cocktail glass. Decorate with a sprig of mint, if desired.

PINK ROSE COCKTAIL

1 ounce dry gin
1 teaspoon grenadine
1 teaspoon lemon juice

1 teaspoon sweet cream
1 egg white

Shake well with cracked ice. Strain into large cocktail glass.

PRINCETON COCKTAIL

1½ ounces dry gin
½ ounce port wine

2 dashes orange bitters

Stir with cracked ice. Strain into cocktail glass. Serve with twist of lemon peel.

QUEEN ELIZABETH COCKTAIL

1 ounce dry gin
½ ounce curaçao or Cointreau

½ ounce lemon juice
Dash of Herbsaint or Pernod

Shake with cracked ice. Strain into cocktail glass.

ROSE OR ROSA COCKTAIL

1½ ounces dry gin
½ ounce kirsch

½ ounce apricot brandy

Stir with cracked ice. Strain into cocktail glass. If desired, dry vermouth may be substituted for dry gin.

SEVENTH HEAVEN COCKTAIL

2 ounces dry gin
¾ ounce maraschino liqueur

1 tablespoon grapefruit juice

Shake with cracked ice. Strain into cocktail glass. Serve with sprig of mint.

SNAPPER COCKTAIL

1½ ounces dry gin

1½ ounces white crème de menthe

Shake with cracked ice. Strain into cocktail glass.

TEXAS JOY COCKTAIL

1½ ounces dry gin
½ ounce sweet vermouth

¼ ounce unsweetened canned grapefruit juice
Dash of Angostura bitters

Stir with cracked ice. Strain into cocktail glass. Serve with twist of lemon peel.

WAIKIKI BEACHCOMBER

¾ ounce dry gin
¾ ounce Cointreau

½ ounce fresh pineapple juice

Shake with cracked ice. Strain into cocktail glass.

WEDDED BLISS COCKTAIL

1 ounce dry gin
1 ounce sweet vermouth

1 ounce brandy
2 dashes orange bitters

Shake with cracked ice. Strain into large cocktail glass.

WHITE LADY COCKTAIL #1

2 ounces dry gin
½ ounce Cointreau

Juice of ½ lemon
1 egg white

Shake well with cracked ice. Strain into large cocktail glass.

WHITE LADY COCKTAIL #2

¾ ounce Cointreau
1½ ounces dry gin

¾ ounce lemon juice

Shake with cracked ice. Strain into cocktail glass.

WHITE CARGO COCKTAIL

Use ½ vanilla ice cream and ½ dry gin. Shake until well mixed. If too thick, add white wine to thin the drink.

WHITE ROSE COCKTAIL

1½ ounces dry gin
Juice of 1 lime
Juice of ¼ orange

¾ ounce maraschino liqueur
1 egg white

Shake well with cracked ice. Strain into large cocktail glass.

WINDSOR COCKTAIL

1½ ounces dry gin

1½ ounces green crème de
menthe

Stir with cracked ice. Strain into cocktail glass. Serve with twist of lemon peel.

YALE COCKTAIL

2 ounces dry gin
Dash of Pernod

Dash of orange bitters

Shake with cracked ice. Strain into cocktail glass. Serve with twist of lemon peel.

rum cocktails

BACARDI COCKTAIL #1

1½ ounces Bacardi rum
Juice of ½ lime

1 teaspoon fine grain sugar

Combine in shaker and stir well. Add finely cracked ice and shake well. Strain into cocktail glass.

BACARDI COCKTAIL #2

1½ ounces Bacardi rum
Juice of 1 lime

½ teaspoon fine grain sugar
Dash of grenadine

Combine in shaker and stir well. Add finely cracked ice and shake well. Strain into cocktail glass.

BEACHCOMBER COCKTAIL

2 ounces white label rum
½ ounce Cointreau or triple sec

Juice of ½ lime
2 dashes maraschino liqueur

Shake vigorously with lots of shaved ice or mix in electric blender with shaved ice. Serve in champagne glass.

BEE'S KNEES COCKTAIL

¾ ounce orange juice
1 teaspoon fine grain sugar

½ ounce lime juice
1½ ounces white label rum

Shake with cracked ice. Strain into cocktail glass.

CAPTAIN'S BLOOD

1½ ounces Jamaica rum or gold
label rum

Juice of 1 lime
3 dashes Angostura bitters

Shake with cracked ice. Strain into cocktail glass.

CUBAN COCKTAIL #1

2 ounces Bacardi rum
¾ ounce apricot brandy

Juice of ½ lime or ¼ lemon

Shake with cracked ice. Strain into cocktail glass.

CUBAN COCKTAIL#2

1 *ounce Bacardi rum*
1 *ounce pineapple juice*

1 *teaspoon grenadine*
5 *drops maraschino liqueur*

Mix ingredients and pour into a goblet filled with shaved ice. Serve with short straws.

CUBANO COCKTAIL

2 *ounces Cuban rum*
Juice of ½ lime

¼ *ounce pineapple juice*

Shake with cracked ice. Strain into cocktail glass.

CUBA LIBRE COCKTAIL

1 *ounce white label rum*
1 *ounce cola drink*

Juice of ½ lime

Shake with cracked ice. Strain into cocktail glass.

DAIQUIRI

2 *ounces white label rum*
Juice of ½ lemon or lime

1 *teaspoon fine grain sugar*

Shake well with finely shaved ice. Strain into cocktail glass.

FROZEN DAIQUIRI

2 *ounces white label rum*
Juice of ½ lemon or lime

1 *teaspoon fine grain sugar*
Dash of maraschino liqueur

Shake very vigorously with 8 to 10 ounces shaved ice or mix in electric blender for 1 minute. Serve unstrained in champagne glass with short straws.

EL PRESIDENTE COCKTAIL

1½ *ounces gold label rum*
½ *ounce curaçao*

½ *ounce dry vermouth*
Dash of grenadine

Shake well with cracked ice. Strain into cocktail glass.

HAVANA COCKTAIL

1½ *ounces white label rum*
1 *ounce pineapple juice*

¼ *ounce lemon juice*

Shake with cracked ice. Strain into cocktail glass.

HAVANA CLUB COCKTAIL

2 ounces Havana gold label rum   1 ounce dry vermouth

Stir well in cracked ice. Strain into cocktail glass. Serve with cherry.

HONEY BEE COCKTAIL

¼ ounce honey   ¼ ounce lemon juice
2 ounces Bacardi rum

Shake with cracked ice. Strain into cocktail glass.

HONEYSUCKLE COCKTAIL

Juice of ½ lemon   1½ ounces gold label rum
1 teaspoon strained honey

Blend the honey in the juice and rum. Add ice and shake well. Strain into cocktail glass.

JAMAICA RUM COCKTAIL

2 ounces Jamaica rum   Juice of ½ lime
1 teaspoon fine grain sugar

Shake with cracked ice. Strain into cocktail glass.

MARY PICKFORD COCKTAIL

2 ounces Cuban rum   2 dashes grenadine
¾ ounce fresh pineapple juice

Shake with cracked ice. Strain into cocktail glass.

MIAMI COCKTAIL

¾ ounce white crème de menthe   2 ounces white label rum
4 dashes lemon juice

Shake with cracked ice. Strain into cocktail glass.

MIAMI BEACH COCKTAIL

2 ounces white label rum   ¼ teaspoon lemon juice
¾ ounce Cointreau

Shake with cracked ice. Strain into cocktail glass.

MORNING ROSE COCKTAIL

¾ ounce white label rum   ¾ ounce curaçao or triple sec
½ ounce lemon juice   ½ ounce grenadine

Shake with cracked ice. Strain into cocktail glass.

NATIONAL COCKTAIL

2 ounces Cuban rum ½ ounce apricot liqueur
½ ounce pineapple juice

Shake with cracked ice. Strain into cocktail glass. Decorate with cherry and pineapple stick. *Note:* Also known as Nacional Cocktail.

OLYMPIA COCKTAIL

1½ ounces gold label rum Juice of ½ lime
1 ounce cherry brandy

Shake with cracked ice. Strain into cocktail glass.

PALMETTO COCKTAIL

1 ounce gold label rum 3 dashes Angostura bitters
1 ounce dry vermouth

Shake well with cracked ice. Strain into cocktail glass.

PARADISE RUM COCKTAIL

1½ ounces white label rum ½ ounce apricot liqueur

Shake with cracked ice. Strain into cocktail glass.

PILGRIM COCKTAIL

Juice of ½ lemon or lime 1½ ounces New England rum
1 teaspoon grenadine

Shake well with cracked ice. Strain into cocktail glass.

PIRATE'S COCKTAIL

1½ ounces gold label rum Dash of Angostura bitters
¾ ounce sweet vermouth

Stir in cracked ice. Strain into cocktail glass.

PLATINUM BLONDE COCKTAIL

1 ounce white label rum ½ ounce sweet cream
1 ounce Cointreau

Shake with cracked ice. Strain into cocktail glass.

RUM DUBONNET

¾ ounce white label rum Juice of ½ lime
¾ ounce Dubonnet

Stir with cracked ice. Strain into cocktail glass.

RUM FRAPPE

1½ ounces Jamaica or New England rum   ½ cup orange sherbet

Put sherbet in a highball glass or large champagne glass. Add rum and stir slowly until smooth.

RUM OLD-FASHIONED

See Old-Fashioned.

RUMMY COCKTAIL

½ ounce Jamaica rum   ½ ounce lemon or lime juice
1 ounce dry vermouth   2 dashes grenadine

Shake well with cracked ice. Strain into cocktail glass.

SANTIAGO COCKTAIL

2 ounces gold label rum   ¼ teaspoon grenadine
Juice of ½ lime

Shake with cracked ice. Strain into cocktail glass.

Santiago Frappé: Combine the same ingredients in a shaker full of shaved ice. Shake until glass frosts. Strain.

SEPTEMBER MORN COCKTAIL

1½ ounces white label rum   Dash of grenadine
Juice of ½ lime   1 egg white

Shake well with cracked ice. Strain into large cocktail glass.

SOUTH SEA DIPPER

1½ ounces white label rum   ¼ ounce lime juice
½ ounce pineapple juice   1 teaspoon fine grain sugar

Shake with cracked ice. Pour without straining into small highball glass. Decorate with sliced fruit. Serve with straws.

TRINIDAD COCKTAIL

2 ounces Trinidad rum   1 teaspoon fine grain sugar
Juice of ½ lime   3 dashes Angostura bitters

Shake with cracked ice. Strain into cocktail glass.

WEST INDIES COCKTAIL #1

Add 5 or 6 dashes pineapple juice to the recipe for Frozen Daiquiri.

WEST INDIES COCKTAIL #2

Juice of ½ lime　　　　　　　　*1½ ounces white label rum*
1 teaspoon honey

Shake with cracked ice. Strain into 8-ounce highball glass. Fill with chilled champagne. Stir slightly and serve.

WHITE LION COCKTAIL

1½ ounces gold label rum　　　*3 dashes Angostura bitters*
Juice of ½ lemon　　　　　　　*3 dashes raspberry syrup*
1 teaspoon fine grain sugar

Shake well with cracked ice. Strain into cocktail glass.

WHITE LILY COCKTAIL

¾ ounce white label rum　　　*¾ ounce Cointreau*
¾ ounce dry gin　　　　　　　*2 dashes anisette*

Stir with cracked ice. Strain into cocktail glass.

vodka cocktails

BLUE MONDAY COCKTAIL

1½ ounces vodka   ½ ounce Cointreau

Shake with cracked ice. Strain into cocktail glass.

KANGAROO COCKTAIL

2 ounces vodka   ¾ ounce dry vermouth

Shake with cracked ice. Strain into cocktail glass. Serve with twist of lemon peel.

RED ROOSTER COCKTAIL

2 ounces well-seasoned tomato   ¾ ounce vodka
   juice

Shake with cracked ice. Strain into cocktail glass.

RUSSIAN COCKTAIL

2 ounces vodka   ¾ ounce crème de cacao

Shake with cracked ice. Strain into cocktail glass.

TOVARICH COCKTAIL

1½ ounces vodka   Juice of ½ lime
  1 ounce kümmel

Shake with cracked ice. Strain into cocktail glass.

VODKA COCKTAIL

1½ ounces vodka   Juice of ½ lime or lemon
  ½ ounce cherry brandy

Shake with cracked ice. Strain into cocktail glass.

VODKA MARTINI

1½ ounces vodka   ½ ounce dry vermouth

Stir well with cracked ice. Strain into cocktail glass. Serve with a twist of lemon peel.

BLACK RUSSIAN

1½ ounces vodka   ¾ ounce Kahlúa (coffee liqueur)

Pour over ice cubes in Old-Fashioned glass.

BLOODY MARY

1½ ounces vodka   1 dash lemon juice
1½ ounces tomato juice

Shake well with cracked ice and strain into Old-Fashioned cocktail glass with cube of ice.

SCREWDRIVER

Put 2 or 3 cubes of ice into a 6-ounce glass. Add 2 ounces of vodka. Fill balance of glass with orange juice and stir.

VODKA GIMLET

1½ ounces vodka   Juice of ½ lime

Stir well with cracked ice and strain into 3-ounce cocktail glass.

VODKA SOUR

2 ounces vodka   ½ teaspoon powdered sugar
Juice of ½ lemon

Shake well with cracked ice and strain into 6-ounce sour glass. Fill with carbonated water and stir. Decorate with half a slice of lemon and a cherry.

VODKA AND TONIC

Put 2 ounces of vodka and cube of ice in 12-ounce Tom Collins glass. Fill balance with quinine tonic and stir.

VODKA STINGER

1 ounce vodka   1 ounce white crème de menthe

Shake well with cracked ice and strain into 3-ounce cocktail glass.

VODKA TWISTER

2 ounces vodka   Juice of ½ lime

Pour into 12-ounce Tom Collins glass. Add several cubes of ice, drop rind into glass. Fill with Seven-Up and stir well.

whisky cocktails

AFFINITY COCKTAIL

1 ounce Scotch whisky
¾ ounce dry vermouth

¾ ounce sweet vermouth
2 dashes Angostura bitters

Stir with cracked ice. Strain into cocktail glass. Twist lemon peel over drink.

BARBARY COAST COCKTAIL

¾ ounce dry gin
¾ ounce Scotch whisky

¾ ounce crème de cacao
½ ounce fresh cream

Shake well with finely cracked ice. Strain into cocktail glass.

BLACKTHORN COCKTAIL

1½ ounces Irish whisky
1 ounce dry vermouth

Dash of Angostura bitters
3 dashes anisette

Stir well with cracked ice. Strain into cocktail glass.

BLOOD AND SAND COCKTAIL

½ ounce Scotch whisky
½ ounce cherry brandy

½ ounce orange juice
½ ounce sweet vermouth

Shake well with cracked ice. Strain into cocktail glass.

BOBBY BURNS COCKTAIL

1½ ounces Scotch whisky
1 ounce sweet vermouth

3 dashes Benedictine

Stir with cracked ice. Strain into cocktail glass. Serve with twist of lemon peel.

BOOMERANG COCKTAIL

1 ounce rye or bourbon
¾ ounce dry vermouth
¾ ounce Swedish Punch

2 dashes lemon or lime juice
Dash of Angostura bitters

Shake with cracked ice. Strain into cocktail glass.

BROOKLYN COCKTAIL

2 ounces rye or bourbon
¾ ounce dry vermouth

Dash of maraschino liqueur
Dash of Angostura bitters

Shake with cracked ice. Strain into cocktail glass.

CANADIAN WHISKY COCKTAIL

1½ ounces Canadian whisky
2 dashes Angostura bitters

1 teaspoon fine grain sugar

Shake with cracked ice. Strain into cocktail glass.

FAN'S SPECIAL COCKTAIL

1 ounce Scotch whisky
½ ounce Cointreau

½ ounce fresh grapefruit juice

Shake with cracked ice. Strain into cocktail glass.

FRISCO COCKTAIL

1½ ounces bourbon

¾ ounce Benedictine

Stir in cracked ice. Strain into cocktail glass. Serve with twist of lemon peel.

HURRICANE COCKTAIL

¾ ounce white crème de menthe
¾ ounce rye or bourbon

¾ ounce dry gin
Juice of 1 lemon

Shake with cracked ice. Strain into cocktail glass.

IRISH COCKTAIL

1½ ounces Irish whisky
2 dashes Pernod
2 dashes curaçao

Dash of maraschino liqueur
Dash of Angostura bitters

Shake with cracked ice. Strain into cocktail glass. Serve with olive and piece of orange peel twisted over drink.

LOCH LOMOND COCKTAIL

1½ ounces Scotch whisky
3 dashes Angostura bitters

1 teaspoon fine grain sugar

Shake well with shaved ice. Strain into cocktail glass.

MANHATTAN

2 ounces rye
¾ ounce sweet vermouth

2 dashes Angostura bitters

Pour over cracked ice in mixing glass. Stir well to blend and dilute slightly. Strain into cocktail glass. Serve with cherry.

Rum or Scotch Manhattan: Use gold label rum or Scotch instead of rye.

Vodka Manhattan: Use 1½ ounces vodka instead of rye.

MANHATTAN (Dry)

2 ounces rye

½ ounce dry vermouth

Pour whisky and vermouth over cracked ice in mixing glass. Stir well to blend and dilute slightly. Strain into cocktail glass. Serve with twist of lemon peel.

DUBONNET MANHATTAN

1½ ounces Dubonnet
1½ ounces rye or bourbon

Dash of Angostura bitters

Pour over cracked ice in mixing glass. Stir well to blend and dilute very slightly. Strain into cocktail glass. Serve with cherry.

MILLIONAIRE COCKTAIL

1½ ounces rye or bourbon
½ ounce curaçao

Dash of grenadine
1 egg white

Shake well with cracked ice. Strain into large cocktail glass.

MIST COCKTAIL

2 ounces rye, bourbon, or Scotch
 whisky

Crushed ice
Twist of lemon peel

Fill Old-Fashioned glass with crushed ice. Pour whisky over it. Serve with twist of lemon peel and straws.

MONTE CARLO COCKTAIL

1½ ounces rye
½ ounce Benedictine

2 dashes Angostura bitters

Shake well with cracked ice. Strain into cocktail glass.

NEW ORLEANS COCKTAIL

1½ ounces bourbon
Dash of orange bitters
2 dashes Angostura bitters

Dash of anisette
2 dashes Pernod
½ lump sugar

Stir well with cracked ice. Strain into cocktail glass. Serve with twist of lemon peel.

NEW YORKER COCKTAIL

2 ounces rye
Juice of ½ lime

2 dashes grenadine
½ teaspoon bar syrup

Shake with cracked ice. Strain into cocktail glass. Serve with twist of lemon peel.

OLD-FASHIONED COCKTAIL #1

1 teaspoon fine grain sugar or bar
   syrup
2 twists lemon peel

1 or 2 dashes Angostura bitters
2 or 2½ ounces bourbon or rye
Several ice cubes

Put sugar, 1 twist of lemon peel, and bitters to taste in glass. Stir well. Add 1 ounce whisky. Allow to blend thoroughly. Add ice cubes. Add remaining whisky and lemon peel. Serve with a small bar spoon and a cherry. If desired, serve with a slice of orange and a stick of pineapple.

Variations: Applejack, gin, brandy, rum, Scotch, or vermouth may be used instead of bourbon or rye.

OLD-FASHIONED COCKTAIL #2

1 lump of sugar
2 or 3 dashes Angostura bitters
Splash of soda
2 ice cubes

Twist of lemon peel
Cherry
1½ ounces desired liquor

Splash the bitters onto the lump of sugar in Old-Fashioned glass. Add soda and muddle thoroughly. Add 2 ice cubes, lemon peel, cherry, and desired liquor (applejack, gin, brandy, rye, bourbon, rum, Scotch, or vermouth). Serve.

ON THE ROCKS

2 or 3 ounces rye, bourbon, or
   Scotch whisky

Several ice cubes
Twist of lemon peel

Pour whisky over ice cubes in an Old-Fashioned glass. Serve with twist of lemon peel.

ROB ROY COCKTAIL

1½ ounces Scotch whisky   2 dashes Angostura bitters
1 ounce sweet vermouth

Stir with cracked ice. Strain into cocktail glass. Serve with cherry or twist of lemon peel.

SHAMROCK COCKTAIL

1½ ounces Irish whisky   ½ ounce dry vermouth
½ ounce green crème de   3 dashes green Chartreuse
menthe

Stir with cracked ice. Strain into cocktail glass.

SCOTCH SIDE CAR

¾ ounce Cointreau   ¾ ounce lemon juice
1½ ounces Scotch whisky

Shake well with cracked ice. Strain into large cocktail glass.
Variations: Rye, bourbon, rum, or gin may be substituted for Scotch.

TIPPERARY COCKTAIL

¾ ounce Irish whisky   ¾ ounce green Chartreuse
¾ ounce sweet vermouth

Shake with cracked ice. Strain into cocktail glass.

T.N.T. COCKTAIL

¾ ounce whisky (rye, bourbon, or   ¾ ounce Pernod
Irish)

Shake with cracked ice. Strain into cocktail glass.

WALDORF COCKTAIL

¾ ounce bourbon   ¾ ounce Pernod
¾ ounce sweet vermouth   Dash of Angostura bitters

Shake well with cracked ice. Strain into cocktail glass.

WARD EIGHT #1

Juice of ½ lemon   ½ ounce grenadine
Juice of ½ orange (optional)   1½ ounces rye or bourbon

Shake with cracked ice. Pour unstrained into an 8 to 10 ounce tumbler. Fill with soda. Garnish with orange slice and cherry.

WARD EIGHT #2

1½ ounces rye or bourbon   Juice of ½ lemon
4 dashes grenadine

Shake with cracked ice. Serve in goblet with finely cracked ice. Serve with straws.

WHISKY COCKTAIL

1½ to 2 ounces rye or bourbon   Dash of bar syrup (optional)
3 dashes Angostura bitters

Stir well with cracked ice and strain into an over-size whisky glass.

ZAZARAC COCKTAIL

3 drops anisette or Pernod   1 ounce water
1½ ounces bourbon   5 drops Angostura or Peychaud's
½ ounce bar syrup   bitters

Add the anisette or Pernod to a well chilled Old-Fashioned glass. Swirl it around to coat glass thoroughly. Add remaining ingredients and 1 ice cube. Stir to blend. Squeeze a twist of lemon over top for oil. Serve with lemon peel in glass.

wine and wine service

WINE may be quite simply defined as the fermented juice of sound, ripe grapes which have been crushed after harvesting. There are many types of wines because there are many types of grapes, variations in soil, climates, and methods of cultivation and production. An extremely small percentage of the wines of any country is considered "fine" wine. A little larger percentage is considered moderately excellent wine and the remainder is just ordinary but wholesome wine.

The wine is "fine" when all elements of it are perfectly balanced. This occurs only when climatic conditions are ideal during the spring, summer, and fall (the so-called "vintage" year), on land situated to take full advantage of these conditions, on soil that contains the requisite chemical properties, and only with grapevines that are receptive to these ideal conditions. For example, in France, the largest producer in the world of "fine" wines, these ideal soil and climatic conditions may exist on one hillside of a small valley and ordinary wine may be produced from the same type of grapes grown on the opposite side of that same valley.

The principal types of wines are red and white, dry and sweet, natural and fortified, still and sparkling, and apéritif wines.

Red Wines: A wine is red (this includes the many shades of pink and brown) when the skins of dark grapes are permitted to remain in the juice during fermentation. The alcohol dissolves the coloring of the skins. Or, it may be red because special coloring wines have been added. Famous red wines include port, claret, cabernet, burgundy, chianti, and zinfandel.

White Wines: A wine is white if made from white grapes or if the skins have been removed from dark grapes before fermentation. Well-known white wines include sherry, Madeira, sauterne, chablis, Malaga, Graves, Rhine wine (also called riesling or hock), Moselle, marsala, tokay, muscatel, and champagne.

Dry Wines: Refers to wines without sweetness; those in which most, if not all of the grape sugar has been converted into alcohol.

Sweet Wines: Refers to wines in which varying amounts of grape sugar remain unconverted, or those to which special sweetening wine has been added.

Natural Wines: Refers to wines that are pure and unadulterated except with certain minor additions that have proven by time and practice to be beneficial and harmless.

Fortified Wines: Refers to wines to which spirits or brandy have been added in order to either achieve a particular result as to character, or to preserve the wines in very hot climates.

Still Wines: Wines are still if the carbonic gas formed through fermentation has completely escaped before the wine is bottled.

Sparkling Wines: Wines are sparkling if the carbonic gas which has been created by an added fermentation or artificially introduced has been retained in the bottle.

Apéritif Wines: Usually refers to the vermouths and such brand name wines as Dubonnet, Byrrh, Amer Picon, etc., which are not true wines but have been modified with the addition of herbs, spices, roots, seed, flowers, and other flavoring materials which have been steeped in the wines for varying periods. Apéritif or appetizer wines are so called because they are favored for cocktail use and before-meal drinking. Dry Sherry, a fortified wine, is also commonly used as an appetizer wine.

SERVING WINES

The amount of misinformation regarding wines is so tremendous and the number of "do's" and "don'ts" about wine service that have been enumerated by so-called connoisseurs are so great in number that the average host or hostess hesitates to serve wines. Yet for hundreds and even thousands of years before this long list of rules was developed, wine added much pleasure to dining and entertaining. It certainly is not necessary, then, to memorize these numerous and complex rules before serving wine.

The few simple suggestions which follow are based on the assumption that one drinks and serves wines for enjoyment. They are based on the preferences of the vast majority of wine drinkers who do abide by certain preferences in order to get the maximum enjoyment from drinking wine. In addition, a chart is offered for the benefit of those people who would like to know the rules laid down for "formal" dinners where a variety of wines may be served, and specific types of wines chosen for each course

1. Remember that really "fine" wines are rare treats for special occasions. The important consideration when choosing a table wine for ordinary occasions is that the wine should be sound—and that does not mean high-priced. Choose good domestic products rather than dubious imported wines. Your guests will be more impressed, if they know anything about wines, with a sound wine rather than one that has a fancy, foreign label. If they are uninformed, you may enjoy the pleasure of starting their education.

2. Unless you have the necessary cool wine cellar, buy only enough wine to fill immediate needs. Wines may deteriorate rapidly in a warm closet.

3. Buy from a well-informed, reputable dealer who may be a storehouse of reliable information in guiding you and helping you avoid impressive names that would just cause you to waste money.

4. It is quite proper to serve only one wine with a meal. For this purpose select a plain wine such as a medium dry sherry or claret. One good wine is far simpler and more palatable than half a dozen of doubtful quality. For formal occasions, champagne or any other sparkling wine is often served throughout a meal.

5. Red or white light wines may be served with almost any dish. Avoid, however, serving dry wines with sweet dishes or foods that have sweet sauces and avoid serving red wines with shellfish. This last is one of the few basic rules that have come down to us that seems to make sense. For some inexplicable reason shellfish seems to have a property that makes red wine taste unpleasantly metallic to some people. If it doesn't have that effect on you then there is no reason why you shouldn't forget about it, insofar as your own preferences are concerned, but remember that such may not be the case with your guests. Your own experience will tell you that a dry wine would not necessarily go well with sweet dishes nor would a very sweet wine go well with the usual foods in a meal, for the same reason that you wouldn't serve candy with roast beef.

6. Experience indicates that most Americans like their wines, whether red or white, slightly chilled. This is quite contrary to the rule that red still wines should always be served at room temperature. Most people like white wines slightly colder than red wines but this, too, is a matter of personal preference. The ideal temperature for white wines is 45° F. to 50° F. Sparkling wines should always be well-chilled. Champagne, for example, is at its best when served at a temperature of 40° F. or slightly less. To chill wine thoroughly, place the bottle in a refrigerator for an hour or two and then in a wine cooler (a bucket of ice) for 20 to 30 minutes. If you plan to serve a wine at room temperature, allow it to stand in the room where it is to be served for several hours. Never warm wine artificially or it will spoil.

7. A few customs have entrenched themselves so well that they have become almost traditional. They include the service of white wines with hors d'oeuvres, fish, and white meats, and the service of red wines with cheeses, salads, and dark meats—the serving of white wines before red wines, and dry wines before sweet wines. The reasons for some of these are obvious as explained in number 5 above. Others have grown out of the fact that white wines are not generally as full flavored as the reds and, as a result, may be a happier choice with the more delicately flavored dishes, and red wines which are usually more fully flavored may make a better accompaniment for the more highly flavored and seasoned dishes. We offer these traditional suggestions only as a guide. Each person should, in the last analysis, be guided by personal preferences.

WINE AND FOOD COMBINATIONS

These are the most popular wine and food combinations. But there are no rules! The "correct" wine is the one **you** like best.

APPETIZER WINES *SUCH AS:* Sherry Vermouth Flavored Wines	*Serve chilled, without food or with* HORS d'OEUVRE NUTS, CHEESES 
RED DINNER WINES *SUCH AS:* Burgundy Claret Rosé (Pink)	*Serve at cool room temperature, with* HEARTY DISHES: STEAKS, CHOPS, ROASTS, GAME, CHEESE DISHES, SPAGHETTI *(Serve Rosé chilled, with any food.)*
WHITE DINNER WINES *SUCH AS:* Chablis Rhine Wine Sauterne	*Serve well chilled, with* LIGHTER DISHES: CHICKEN, FISH, SHELLFISH, OMELETS, ANY WHITE MEATS 
DESSERT WINES *SUCH AS:* Port Muscatel Tokay Cream (Sweet) Sherry	*Serve chilled or at cool room temperature, with* FRUITS, COOKIES, NUTS, CHEESES, FRUIT CAKES, POUND CAKES
SPARKLING WINES *SUCH AS:* Champagne Sparkling Burgundy	*Serve well chilled, with any food:* APPETIZERS, THE MAIN COURSE, OR DESSERTS  *(And especially good in festive party punches)*

WINES AND WINE SERVING

Left-hand column shows how to serve various wine types using the *all-purpose 9-ounce glass* recommended by California's wine growers. Right-hand column shows traditional glasses for these wine types.

ALL-PURPOSE GLASS (9-oz.)	WINE TYPES	TRADITIONAL GLASSES
APPETIZER WINES	SHERRY VERMOUTH FLAVORED WINES	2½ to 4-ounce capacity
RED DINNER WINES (INCLUDING ROSÉ WINE)	BURGUNDY Pinot Noir (pea-no no-ahr) CLARET Cabernet (kab-er-nay) Zinfandel (zin-fan-dell) "VINO" TYPES (vee-no) ROSE (Pink) (roh-zay) Red Chianti (kee-ahn-tee)	6 to 9-ounce capacity
WHITE DINNER WINES	SAUTERNE (so-tairn) Semillon (say-mee-yonh) Sauvignon Blanc (so-vee-nyonh blanh) RHINE WINE Riesling (reez-ling) Sylvaner (sil-vah-ner) CHABLIS (shah-blee) Pinot Blanc (pea-no blanh) Chardonnay (shar-doh-nay)	5 to 8-oz. capacity Rhine Wines Other White Wines
DESSERT WINES	PORT MUSCATEL (muss-kah-tell) TOKAY (toh-kay) CREAM (SWEET) SHERRY	2½ to 4-ounce capacity
SPARKLING WINES	CHAMPAGNE (sham-pain) Brut (very dry) (brewt) Sec (semi-dry) (sehk) Doux (sweet) (doo) SPARKLING BURGUNDY	5 to 8-oz. Saucer Tulip

Wine experts agree that no wine glass should ever be filled completely. Air space left above the wine helps to concentrate the wine's bouquet, to add to your enjoyment. It is recommended that you fill the glasses to the levels shown above. Levels in the all-purpose glass in the left-hand column show the usual amount served of each wine type, when this glass is used.

HOW TO KEEP WINES

In caring for wines you must distinguish between natural and fortified wines. Natural wines continue to change after being bottled. They have to be kept tightly sealed to keep out all air. If these wines are allowed to stand up for any length of time the corks will dry up enough to allow air to come in and permit additional fermentation which, in time, will cause the wine to turn sour. For this reason it is necessary to store all wines which have an alcoholic content of 14 per cent or less with the bottles on their sides and with the corks slightly down so that they will be kept moist by the wine. After a bottle is opened, keep it in the refrigerator or it may turn sour in just a few days. Fortified wines have had sufficient alcohol added to them to prevent further fermentation. On opening there is no danger from further fermentation.

wine cocktails

ADONIS COCKTAIL

¾ *ounce sweet vermouth*   2 *dashes orange bitters*
1½ *ounces dry sherry*

Stir well in cracked ice. Strain into cocktail glass.

BAMBOO COCKTAIL

1½ *ounces sherry*   2 *dashes Angostura bitters*
1½ *ounces dry vermouth*

Stir well with cracked ice. Strain into cocktail glass.

BRAZIL COCKTAIL

1½ *ounces sherry*   *Dash of Angostura bitters*
1 *ounce dry vermouth*   *Dash of Pernod*

Combine in cocktail glass. Add a squeeze of lemon peel on top for oil. Stir gently.

BYRRH COCKTAIL

¾ *ounce Byrrh*   ¾ *ounce whisky*
¾ *ounce dry vermouth*

Stir well with cracked ice. Strain into cocktail glass. Serve with twist of lemon peel.

CHAMPAGNE COCKTAIL #1

1 *lump sugar*   *Stick of pineapple*
Angostura or Peychaud's bitters   *Champagne*
Half slice of orange

Serve in "saucer" champagne glass. Place lump of sugar in glass. Saturate it with bitters. Fill with chilled champagne. Serve with orange slice and pineapple stick against opposite sides of glass.

CHAMPAGNE COCKTAIL #2

1 ounce Southern Comfort
Dash of Angostura or Peychaud's
    bitters

Twist of lemon peel
Cherry

Combine in a large "saucer" champagne glass. Fill with well chilled champagne.

COFFEE COCKTAIL #1

2 ounces port wine
½ ounce brandy

Dash of curaçao
1 teaspoon fine grain sugar

Shake with cracked ice. Strain into large cocktail glass or wine glass. Serve with grating of nutmeg on top.

COFFEE COCKTAIL #2

1½ ounces port wine
½ ounce brandy

¼ teaspoon fine grain sugar
1 whole egg

Shake well with cracked ice. Strain into large cocktail glass.

DIPLOMACY COCKTAIL

1½ ounces dry vermouth
¾ ounce sweet vermouth

Dash of maraschino liqueur

Stir with cracked ice. Strain into cocktail glass.

DUBONNET COCKTAIL

1 ounce Dubonnet

1 ounce dry gin

Stir with large pieces of ice. Strain into glass. If desired, twist lemon peel over glass and add a dash of orange bitters or of dry vermouth.
Dubonnet Dry Cocktail: Use 1½ ounces dry gin and ¾ ounce Dubonnet.

FIG LEAF COCKTAIL

1½ ounces sweet vermouth
1 ounce white label rum

Juice of ½ lime
Dash of Angostura bitters

Shake with cracked ice. Strain into cocktail glass.

HARVARD WINE COCKTAIL

1 ounce dry vermouth   Dash of orange bitters
¾ ounce brandy

Stir with cracked ice. Strain into cocktail glass. Fill with soda.

MERRY WIDOW COCKTAIL #1

1½ ounces Dubonnet or Byrrh   1½ ounces dry vermouth or dry
     gin

Stir well with cracked ice. Strain into cocktail glass. Serve with twist of lemon peel.

MERRY WIDOW COCKTAIL #2

1 ounce dry gin   2 dashes Benedictine
1 ounce dry vermouth   2 dashes Angostura or Peychaud's
2 dashes Pernod   bitters

Stir with cracked ice. Strain into cocktail glass. Serve with twist of lemon peel.

PERFECT COCKTAIL

¾ ounce dry vermouth   ¾ ounce dry gin
¾ ounce sweet vermouth

Shake well with cracked ice. Strain into cocktail glass. Serve with twist of lemon peel.

PORT WINE SANGAREE

½ teaspoon fine grain sugar   2¼ ounces port wine
¾ ounce water

Stir with cracked ice. Strain into cocktail glass.

QUEEN ELIZABETH WINE COCKTAIL

1 ounce dry vermouth   ½ ounce lime or lemon juice
½ ounce Benedictine

Shake with cracked ice. Strain into cocktail glass.

SHERRY COCKTAIL

2½ ounces sherry   3 dashes orange bitters
3 dashes dry vermouth

Stir with cracked ice. Strain into cocktail glass.

SHERRY AND EGG

Place 1 teaspoon sherry in a cocktail glass. Add a whole fresh egg, keeping yolk intact. Fill the glass with chilled sherry wine until egg floats.

SHERRY TWIST COCKTAIL

1½ ounces sherry
½ ounce dry vermouth
½ ounce brandy

½ ounce Cointreau
¼ teaspoon lemon juice
1 small piece of cinnamon

Shake with cracked ice. Strain into large cocktail glass.

TROPICAL COCKTAIL

1 ounce dry vermouth
½ ounce crème de cacao
½ ounce maraschino liqueur

Dash of orange bitters
Dash of Angostura bitters

Shake with cracked ice. Strain into cocktail glass.

VERMOUTH COCKTAIL #1

1½ ounces dry or sweet vermouth   3 dashes Angostura bitters

Stir with cracked ice. Strain into cocktail glass. Serve with slice ot lemon.

VERMOUTH COCKTAIL #2

2 ounces sweet vermouth
½ teaspoon curaçao
1 teaspoon Amer Picon

½ teaspoon fine grain sugar
Dash of Angostura bitters

Shake with cracked ice. Strain into cocktail glass. Serve with twist of lemon peel and a cherry.

VERMOUTH FRAPPE

2 *ounces sweet vermouth*   *Dash of Angostura bitters*

Shake with shaved ice until glass frosts. Strain and serve.

VERMOUTH APERITIF

Serve 3 ounces sweet vermouth, chilled or with cracked ice, in a cocktail glass. Twist a piece of lemon peel over drink, or add a couple of drops of lemon bitters.

VERMOUTH HALF 'N' HALF

½ *dry vermouth*   ½ *sweet vermouth*

Stir and serve with cracked ice in a cocktail glass.

ZAZA COCKTAIL #1

1 *ounce sherry*   1 *ounce Dubonnet*

Stir with cracked ice. Strain into cocktail glass.

ZAZA COCKTAIL #2

1 *ounce Byrrh*   1 *ounce sloe gin*

Stir with cracked ice. Strain into cocktail glass.

miscellaneous cocktails

AKVAVIT COCKTAIL

2 ounces akvavit   ¾ ounce dry vermouth

Stir with cracked ice. Strain into cocktail glass.

ALLIES COCKTAIL

¾ ounce sweet vermouth   ¾ ounce kümmel
¾ ounce dry gin

Stir with cracked ice. Strain into cocktail glass.

AMERICAN BEAUTY COCKTAIL

½ ounce brandy   ½ ounce orange juice
½ ounce dry vermouth   Dash of white crème de menthe
½ ounce grenadine

Shake with cracked ice. Strain into cocktail glass. Top with port wine.

BETWEEN-THE-SHEETS #1

¾ ounce gold label rum   ¾ ounce brandy
¾ ounce Cointreau   Juice of ½ lime or lemon

Shake with cracked ice. Strain into cocktail glass.

BETWEEN-THE-SHEETS #2

¾ ounce triple sec   ¾ ounce cognac
¾ ounce white label rum   Dash of lemon juice (optional)

Shake with cracked ice. Strain into cocktail glass.

CAFE AU KIRSCH #1

1 ounce kirsch   1 egg white
1 ounce cognac   1 ounce cold black coffee

Shake very thoroughly with shaved ice. Strain into wine glass.

CAFE AU KIRSCH #2

1 ounce kirsch   1 teaspoon fine grain sugar
1 ounce cold black coffee   1 egg white

Shake well with cracked ice. Strain into large wine glass.

COFFEE COCKTAIL #3

¾ ounce brandy   ¾ ounce cold black coffee
¾ ounce Cointreau

Shake with cracked ice. Strain into cocktail glass.

CORONATION COCKTAIL

1 ounce dry gin   1 ounce Dubonnet
1 ounce dry vermouth

Stir well with cracked ice. Strain into cocktail glass.

TEQUILA COCKTAIL #1

2 ounces tequila   Juice of ½ lime
1 teaspoon fine grain sugar

Shake with cracked ice. Strain into cocktail glass.

TEQUILA COCKTAIL #2

2 ounces tequila   4 dashes curaçao
Juice of ½ lime

Shake well with cracked ice. Strain into cocktail glass.

after dinner drinks

THE group of drinks offered in this section include the most popularly accepted versions of many old-time favorites; however, they should serve only as a guide. Actually any of the vast variety of cordials may be served "neat" in a cordial glass or as a frappé in a large cocktail glass as suggested in the recipe for Frappés. Many new and interesting flavors are developed each year in cordials and many of them may be substituted in the recipes that follow. If you plan to serve cordials after dinner see the suggestions in the entry on cordials and liqueurs in the Bartender's Dictionary.

AFTER DINNER COCKTAIL

1 ounce apricot brandy   4 dashes lemon juice
1 ounce curaçao

Shake with cracked ice. Strain into cocktail glass.

AFTER DINNER SPECIAL

¾ ounce peach liqueur   ¾ ounce curaçao or triple sec

Shake well with cracked ice. Strain into cocktail glass.

ANGEL'S KISS

¼ ounce crème de cacao   ¼ ounce sweet cream
¼ ounce crème yvette   ¼ ounce brandy

Pour ingredients carefully off the back of a teaspoon into a liqueur glass so that ingredients will form separate layers.

ANGEL'S TIP #1

⅓ crème de cacao   ⅓ heavy cream
⅓ maraschino liqueur

Use a cordial glass and add each of the 3 ingredients in the order listed, gently floating one on top of the other to form 3 layers.

ANGEL'S TIP #2

1½ ounces maraschino liqueur   Red maraschino cherry
1 tablespoon whipped cream

Pour liqueur into sherry glass. Top with whipped cream. Place a red cherry in the exact center.

ANISETTE COCKTAIL #2

¾ ounce anisette   ¾ ounce triple sec

Shake with shaved ice. Strain into cocktail glass.

APRICOT BRANDY AFTER DINNER SPECIAL

1 ounce apricot brandy   1 ounce triple sec or orange
                               curaçao

Shake with cracked ice. Strain into cocktail glass.

B & B

½ ounce Benedictine   ½ ounce brandy

Blend in a liqueur glass.

CREME DE MENTHE FRAPPE #1

Add 2 ounces crème de menthe to a shaker full of shaved ice. Shake until glass is frosted. Strain into cocktail glass.

CREME DE MENTHE FRAPPE #2

Fill a cocktail glass with finely shaved ice. Add 2 ounces crème de menthe. Serve with short straws.

DIANA

Use a tall narrow-stemmed glass. Fill with shaved ice. Add 1½ ounces white crème de menthe. Top with 1 ounce brandy. Serve with short straws.

FLOATS

Fill a small liqueur glass ¾ full of crème de cacao, peach brandy, or other brandies or liqueurs. Float sweet cream on top.

FRAPPES

Fill a large cocktail glass with finely shaved ice. Add desired liqueur and serve with straws. Garnish with fruit.

GRASSHOPPER #1

1 *ounce crème de menthe*   1 *ounce crème de cacao*

Pour slowly into liqueur glass.

GRASSHOPPER #2

1 *ounce white crème de menthe*   1 *ounce heavy sweet cream*
1 *ounce green crème de menthe*

Shake with finely cracked ice. Strain into large cocktail glass.

POUSSE CAFE

Pour 5 to 7 different cordials off the back of a spoon into a liqueur glass so that they form colorful layers. It requires a steady hand and patience. Start with the heaviest cordials first. Top with a float of brandy. Suggested combinations follow.

POUSSE CAFE #1

$\frac{1}{6}$ *grenadine* $\frac{1}{6}$ *orange curaçao*
$\frac{1}{6}$ *crème de cacao* $\frac{1}{6}$ *crème yvette*
$\frac{1}{6}$ *maraschino liqueur* $\frac{1}{6}$ *brandy*

POUSSE CAFE #2

$\frac{1}{7}$ *raspberry liqueur* $\frac{1}{7}$ *yellow Chartreuse*
$\frac{1}{7}$ *anisette* $\frac{1}{7}$ *green Chartreuse*
$\frac{1}{7}$ *Parfait Amour* $\frac{1}{7}$ *brandy*
$\frac{1}{7}$ *crème yvette*

RAINBOW

$\frac{1}{7}$ *crème de violette* $\frac{1}{7}$ *green Chartreuse*
$\frac{1}{7}$ *crème de cacao* $\frac{1}{7}$ *maraschino liqueur*
$\frac{1}{7}$ *yellow Chartreuse* $\frac{1}{7}$ *brandy*
$\frac{1}{7}$ *Benedictine*

Pour carefully off the back of a spoon into a liqueur glass so that the liqueurs form separate layers.

SAM WARD

Fill a cocktail glass with fine ice. Put inside glass, around the edge, a circle of lemon peel. Fill with yellow Chartreuse.

STARS AND STRIPES

⅓ *crème de cassis*   ⅓ *green Chartreuse*
⅓ *maraschino liqueur*

Pour ingredients carefully into a liqueur glass so that they do not mix.

UNION JACK

⅓ *grenadine*   ⅓ *green Chartreuse*
⅓ *maraschino liqueur*

Pour ingredients carefully into liqueur glass so that they do not mix.

WINDY CORNER

Stir 2 ounces blackberry liqueur with ice. Strain into cocktail glass. Top with grated nutmeg.

miscellaneous drinks

BRANDY FLOAT

Fill an Old-Fashioned glass nearly full of soda. Put the bowl of a tea-spoon on top and pour 1 ounce of brandy slowly into the spoon, allowing it to flow gently over the top of the soda. Slide the spoon out carefully so as not to disturb the floating brandy.

BRANDY CRUSTA COCKTAIL

Moisten the edge of a small wine glass with lemon and rub edge into powdered sugar to frost edge. Combine in a mixing glass:

1½ ounces brandy
½ ounce curaçao
3 dashes maraschino liqueur

1 dash Angostura bitters
4 dashes lemon juice

Add cracked ice, stir, and strain into prepared glass. Serve with a slice of orange.

Gin or Rum Crusta: Substitute dry gin or gold label rum for brandy.

COBBLERS

Cobblers are attractive tall drinks made with lots of finely cracked ice, attractively garnished with fruit and berries. To make the standard cobbler fill a large goblet with finely cracked ice. Add 3 ounces of burgundy, claret, sauterne, sherry, port, or Rhine wine; brandy, white label rum, or your favorite whisky. Add a teaspoon of fine grain sugar or bar syrup. Stir well. Decorate with slices of orange, small sticks of pineapple, and if desired berries and a sprig of mint. Serve with straws and a small spoon.

CHAMPAGNE COBBLER

½ teaspoon lemon juice
½ teaspoon curaçao

Champagne to fill glass

Fill a large goblet ⅔ full of finely cracked ice. Add lemon juice and curaçao. Stir well. Decorate with a slice of orange and pineapple stick. Fill with chilled champagne. Stir slightly. Serve with straw.

RUM COBBLER

2 ounces gold label rum   2 dashes curaçao
2 dashes lemon juice

Fill a large goblet with finely cracked ice. Add the ingredients and stir well. Garnish with fruits and berries and, if desired, a sprig of mint.

SHERRY COBBLER

3 ounces medium or sweet sherry   1 teaspoon orange juice
1 teaspoon fine grain sugar

Dissolve the sugar in the orange juice in a tall tumbler. Add enough finely cracked ice to fill glass about ¾ full. Add sherry and fill glass with soda. Garnish with fruit. Serve with straw.

FLIPS

2 ounces liquor or wine   1 egg
1 teaspoon fine grain sugar

Shake vigorously with cracked ice. Strain into large wine glass. Top with grating of nutmeg.

Variations: Use any of the following liquors or wines in flips: claret, port, or sherry wine, bourbon or rye whisky, white or gold label rum, brandy or blackberry or cherry brandy.

PORTO FLIP

4 ounces port wine   1 ounce heavy cream
1 egg   Dash of Benedictine

Shake vigorously with cracked ice. Strain into goblet. Top with grating of nutmeg.

WHISKY-PEPPERMINT FLIP

Add ¼ ounce of essence of peppermint to a regular flip made with rye whisky.

SMASHES

1 teaspoon fine grain sugar   1½ ounces dry gin
2 sprigs fresh mint

Combine sugar and mint in an Old-Fashioned glass. Add just enough water to dissolve sugar. Crush mint with a muddler. Add ½ glass cracked ice and the gin. Add a squirt of soda. Stir slightly.

Variations: Use brandy, rye, bourbon, Scotch or rum instead of gin.

SOURS

2 ounces rye or bourbon   ½ teaspoon fine grain sugar
½ ounce lemon or lime juice

Shake with cracked ice. Strain into Delmonico glass. Garnish with slice of orange and a cherry. If desired, add a squirt of soda water.

Variations: Use applejack, brandy, gin, Scotch, or rum instead of rye or bourbon.

Note: A large cocktail glass will serve the purpose if you don't have Delmonico glasses.

COGNAC SOUR

1½ ounces cognac   ¾ ounce lemon juice
 2 dashes Angostura bitters 1 teaspoon fine grain sugar

Shake with cracked ice. Strain into sour glass. Garnish with fruit.

FIREMAN'S SOUR

2 ounces Bacardi rum   ½ ounce grenadine
Juice of 1 lime   ½ teaspoon fine grain sugar

Shake with cracked ice. Strain into sour glass. Garnish with slice of orange and a cherry. If desired, add a squirt of soda water.

ROCK AND RYE SOUR

1½ ounces rock and rye   Juice of ½ lemon

Shake in finely cracked ice. Strain into sour glass. Garnish with fruit.

SARATOGA SOUR

Add 1 egg white to Sour recipe.

SLOE GIN SOUR

1½ ounces sloe gin   ¼ teaspoon fine grain sugar
Juice of ½ lemon

Shake with cracked ice. Strain into sour glass. Fill with soda. Garnish with fruit.

BRANDY SHRUB

Rinds of 2 lemons
Juice of 5 lemons
2 quarts brandy

1 quart sherry
2 pounds sugar

Cut the rinds into very thin pieces. Combine with juice and brandy. Cover and let stand for 3 days. Then add sherry and sugar. Mix thoroughly until sugar has dissolved. Run through a jelly bag, then bottle for use. Serve hot or cold, diluting with hot or cold water.

RUM SHRUB

1½ quarts orange juice
1 pound sugar

1 gallon rum

Mix together and pour into a small cask. Let stand for 6 weeks, then bottle for use. Serve hot or cold, diluting with hot or cold water.

BRANDY FIX

1 ounce brandy
1 ounce cherry brandy

½ ounce lemon juice
1 teaspoon fine grain sugar

Fill an 8-ounce tumbler ⅔ full of shaved ice. Add the ingredients. Stir slowly to dissolve sugar. Serve with a slice of lemon.

GIN FIX

2 ounces dry gin
1 ounce water

1 teaspoon fine grain sugar
½ ounce lemon juice

Fill an 8-ounce tumbler ⅔ full of shaved ice. Add the ingredients. Stir slowly to dissolve sugar. Decorate with a variety of fruits.

WHISKY FIX

Substitute rye or bourbon in Gin Fix.

RUM FIX

2 ounces white label rum
½ ounce lemon juice

1 teaspoon fine grain sugar
Dash of curaçao

Fill an 8-ounce tumbler ⅔ full of shaved ice. Add the ingredients. Stir slowly to dissolve sugar. Decorate with a variety of fruits.

eggnogs and milk punches

EGGNOG

1 egg
1 teaspoon fine grain sugar

2 ounces brandy
8 ounces fresh milk

Shake well with cracked ice. Strain into a tall glass. Serve with grated nutmeg on top.

Variations: Substitute gin, port, rum, sherry, or whisky for brandy.

BREAKFAST EGGNOG

1½ ounces brandy
½ ounce curaçao

1 whole egg
4 ounces milk

Shake with cracked ice. Strain into highball glass. Serve with grated nutmeg on top.

EGGNOG BALTIMORE

1 egg yolk
Grated nutmeg
1 tablespoon fine grain sugar
½ ounce brandy

¼ ounce Madeira wine
¼ ounce white label rum
Milk

Beat egg yolk with nutmeg until creamy. Combine with other ingredients except milk in a shaker. Add a few large pieces of cracked ice. Shake well. Strain into a highball glass. Fill with chilled milk.

NEW YEAR'S EGGNOG

10 eggs, separated
1¼ pounds fine grain sugar
1 quart brandy

12 ounces white label rum
1 gallon milk

Beat egg yolks until light. Add sugar, brandy, and rum. Stir until sugar is dissolved. Add milk, slowly, stirring continually. Beat whites of eggs to a stiff froth and add to top of mixture. Fill glasses, putting some egg white on top. Grate a little nutmeg over each serving. Makes about forty-eight 4-ounce servings.

CRAZY COW PUNCH

1½ ounces whisky
1 teaspoon fine grain sugar

Milk

Dissolve sugar in whisky. Add finely shaved ice. Shake until glass frosts. Strain into 10-ounce highball glass. Add 2 ice cubes and milk to fill glass. Top with grated nutmeg.

Variations: Use applejack, brandy, or gold label rum instead of whisky.

MILK PUNCH

2 ounces whisky, brandy, or gold label rum
8 ounces milk
1 teaspoon fine grain sugar

Shake with cracked ice. Strain into a tall glass. Serve with grated nutmeg on top.

long drinks

BLACK VELVET

Use ½ chilled champagne and ½ chilled stout. Pour simultaneously and slowly into a 14-ounce collins glass.

BRANDY AND SODA

Pour 1½ ounces brandy into an 8-ounce glass. Add 2 ice cubes and fill with soda. Stir slightly.

GIN BUCK

2 ounces dry gin   Juice of ½ lime or lemon

Pour into 10-ounce highball glass. Add ice cubes and fill with ginger ale.

RUM BUCK

2 ounces gold label rum   ½ teaspoon lemon juice
1 ounce Cointreau   ½ teaspoon fine grain sugar

Shake with cracked ice. Strain into highball glass. Add lump of ice. Fill with soda.

BYRRH CASSIS

3 ounces Byrrh   1½ ounces créme de cassis

Add to ice cubes in a small highball glass. Fill with soda. Stir slightly.

APPLEJACK COOLER

1 tablespoon fine grain sugar 1½ ounces applejack
Juice of ½ lemon or 1 lime

Shake well with cracked ice. Strain into highball glass. Add ice cubes. Fill with soda.

APRICOT COOLER

Juice of ½ lemon 2 dashes grenadine
Juice of ½ lime 1 ounce apricot brandy

Shake well with cracked ice. Strain into highball glass. Add ice cubes. Fill with soda.

BISHOP'S COOLER

3 ounces burgundy wine ½ ounce lemon juice
½ ounce Jamaica or gold label 1 teaspoon fine grain sugar
  rum 2 dashes Angostura bitters
1 ounce orange juice

Pour all ingredients into 10-ounce highball glass. Add fine ice to fill glass and stir.

CLARET LEMONADE

Juice of 1 lemon 3 ounces claret wine
2 teaspoons fine grain sugar 3 ounces water

Shake well with cracked ice. Strain into 10-ounce highball glass. Add ice cubes and serve.

CUBAN COOLER

Pour 2 ounces Cuban rum over ice cubes in a highball glass. Fill with ginger ale. Twist a piece of lemon or lime peel over top and drop into glass.

GIN COOLER

2 ounces dry gin 1 teaspoon fine grain sugar

Dissolve sugar in gin. Add to tumbler with cracked ice. Fill with soda.

Variations: Substitute 2 ounces gold label rum or whisky, or 3 ounces wine for gin.

LONE TREE COOLER

Juice of 1 lemon
Juice of ¼ orange
1 ounce grenadine

1 ounce dry gin
½ ounce dry vermouth

Shake well with cracked ice. Strain into a highball glass. Add ice cubes. Fill with soda.

MANHATTAN COOLER

Juice of ½ lemon or lime
½ tablespoon fine grain sugar

4 ounces claret wine
3 dashes gold label rum

Stir well with cracked ice. Strain into a highball glass. Add ice cubes. Fill with soda. Garnish with fruit.

ORANGE BLOSSOM COOLER

Juice of ½ orange
1 teaspoon fine grain sugar

1½ ounces dry gin

Shake with cracked ice. Strain into a highball glass. Add ice cubes. Fill with soda. Garnish with fruit.

REMSEN COOLER

1½ ounces Scotch whisky

Peel of ½ lemon

Cut the lemon peel in spiral form. Place in highball glass with 2 ice cubes and whisky. Fill with chilled soda.

WHISKY COOLER

Juice of ½ lemon
1 teaspoon fine grain sugar

3 ounces rye or bourbon
Ginger ale

Dissolve the sugar in the lemon juice in a highball glass. Add ice cubes and the rye or bourbon. Fill with ginger ale. Stir slightly.

WHITE WINE COOLER

1 tablespoon bar syrup
3 ounces soda

White wine

Pour bar syrup over ice cubes in a highball glass. Add soda. Fill glass with white wine. Garnish with a half slice of orange and a sprig of mint.

RED WINE COOLER

2 teaspoons fine grain sugar   Red wine
4 teaspoons orange juice

Dissolve sugar in a little water. Add orange juice. Pour over ice cubes in a highball glass. Fill with red wine. Garnish with a lemon slice.

CUBA LIBRE

Juice and whole rind of ½ lime   1½ ounces white label rum

Squeeze the juice into a 10-ounce collins glass. Drop in the lime rind. Add ice cubes. Fill with cola beverage. Stir slightly.

GIN DAISY

1½ ounces dry gin   3 dashes grenadine or raspberry
Juice of ½ lemon   syrup

Stir into a large goblet half filled with shaved ice. Add a squirt of soda. Garnish with fruit and a sprig of mint.

Variations: Substitute applejack, brandy, gold label rum, or whisky for gin.

RUM DAISY SPECIAL

Juice of ½ lemon   1 teaspoon fine grain sugar
Juice of ½ lime   1 teaspoon raspberry syrup
Juice of ½ orange   1½ ounces white label rum

Shake with cracked ice. Strain into a highball glass. Fill with soda.
June Daisy: Substitute dry gin for rum in Rum Daisy Special.

GIN FIZZ

2 ounces dry gin   Juice of ½ lime
Juice of ½ lemon   1 teaspoon fine grain sugar

Shake well with cracked ice. Strain into an 8-ounce highball glass. Add 1 ice cube. Fill with soda.

ALABAMA FIZZ

Garnish Gin Fizz with a sprig or two of mint.

BRANDY FIZZ

Substitute brandy for gin in Gin Fizz.

GOLDEN FIZZ

Add yolk of 1 egg to Gin Fizz.

SILVER FIZZ

Add white of 1 egg to Gin Fizz.

SLOE GIN FIZZ

Substitute sloe gin for dry gin in Gin Fizz.

SOUTHSIDE FIZZ

Same as Alabama Fizz.

DUBONNET FIZZ

2 ounces Dubonnet   ½ ounce lemon juice
1 ounce cherry brandy   1½ ounces orange juice

Shake with cracked ice. Strain into an 8-ounce highball glass. Fill with soda.

MORNING GLORY FIZZ

1½ ounces Scotch or bourbon   1 egg white
Juice of 1 lemon   2 dashes Pernod
1 teaspoon fine grain sugar

Shake with cracked ice. Strain into glass. Add ice cube and soda.

NEW ORLEANS FIZZ

2 ounces dry gin   1 teaspoon fine grain sugar
Juice of ½ lime   1 egg white
Juice of ½ lemon   1 ounce sweet cream

Shake vigorously with cracked ice. Strain into a 10-ounce glass. Add a couple of squirts of soda. This drink should be thick.

RAMOZ FIZZ

Juice of ½ lime   2 ounces dry gin
Juice of ½ lemon   3 dashes orange flower water
1 ounce sweet cream   1 egg white

Shake vigorously with cracked ice until glass frosts. Pour into a 10-ounce glass with the edge frosted by rubbing with a piece of lemon and then dipping in powdered sugar. Add soda, if desired.

ROYAL FIZZ

2 ounces dry gin
1½ teaspoons fine grain sugar

Juice of ½ lemon or lime
1 egg

Shake with cracked ice. Strain into 8-ounce glass. Fill with soda.

SARATOGA FIZZ

1½ ounces rye or bourbon
½ ounce lemon juice
¼ ounce lime juice

1 teaspoon fine grain sugar
1 egg white

Shake with cracked ice. Serve without straining in an 8-ounce highball glass. Garnish with a cherry.

FRENCH "75"

2 ounces dry gin or brandy
Juice of 1 lemon

1 teaspoon fine grain sugar

Shake well with cracked ice. Pour into an 8-ounce highball glass. Fill with chilled champagne. Stir very slightly.

GIMLET

1½ ounces dry gin
Juice of ½ lime

1 teaspoon fine grain sugar

Dissolve sugar in the lime juice in a 6-ounce glass. Add gin, and ice if desired. Fill with chilled soda. Stir slightly.

GIN AND TONIC

Rub peel of lime or lemon around inside edge of an 8-ounce highball glass. Pour in 1½ ounces dry gin. Add ice cubes and a slice of lime or lemon. Fill with quinine water.

HIGHBALLS

Serve highballs in 8- or 10-ounce highball glasses. To prepare any highball, place 1 or 2 ice cubes in the glass. Add 1½ to 3 ounces of desired liquor. Fill glass with soda or ginger ale. Serve with a small bar spoon in glass and a twist of lemon peel if desired. Use any of the following liquors: applejack, bourbon, brandy, gin, rye, rum, Scotch, and cordials. Scotch is generally served with plain or soda water and you determine your guest's choice of soda or ginger ale with the other liquors.

ABSINTHE HIGHBALL

1½ ounces Pernod or Herbsaint   2 dashes Angostura bitters
4 dashes curaçao

Shake with cracked ice. Strain into an 8-ounce highball glass. Add ice cubes and soda to fill glass. Stir very slightly.

AMERICANO HIGHBALL

3 ounces sweet vermouth   3 dashes Angostura bitters

Combine in an 8-ounce highball glass. Add cracked ice. Fill with soda. Stir slightly. Top with dash of lemon bitters. Serve with twist of lemon peel.

DUBONNET HIGHBALL

3 ounces Dubonnet   1 teaspoon lemon juice

Stir with cracked ice in highball glass. Fill with soda.

POMPIER HIGHBALL

3 ounces dry vermouth   ½ teaspoon créme de cassis

Pour into highball glass. Add ice cubes and fill with soda. Twist lemon peel over top. Stir slightly.

HORSE'S NECK

Peel the whole rind of a lemon spiral fashion in one piece. Place one end of the lemon peel on the lip of a 10-ounce glass and let the remainder curl inside the glass. Add ice cubes and 1½ ounces of gin or whisky. Fill with ginger ale. This drink is traditionally served without spirits for the teetotaler.

MAJOR BAILEY

2 ounces dry gin   ¼ ounce lime juice
1 teaspoon fine grain sugar   ¼ ounce lemon juice
6 to 7 sprigs of mint

Combine in an Old-Fashioned glass and muddle thoroughly. Pour into a tall highball glass filled with shaved ice. Stir until glass frosts. Decorate with a couple of sprigs of mint. Serve with straws.

MAMIE TAYLOR

1½ to 2 ounces Scotch whisky   ¼ teaspoon fine grain sugar
Juice of ½ lime or lemon

Pour into a 10-ounce highball glass. Add ice cubes and fill with ginger ale.

MOJITO

2 ounces white label rum   Juice and rind of ½ lime
1 teaspoon fine grain sugar   Few sprigs of mint

This drink is similar to a Mint Julep except that it is made with rum. Muddle a few sprigs of mint and the sugar in a tall highball glass. Add rum, juice, and whole rind of lime. Fill with shaved ice and stir until glass frosts. Garnish with an additional few sprigs of mint.

MOSCOW MULE

2 ounces vodka   ½ lime
8 ounces ginger beer

Squeeze and drop lime and juice into a 12- or 14-ounce tumbler. Add vodka, ginger beer, and ice cubes. Stir and serve.

AMERICAN PUNCH (To serve 1)

Juice of ½ orange   1 ounce dry vermouth
½ teaspoon fine grain sugar   1 teaspoon créme de menthe
1 ounce brandy

Combine juice, sugar, brandy, and vermouth. Shake well with cracked ice. Strain into a goblet filled with crushed ice to which the crème de menthe has been added.

BLACKBERRY PUNCH (To serve 1)

2 ounces blackberry liqueur   Juice of 1 lime
1 ounce gold label rum   1 teaspoon fine grain sugar

Shake well with cracked ice. Strain into large goblet filled with shaved ice. Garnish with fresh fruit. Serve with straw.

CLARET PUNCH #1 (To serve 1)

4 ounces claret wine   1 teaspoon Benedictine
1 teaspoon brandy   Champagne to fill
1 teaspoon curaçao

Pour into tall glass over ice cubes. Fill glass with champagne. Decorate with fresh fruit.

CLARET PUNCH #2 (To serve 1)

4 ounces claret wine
1 ounce lemon juice
½ ounce curaçao

Dash of grenadine
2 dashes Angostura bitters

Shake well with cracked ice. Pour unstrained into large collins glass. Fill with soda. Garnish with fruit. Serve with straw.

FISH HOUSE PUNCH #1 (To serve 1)

Juice of ½ lemon
1 teaspoon fine grain sugar
1 ounce brandy
1 ounce peach liqueur

1 ounce Jamaica rum
Dash of Angostura bitters
    (optional)

Mix lemon juice and sugar in a 12-ounce tall glass. Add 2 ice cubes, brandy, peach liqueur, rum, and bitters. Stir and fill with chilled soda.

FISH HOUSE PUNCH #2 (To serve 1)

Juice of ½ lemon
½ teaspoon fine grain sugar

¾ ounce whisky
¾ ounce rum (gold label)

Mix and shake with ice the lemon juice, sugar, and whisky. Pour into a tall glass. Add soda. Decorate with fruit. Top with rum.

PLANTER'S PUNCH #1

2 ounces Jamaica rum   Dash of grenadine
Juice of ½ lemon

Fill 10-ounce glass with crushed ice. Add all ingredients and stir. Fill
glass with soda. Decorate with a maraschino cherry, a slice of orange,
a sliver of pineapple, and a sprig of mint.

PLANTER'S PUNCH #2

2 ounces gold label rum   1 ounce bar syrup
1 ounce fresh lime juice   5 dashes Angostura bitters

Combine in mixing glass with lots of shaved ice. Shake vigorously.
Pour unstrained into a 10-ounce highball glass. Fill with soda. Stir
slightly. Garnish with slice of lemon and grating of nutmeg. Serve
with straw.

PLANTER'S PUNCH #3

Juice of ½ lemon or lime   1 teaspoon grenadine
1 teaspoon sugar   1½ ounces New England rum

Shake well with cracked ice. Pour into a 12-ounce glass filled with
finely cracked ice. Decorate with fruit.

RUM PUNCH #1 (To serve 1)

Juice of ¼ lemon   1½ ounces gold label rum
¼ teaspoon fine grain sugar   ¾ ounce chilled water

Pour into a tall glass ⅔ full of fine cracked ice. Add fruit in season.
Serve with straw.

RUM PUNCH #2 (To serve 1)

Juice of ½ lemon   2 ounces gold label rum
½ ounce pure maple syrup   2 dashes grenadine

Shake well with ice. Pour into a 10-ounce tumbler filled with crushed
ice. Garnish with sliver of pineapple, slice of orange, and a cherry.

WHISKY PUNCH (To serve 1)

Juice of ½ lemon   1½ ounces whisky
½ teaspoon fine grain sugar

Shake with cracked ice. Strain into goblet. Add fruit in season. Fill
with chilled soda.

GIN RICKEY

2 ounces dry gin   Soda water
Juice and whole rind of ½ lime

Squeeze lime juice into an 8-ounce highball glass. Drop in lime rind.
Add gin and ice cubes. Fill with soda. Stir very slightly.

Variations: Substitute applejack, bourbon, brandy, any desired cordial,
rum, rye, Scotch, or sloe gin for dry gin in above recipe to make other
types of rickeys.

SANGAREES

Sangarees are tall drinks made with port, sherry, or sauterne wine.
Combine 3 or 4 ounces of desired wine in a tall glass. Add 1 teaspoon
fine grain sugar or bar syrup, lots of cracked ice, and a slice of lemon.
Fill glass with water. Stir and sprinkle a little grated nutmeg on top
before serving.

SHANDY GAFF

Use ½ ale or beer and ½ ginger ale. Pour the ale into a highball glass.
Add ice cubes and fill with ginger ale.

SLINGS

Serve 1½ ounces dry gin, brandy, rum, Scotch, rye, or bourbon in a
highball glass with cracked ice. Fill with soda. Add 2 or 3 dashes
Angostura bitters. Garnish with a twist of lemon peel.

SINGAPORE GIN SLING

2 ounces dry gin   Juice of ½ lemon
1 ounce cherry brandy   Dash of Angostura bitters
1 teaspoon fine grain sugar

Shake with cracked ice. Strain into a tall highball glass. Add ice
cubes. Fill with soda. Stir slightly. Twist a piece of lemon peel over
drink. Garnish with a sprig of mint.

WHISKY SLING SPECIAL

1 lump sugar   1½ ounces Scotch whisky
1 lime

Place the lump of sugar in a highball glass. Add enough water to dissolve sugar. Squeeze the lime and drop in the rinds with the juice.
Add the Scotch and a couple of ice cubes. Fill with soda.

SWIZZLES

1½ ounces dry gin
Juice of 1 lime

3 dashes Angostura bitters
1 teaspoon fine grain sugar

Turn ingredients into a glass pitcher. Add 8 to 10 ounces finely shaved ice. Churn vigorously with a swizzle stick until it foams and the pitcher frosts. Strain into cocktail glass.

Note: The swizzle stick is the dried stem of a plant that has radiating branches. It comes from the West Indies. When twirled rapidly between the palms of the hand the forked branch ends assure the traditional perfect mixture of the drink. Similar results may be obtained by shaking very vigorously in a cocktail shaker.

Variations: Use applejack, Jamaica rum, or whisky instead of dry gin.

APPLE SWIZZLE

1½ ounces applejack
1 ounce gold label rum
Juice of ½ lime

1 teaspoon fine grain sugar
5 dashes Angostura bitters

Follow method for Swizzles.

TOM COLLINS

2 ounces dry gin
1 tablespoon fine grain sugar

Juice of ½ lemon or lime

Shake well with cracked ice. Strain into 10- to 14-ounce collins glass. Add 2 or 3 ice cubes. Garnish with fruit. Fill with soda. Stir slightly and serve with straw.

Variations: Applejack, bourbon, brandy, rum, rye, Scotch, or vodka may be substituted for dry gin. With bourbon or rye it is called a John Collins.

TEXAS COLLINS

2 ounces dry gin
Juice of ½ grapefruit

1 tablespoon honey

Stir in a collins glass to blend. Add ice cubes. Fill glass with soda.

HOLLAND GIN COLLINS

Substitute Holland gin for dry gin in Tom Collins for surprisingly different-tasting collins.

VERMOUTH CASSIS

2 *ounces dry vermouth*   1 *ounce crème de cassis*

Stir with cracked ice. Strain into a small highball glass. Fill with soda.
Stir very slightly.

ZOMBIE

1 *ounce heavy rum*   ¾ *ounce unsweetened pineapple*
2 *ounces gold label rum*   *juice*
1 *ounce white label rum*   ¾ *ounce papaya juice*
2 *teaspoons apricot brandy*   1 *teaspoon fine grain sugar*
                                 Juice of 1 lime

Shake well with lots of cracked ice. Pour unstrained into a 14-ounce
zombie glass (a tall glass with straight sides). Float a splash of heavy-
bodied 151-proof rum on top. Skewer on a toothpick in the order
named, 1 green cherry, ½ inch of pineapple stick, and 1 red cherry.
Garnish with this and a sprig of mint. Sprinkle powdered sugar over
all.

juleps

MINT JULEPS

There are almost as many versions of the mint julep as there are julep
fanciers. The traditional liquor for a mint julep is bourbon, but brandy,
rye, Jamaica rum, gin, champagne, and even sherry and fruit brandies
are used. Actually these latter variations cannot be called true mint
juleps. The secret of the superb julep is to use plenty of liquor and
allow enough time for the glass to frost properly. By handling the glass
with a towel wrapped around it you avoid warming it with your hands
and in that way facilitate frosting. The following recipe for a true
Mint Julep will satisfy the most discriminating "julep lover." In addition, several other favorite versions of this famous drink follow.

MINT JULEP

6 or 7 mint leaves
1 teaspoon fine grain sugar or bar syrup
Shaved ice

2 to 3 ounces bourbon
Several sprigs of mint dusted with powdered sugar

Place mint leaves in the bottom of a tall glass. Add bar syrup or sugar. Crush well with spoon or muddler and fill with shaved ice. Pour 2 or 3 ounces bourbon over ice and stir until glass begins to frost. Refill to top with ice. If time allows, place in refrigerator for 15–20 minutes. When ready to serve, remove from refrigerator and top with a little whisky. Add sprigs of mint. Serve with straws.

BRANDY JULEP

½ teaspoon fine grain sugar
4 sprigs mint

1½ ounces brandy

Muddle sugar and mint in mixing glass. Empty into goblet. Add brandy and half fill with ice. Decorate with slices of fruit and additional sprigs of mint which have been dusted with powdered sugar.

CHAMPAGNE JULEP

4 sprigs of mint
1 lump sugar

Chilled champagne

Crush 1 or 2 sprigs of mint with lump of sugar and 1 tablespoon cold water in a tall glass. Half fill glass with finely crushed ice and fill with chilled champagne. Garnish glass with sprigs of mint and fruit.

GIN JULEP

1 teaspoon fine grain sugar or bar syrup
1 teaspoon lemon juice

6 or 7 sprigs of mint
3 to 4 ounces dry gin

Crush the mint with the sugar and lemon juice in a tall glass. Fill the glass with finely crushed ice. Add the gin and stir until glass frosts. Garnish glass with mint leaves which have been dusted with powdered sugar and with fruit in season.

hot drinks

BLUE BLAZER

3 ounces Scotch whisky
3 ounces boiling water

1 teaspoon fine grain sugar

Use 2 large mugs with handles. Put the Scotch in one mug, the boiling water in the other. Light the Scotch with a match. While blazing, pour the ingredients several times from 1 mug to the other. If it is well done, it will look like a stream of liquid fire. Add 1 teaspoon fine grain sugar. Serve in a small heated tumbler with a piece of lemon peel.

BRANDY BLAZER COCKTAIL

3 ounces brandy
1 lump sugar

1 piece of orange peel

Combine in a small thick glass. Light with match. Stir with long spoon. Strain into cocktail glass.

CAFE BRULOT COCKTAIL

Moisten the edge of a heavy glass with a piece of lemon. Dip in powdered sugar. Add several ounces hot coffee, then float 1 ounce of cognac on top. Set fire to the cognac.

CAFE BRULOT

8 lumps sugar
2 demitasses of cognac
2 sticks cinnamon, broken
2 small pieces lemon peel
    (about ¼ lemon)

12 whole cloves
5 pieces of orange rind
    (about ½ orange rind)
5 demitasses double-strength
    fresh black coffee

Place all ingredients, except coffee, in a chafing dish. Light the flame and stir constantly with a metal ladle until warmed. Touch the cognac with a flame to ignite. Burn about 1 minute, then slowly add the black coffee. Ladle at once into demitasse cups. Serves 6.

CAFE DIABLE

12 *lumps of sugar*
Grated rind of 1 orange
1 *stick cinnamon, broken*
1 *teaspoon coriander seed*

1 *tablespoon whole cloves*
1 *tablespoon whole roasted coffee
beans*
4 *ounces brandy*
1 *quart hot black fresh coffee*

Heat a chafing dish slightly, then drop in all ingredients except the brandy and hot coffee. Let them heat for about 1 minute. Add 2 ounces brandy and heat all together for about 1 minute. Touch the brandy with a flame. Ladle the liquid fire with a metal ladle to mix gently. Slowly add the hot coffee. Pour a little brandy into the ladle and ignite. Gently blend into the coffee mixture. Repeat until remaining brandy is used up. Serve in demitasse cups. Serves 8 or more.

CAFE DIABLIQUE

1 *cup brandy*
3 *dozen whole cloves*
2 *sticks cinnamon, broken*
½ *orange rind, thinly sliced*

8 *teaspoons sugar*
1 *quart hot fresh strong black
coffee*

Pour brandy into a heat-proof bowl or chafing dish. Add the spices, rind, and sugar. Ignite a little brandy in a metal ladle and lower into the brandy-spice mixture. Let it burn a few minutes and slowly add the hot black coffee. Ladle into demitasse cups. Serves 8 or more.

CAFE ROYAL

Dissolve 1 cube of sugar in 1 teaspoon brandy or other desired liquor. Pour into cup of black coffee and serve.

ENGLISH BISHOP

Stick an orange full of cloves. Roll in brown sugar. Broil under moderate heat or roast in the oven until soft and moderately browned. Cut into quarters and place in heavy saucepan. Pour over 1 quart hot port wine and simmer 20 to 30 minutes. Serve in heated punch glasses. If desired, add about 3 ounces brandy just before serving. Serves 6.

FESTIVAL RUM PUNCH

1 *quart Jamaica rum*
1 *quart apple cider*
3 *sticks cinnamon*

2 *teaspoons allspice*
1 *tablespoon butter*

Combine in a heavy saucepan. Heat almost to boiling point. Serve hot in heated punch cups or mugs. Serves about 10.

GLOGG

The famous Swedish cold weather drink

¾ cup granulated sugar
2 ounces Angostura bitters
8 ounces claret wine

8 ounces sherry wine
4 ounces brandy

Combine and heat all ingredients in a heavy pan until piping hot. Place in heated Old-Fashioned glasses. Fill ¾ full with the hot mixture.

Note: Placing a spoon in the glass before pouring in mixture prevents glass from cracking. Serves about 12.

HOT BUTTERED RUM

1½ ounces Jamaica or New
England rum
1 teaspoon sugar

1 teaspoon butter
Grated nutmeg
Freshly boiling water

Place rum, sugar, and butter in a hot tumbler or mug. Fill with boiling water and stir well. Top with freshly grated nutmeg.

Variations: Early New England recipes usually called for 2 to 3 ounces of rum per serving with as much as 1 tablespoon butter and the addition of 3 or 4 cloves and a stick of cinnamon.

HOT BUTTERED RUM BOWL

1 cup brown sugar
1 cup boiling water
3 quarts apple cider

1 quart Jamaica or New England
rum
Butter
Freshly grated nutmeg

Dissolve sugar in boiling water. Add cider and heat to boiling point. Add rum and enough butter to dot the surface. Turn into a heated bowl. Sprinkle nutmeg generously over top. Serve in heated mugs. Serves about 20.

HOT LOCOMOTIVE

1 egg yolk
1½ teaspoons fine grain sugar
1 ounce honey

6 ounces burgundy or claret
wine
½ ounce curaçao

Combine egg yolk, sugar, and honey in a saucepan. Stir to blend well. Add wine and curaçao. Heat to simmering point. Pour into heated mug and pour back into pan. Repeat several times. Serve in heated mugs with a thin slice of lemon or lime and a dash of cinnamon.

HOT MILK PUNCH

1½ ounces white label rum 1 teaspoon fine grain sugar
1½ ounces brandy Hot milk

In a tall glass stir the sugar in the rum and brandy. Add hot milk to fill glass. Top with grated nutmeg.

HOT RUM LEMONADE

About 1 teaspoon fine grain sugar 1 ounce white label rum
Juice of ½ lemon Slice of lemon

Combine sugar, lemon juice, and rum in hot tumbler or mug. Add freshly boiling water as desired and the slice of lemon.

HOT WINE LEMONADE

About 1½ teaspoons fine grain 2 ounces red or white wine
sugar Slice of lemon
Juice of 1 lemon

Combine sugar, juice, and wine in hot tumbler or mug. Add freshly boiling water as desired and top with slice of lemon.

HOT TODDIES (To serve 1)

1 teaspoon fine grain sugar Piece of cinnamon stick
2 cloves 1½ ounces rye or bourbon
Slice of lemon

Combine all in an Old-Fashioned glass or a mug. Add 1½ ounces or more boiling water. Stir.

Variations: Applejack, brandy, Scotch or gold label rum may be substituted for rye or bourbon.

HOT TODDY (Bowl)

1 quart liquor Lemon slices
2 quarts boiling water Whole cloves
Sugar to taste Small pieces of stick cinnamon

Stud the lemon slices with whole cloves. Combine the liquor, sugar to taste, lemon slices, and cinnamon in a heated bowl. Pour over the boiling water. Serve in hot mugs with a lemon slice in each serving. For the liquor use applejack, brandy, rye, bourbon, or Scotch. Serves about 16.

HOT BUTTERED TODDY

2 *ounces rye or bourbon*	1 *teaspoon fine grain sugar*
1 *ounce orange juice*	½ *teaspoon butter*

Combine in a heated mug. Add boiling water to fill mug. Stir well and serve.

JERSEY FLAMING BOWL

1 *quart applejack*	*Lemon peel pieces*
1 *ounce Angostura bitters*	1 *quart boiling water*
1 *cup fine grain sugar*	

Combine the applejack, bitters, sugar, and enough lemon pieces for each serving. Heat slightly and stir to dissolve sugar. Turn into a heated earthenware bowl. Ignite and stir while flaming. Extinguish flame with the boiling water. Serve in heated mugs. Serves 8 to 10.

JERSEY FLAMING MUG (To serve 1)

3 *ounces applejack*	4 *whole cloves*
3 *dashes Angostura bitters*	2 *pieces lemon peel*

Combine in a heated mug. Fill with boiling water. Top with a float of applejack. Ignite and serve while blazing.

MARINER'S GROG

2 *ounces Jamaica rum*	3 *cloves*
Juice of ½ lemon	*Small stick of cinnamon*
1 *lump sugar*	*Slice of lemon*

Turn all ingredients into a thick small glass or mug. Fill with boiling water. Stir well.

TOM AND JERRY (To serve 1)

1 *egg, separated*	¾ *ounce Jamaica rum*
1 *tablespoon fine grain sugar*	¾ *ounce brandy or rye*

Beat the yolk and white of egg separately, then mix together blending in the sugar. Add the spirits and fill with boiling water. Serve with grating of nutmeg on top.

TOM AND JERRY (To serve 12)

12 *whole eggs*
About 12 ounces fine grain sugar
4 *ounces Jamaica rum*

Whisky or rum as needed
Boiling Water
Nutmeg

Beat whole eggs until very light. Gradually beat in the sugar until batter is thick. Add more sugar if necessary. Add rum to flavor and set aside to ripen (2 to 3 hours). To serve, place a heaping tablespoon of batter in heavy glass or mug. Add 2 ounces or more whisky or rum. Fill with boiling water. Stir and top with grating of nutmeg.

HOT WHISKY LEMONADE

1½ *ounces whisky*
Juice of 1 lemon

Sugar to taste

Combine in a 10-ounce highball glass. Fill glass with hot water.

Note: Put a spoon in glass before pouring in hot water to prevent glass from cracking.

HOT PORT NEGUS

3 *ounces port wine*
1 *teaspoon fine grain sugar*

Boiling water

Dissolve sugar in 1 tablespoon hot water in a warm wine glass. Add port and fill glass with boiling water. Sprinkle with nutmeg.

Note: Place a teaspoon in glass before pouring in hot liquid to prevent glass from cracking.

Hot Sherry Negus: Substitute sherry for port.

HOT RUM PUNCH

Grated rind of 3 lemons
¼ *pound granulated sugar*
Juice of 3 lemons
 1 *tablespoon ground ginger*

1 *pint gold label rum*
1 *pint brandy*
8 *ounces sherry wine*
1 *quart boiling water*

Combine rind and sugar. Grind it with a wooden muddler or the back of a large spoon. Add lemon juice and ginger. Mix well together. Turn into a large casserole. Add rum, brandy, sherry, and boiling water. Add additional sugar, if desired. Allow to ripen over very low heat (do not boil) for about 20 minutes. Serves about 15.

MULLED CLARET (Gluhwein) (To serve 1)

3 *ounces claret wine*
8 *ounces water*
2 *dashes Angostura bitters*
1 *teaspoon fine grain sugar*

1 *piece of cinnamon*
3 *cloves*
½ *teaspoon allspice*
1 *piece of lemon peel*

Combine in a saucepan. Heat to just below boiling point. Strain into large tumbler.

Note: Place spoon in glass before pouring in liquid to prevent glass from cracking.

punch bowl and cup mixes

PUNCH is the traditional cooling drink for dances and parties. It can be anything from a very mild drink to some genuinely strong potion. Punches and cups are very much alike, although the former are usually mixed in a bowl to be served buffet style by the cup or glass, while the latter are served in garnished pitchers at the table. Some people think of punches as going only with satin breeches and lacy ruffles, but it is well to remember that the use of the punch bowl solves the problems of bartending to a very large degree. There is no reason why some of the more popular cocktails such as Martinis or Manhattans can't be served in a punch bowl if you remember to use a large block of ice so that there isn't too much dilution, or set a smaller bowl of thoroughly chilled cocktail mixture into a larger bowl lined with cracked ice. A group of specific recipes is given for a large variety of punches and cups. They are preceded, however, by a basic recipe from which you may make your own variations.

BASIC RED PUNCH BOWL

Juice of 6 lemons
  *2 tablespoons or more of sugar
    or honey*
4½ ounces liquor (3 jiggers)

3 bottles claret wine (fifths)
2 bottles soda water
Sliced fruit or berries
Block of ice

Mix together the juice, sweetening, liquor, and claret. Allow to stand until serving time. Place a large block of ice in a punch bowl. Pour the mixture over the ice. Add the soda and decorate with sliced fruit or berries. This makes a weak punch and serves about 15. Strength can be increased by raising the proportion of liquor.

Variations: Brandy, gin, or rum may be used for the liquor. For a white wine punch instead of the red, substitute a Rhine wine or a white Bordeaux such as Graves or a sauterne.

BACCIO PUNCH

8 ounces fresh grapefruit juice
8 ounces dry gin
4 ounces anisette
8 ounces champagne

8 ounces soda water
Fresh fruit slices
Sugar syrup to taste

Combine juice, gin, and anisette. Pour over block of ice. Add fruit. Add champagne and soda just before serving. Add sugar syrup to taste and stir slightly. Serves 8.

BUDDHA PUNCH

1 quart Rhine wine
6 ounces orange juice
6 ounces lemon juice
3 ounces orange curaçao

3 ounces gold label rum
1 quart champagne
1 quart soda water
Angostura bitters to taste

Mix wine, fruit juices, curaçao, and rum. Pour over block of ice in punch bowl. Add champagne and soda just before serving. Garnish with small slices of lemon, orange, pineapple, and mint leaves. Add bitters to taste. Serves about 10.

BURGUNDY PUNCH

2 quarts Burgundy
8 ounces port wine
4 ounces cherry brandy
Juice of 3 lemons

Juice of 6 oranges
4 ounces fine grain sugar
2 quarts soda water

Mix all but the soda. Pour over block of ice in punch bowl. Decorate with fresh fruit. Just before serving add the soda. Serves about 15.

CHAMPAGNE PUNCH

4 ounces brandy
4 ounces maraschino liqueur
4 ounces curaçao
½ pound fine grain sugar
2 quarts champagne
1 quart carbonated mineral water

Stir the sugar with the brandy, maraschino, and curaçao to dissolve sugar. Pour over a block of ice in a punch bowl. Add and gently stir in champagne and mineral water just before serving. Serves 20 to 25.

CHAMPAGNE CUP

1½ ounces maraschino liqueur
1½ ounces Chartreuse
1½ ounces brandy
1 orange, sliced thin
1 lemon, sliced thin
6 very thin slices pineapple
1 quart chilled champagne

Half fill a 2-quart pitcher with cracked ice. Add fruit, maraschino, Chartreuse, and brandy. Chill thoroughly. Add chilled champagne just before serving. Serve in champagne glasses.

CLARET CUP

1½ ounces curaçao
1½ ounces brandy
1½ ounces bar syrup
Dash of maraschino syrup
6 maraschino cherries
1 ounce lemon juice
1 lemon, sliced thin
1 orange, sliced thin
6 thin slices fresh pineapple
1 quart claret wine
8 ounces soda water

Use a large pitcher. Add cracked ice, liqueur, brandy, sweetening, and fruit. Add claret. Stir well. Just before serving add soda and stir slightly.

CLARET PUNCH

½ pound fine grain sugar
8 ounces lemon juice
3 ounces curaçao
3 quarts claret wine
2 quarts soda water

Mix sugar, lemon juice, curaçao, and claret. Pour into a punch bowl. Set bowl in a larger bowl in a bed of cracked ice. Add a garnish of sliced orange, pineapple, and cherries. Just before serving add soda. Serve in wine glasses. Serves 25.

FISH HOUSE PUNCH

8 ounces brandy
4 ounces peach liqueur
8 ounces Jamaica or gold label rum
4 ounces lemon juice
¾ pound fine grain sugar
2 tablespoons Angostura bitters (optional)
1 quart or more soda water

Dissolve the sugar in a little water. Pour all ingredients except the soda over a block of ice in a large punch bowl. Stir well. Add soda just before serving. Serves 10 or more.

RHINE WINE CUP

2 ounces brandy
1 ounce orange curaçao
1 ounce maraschino liqueur

1 quart Rhine wine
8 ounces soda water

Use a large glass pitcher. Add the ingredients in order listed. Add lots of fine cracked ice. Stir to blend.

RHINE WINE PUNCH

4 ounces brandy
4 ounces maraschino liqueur
½ pound fine grain sugar

3 quarts Rhine wine
1 quart soda water
2 tablespoons tea leaves

Mix brandy and maraschino with sugar and stir to dissolve sugar. Add wine and soda and pour over a block of ice in a punch bowl. Tie tea leaves in a piece of cheesecloth and leave in the mixture about 10 minutes. Garnish with slices of fruit. Serves 20 to 25.

ROMAN PUNCH

1 pound fine grain sugar
Juice of 6 lemons
Juice of 3 oranges
1 quart gold label rum

3 ounces Angostura bitters
6 egg whites, well beaten
1 quart chilled champagne

Dissolve sugar in fruit juices and combine with bitters and rum. Stir to mix well. Add well beaten egg whites and pour over block of ice in punch bowl. Just before serving add champagne. Serves 10.

RUM PUNCH

2 bottles New England or Puerto
    Rican rum
Juice of 12 lemons
1 cup sugar

2 cups very strong tea
2 quarts soda water

Mix all but soda and pour over block of ice in punch bowl. Decorate with fruit. Add soda just before serving. Makes 45 (4-ounce) servings.

SAUTERNE CUP

1 ounce brandy
1 ounce curaçao
1 ounce maraschino liqueur

1 quart chilled sauterne wine
8 ounces chilled soda water

Set a large pitcher in a bed of ice in a bowl. Combine the ingredients in the order listed. Stir slightly. Garnish with slices of lemon and orange. Serves 10.

non-alcoholic beverages

LEMONADE

Juice of 6 lemons
1 quart water

1 cup of basic sugar syrup
(or to taste)

Combine sugar syrup, juice, and water. Chill. Pour over cracked ice in tall glasses.

Variations: Substitute soda water, ginger ale, grape juice (reduce sugar syrup to taste), or orange juice. To serve, garnish with lemon or orange slices, mint leaves, fresh berries, crushed fruit, etc.

Limeade: Use 1 cup lime juice, 1 cup sugar syrup, and 1 quart water.

Orangeade: Use juice of 5 oranges, juice of 1 lemon, 1 cup sugar syrup, and 1 quart water.

Basic Sugar Syrup: Boil 1 cup sugar with 1 cup water for 5 minutes. Chill.

SPICED LEMONADE

1 cup sugar syrup
12 whole cloves
1 (3-inch) stick cinnamon

Juice of 6 lemons
1 quart water

Combine sugar syrup, cloves, and cinnamon. Cook 5 minutes. Strain and add lemon juice and water. Chill and serve over crushed ice.

BASIC TEA PUNCH

2 cups hot tea infusion   6 cups fruit juice
  (pour 1 pint boiling water over   4 cups ginger ale or soda water
  1 teaspoon tea)   Sugar

Just before serving combine, sweeten to taste, and pour over ice block in punch bowl. Serves 25.

Royal Punch: Use 4 cups grape juice and 2 cups grapefruit juice as the fruit juice.

Golden Punch: Use 1 cup lime juice, 2 cups orange juice, and 3 cups pineapple juice as the fruit juice.

California Punch: Use 3 cups loganberry juice, 2½ cups orange juice, and ½ cup lemon juice as the fruit juice.

LIGHT PUNCH

½ cup orange juice   ½ cup strong tea
¼ cup lemon juice   1½ cups water
1 cup pineapple juice   ½ cup sugar syrup
½ cup grapefruit juice

Combine ingredients, stir and chill. Serve with mint cubes. Serves 6 to 8.

DARK PUNCH

1 cup strong tea   1 cup pineapple juice
½ cup lemon juice   ½ cup blackberry juice
1 cup orange juice   ½ cup raspberry juice
2 cups water   ¾ cup sugar syrup

Combine ingredients, stir and chill. Serve over Tea Ice Cubes (page 107). Garnish with slices of orange and lemon, berries and mint leaves.

ORANGE SHERBET PUNCH

Place a large piece of ice in punch bowl. For each 12 servings allow 1 pint orange sherbet to 1 quart ginger ale. Arrange large chunks of sherbet around ice. Pour chilled ginger ale over all. Stir just enough to blend a little of the sherbet into ginger ale.

SUMMER FIZZ

12 sprigs mint   ½ cup lemon juice
1 cup currant jelly   1 quart ginger ale
1 cup hot water   3 cups orange juice
1 cup cold water

Crush mint in a bowl with the back of a silver spoon. Add boiling water and then a glass of currant jelly. When jelly is melted, add cold water. When cold, strain out crushed mint. Add fruit juice and just before serving, the ginger ale. Serve with sprigs of fresh mint or pour over ice cubes which have had mint leaves frozen in them. Serves 8 to 10.

GRAPEFRUIT-ADE

Blend together ½ cup sugar, 3 tablespoons lemon juice, 1½ cups orange juice, and 1½ cups canned or fresh grapefruit juice. Pour over cracked ice in tall glasses.

GRAPE-ADE

Squeeze juice of half a lime over ice cubes placed in a tall glass. Fill glass half full of grape juice and then fill it up with ginger ale. Serve garnished with generous sprig of fresh mint.

COUNTRY CLUB PUNCH

3 cups sugar	Juice of 12 oranges
3 quarts water	1 quart grape juice
1 cup strong tea	1 small can crushed pineapple
Juice of 12 lemons	2 quarts ginger ale

Boil sugar and water together for 8 minutes. Add tea, then chill. Add orange, lemon, and grape juice, and pineapple. Place in refrigerator to mellow for about 2 hours. Before serving, add 2 quarts of ginger ale and ice cubes. For small parties, this recipe may be divided into thirds. If served in a punch bowl, add quarter slices of orange and lemon and 1 small bottle of maraschino cherries. Serves about 50.

HONEY FRUIT PUNCH

Crush 1 large orange to a pulp. Combine with 1 cup honey, 1 finely chopped banana, 1 cup chopped pineapple, and 1 quart grape juice. Pour over ice. Let stand 20 minutes, then serve. Serves 6.

PUNCH PIQUANT

6 lemons	2½ cups water
1 pint grape juice	Ice cubes
½ cup sugar syrup (about)	

Strain the lemon juice. Combine with grape juice and sugar syrup. Add chilled water and chill thoroughly. Pour over ice cubes in tall glasses. Makes 1½ quarts.

RASPBERRY-ADE

½ cup sugar
2½ cups water
2 teaspoons tea leaves
½ cup boiling water
¼ cup lemon juice

2 cups grapefruit juice
1 cup raspberry juice
1 cup pineapple juice
3 cups ginger ale

Combine sugar and ½ cup water; boil for 5 minutes and let cool. Combine tea and ½ cup boiling water, let stand 5 minutes and strain. Combine fruit juices, syrup, tea, 2 cups cold water, and ginger ale. Mix thoroughly and pour into generously iced glasses.

MINT TINKLE

1½ cups water
½ cup granulated sugar
6 tablespoons lemon juice

⅛ teaspoon mint extract
Green vegetable coloring
1 quart ginger ale

Combine water and sugar; bring to a boil, stirring constantly. Remove from heat and cool. Add lemon juice, mint extract, and enough green vegetable coloring to tint mixture a very delicate green. Just before serving add ginger ale and serve with chopped ice or ice cubes. Garnish each glass with thin slice of lemon and sprig of mint. Makes 1½ quarts.

CURRANT FIZZ

2 (8-ounce) glasses currant
jelly
2 cups boiling water
2½ cups orange juice

⅔ cup lemon juice
1 quart ginger ale

Beat currant jelly until frothy. Add boiling water and continue beating until jelly is dissolved. Add fruit juices and stir well. Chill. Just before serving, add ginger ale. Makes almost 2 quarts.

SPICED TEA FROST

⅔ cup granulated sugar
2 cups cold water
Grated rind 1 lemon
8 whole cloves
2 (1-inch) pieces stick cinnamon

¼ teaspoon ginger
5 cups freshly made hot tea
Lemon sections
Ice

Combine all ingredients but the tea, lemon sections, and ice. Boil 15 minutes, then strain. Cool; add tea, mix well and pour over ice in tall glasses. Serve with lemon sections.

EGGNOG

1 *egg*	¼ *teaspoon vanilla*
1 *tablespoon sugar*	1 *cup cold milk*
Dash of salt	*Dash of nutmeg*

Beat salt, egg, and sugar. Add vanilla and milk. Beat thoroughly. Pour into glass and sprinkle lightly with nutmeg. Serves 1.

Honey Eggnog: Substitute 2 tablespoons honey for sugar.

Chocolate Eggnog: Omit sugar. Add 1½ tablespoons chocolate syrup and 1 tablespoon malted milk (optional). Beat well and top with whipped cream.

Fruit Juice Eggnog: Flavor eggnog with 2 tablespoons fresh or canned fruit juice.

Sherry Eggnog: Flavor eggnog with 2 tablespoons sherry wine or other favorite wine.

Malted Milk Eggnog: Add 1 to 2 tablespoons malted milk to eggnog.

Almond Eggnog: Omit vanilla. Flavor eggnog with 6 drops almond extract.

FRUIT MILK SHAKES

Use thoroughly chilled milk, fruit juices, or pulps. Shake or beat with fruit or syrup until well blended and sweeten to taste. Garnish with whipped cream if desired. Evaporated milk diluted with an equal amount of water may be used instead of fresh milk. Each of the following makes 4 generous servings.

Banana Shake: Combine 3 mashed ripe bananas with 3 cups milk.

Fruit Juice Shake: Combine 4 cups milk with ½ cup fruit syrup from cooked or canned fruit. Use apricot, peach, plum, pineapple, prune, or fruit nectar.

Grape Juice Shake: Use 2½ cups milk, 1½ cups grape juice, and 1 teaspoon lemon juice.

Orange Shake: Use 2 cups of milk, 2 cups orange juice, and ¼ teaspoon almond extract.

Prune Shake: Use 2 cups milk, 2 cups prune juice, and 1 teaspoon lemon juice.

Strawberry Shake: Use 4 cups of milk and 1 cup crushed sweetened strawberries.

CHOCOLATE MILK SHAKES

Use 2 tablespoons chocolate or cocoa syrup for each cup of milk. Shake or beat well. Garnish with whipped cream if desired.

Chocolate Frosted: Beat dip of vanilla or chocolate ice cream into chocolate milk shake.

Minted Chocolate Shake: Flavor each chocolate milk shake with 3 drops of peppermint extract. Garnish with whipped cream and sprig of fresh mint.

Chocolate-Mocha Shake: Mix ¼ cup hot double strength coffee, 1 cup milk, and 2 tablespoons chocolate syrup. Cool and pour over cracked ice in glasses. Top with whipped cream. Serves 2.

SPICED GRAPE JUICE

1 *quart grape juice*	12 *whole cloves*
½ *cup sugar*	⅛ *teaspoon salt*
8 *short pieces stick cinnamon*	*Lemon juice (optional)*

Mix all ingredients and bring to boiling point. Cool and let stand several hours. When ready to serve, reheat, remove spices, and add lemon juice if desired. Serve hot.

SPICED CIDER

1 *quart sweet cider*	8 *short pieces stick cinnamon*
¼ *cup sugar*	12 *whole cloves*
⅛ *teaspoon salt*	8 *whole allspice*

Mix all ingredients, bring to boiling point, cool, and let stand several hours. Reheat, remove whole spices and serve hot.

DECORATIVE ICE CUBES

To add a touch of color and interest to cool summer beverages, color the ice cubes which you use. To make decorated ice cubes with the decorations in the center, fill a freezing tray half full of water, freeze slowly, and add decorations. These may be small flowers, such as rosebuds, green and red cherries, mint leaves, or sections of orange and lemon slices. A tablespoon more water may be added and frozen to keep the decorations in place before the tray is filled with chilled water. If using colored cubes, be careful not to use too much coloring matter, so cubes will be a delicate color.

Coffee Ice Cubes: Prepare strong black coffee, let cool, and freeze in ice-cube tray.

Tea Ice Cubes: Prepare hot tea, cool, and freeze.

Berry Ice Cubes: Add 1 strawberry, raspberry, or blackberry to the water in each section of ice-cube tray. Freeze.

Ginger Ale Cubes: Freeze ginger ale in ice cube trays.

Half-'n'-Half Cubes: Freeze ½ part ginger ale and ½ part loganberry juice.

snacks

canapes, hors d'oeuvres, other snacks

APPETIZERS were once savory trifles to be served with cocktails or sherry before dinner. In recent years they have gained new importance. Influenced by the French hors d'oeuvres, the Swedish smörgasbord, the Russian zakuska, the Italian antipasto or the Greek oretika, they are now more varied, more elaborate, and some of them are hearty enough to appear as the principal fare for a special luncheon or a late evening buffet. In any language they must always spell the same charm—be alluring to the eye and the stomach. They must make you want to eat more and more. To the French hors d'oeuvres is a general term for appetizers but Americans tend to apply the term to any "taste-teasing" bit of food that can be eaten with the fingers. If it is hot or has a sauce or marinade, it will be speared on a cocktail pick, but it is usually tiny enough not to require a fork. Canapés are simply hors d'oeuvres served on a bread or other edible base. Toast cut in fancy shapes, cocktail puffs, crêpes, tiny biscuits, timbale cases, crackers and potato chips serve the same purpose as the tiny shapes of bread. Canapés along with piquant bits of food on picks, peanuts, cheese popcorn, olives, crisp vegetables and the like are standbys for cocktail parties.

When the occasion calls for it, they may be extremely elaborate, varied, attractively garnished. The extreme example would be the Swedish smörgasbord—the beautifully appointed table laden with countless varieties of food. Many of them are far too heavy to be classified as appetizers. In fact restaurants in this country which offer Swedish food often list the smörgasbord as a meal in itself. Foods on a typical smörgasbord will include several varieties of bread, imported and domestic cheeses, all sorts of cold cuts of meat, three or four varieties of herring, several sweet and sour dishes, tiny meat balls, spaghetti, egg dishes, anchovies, caviar, crisp vegetables, shrimp and other seafood, and even a variety of salads.

Russian appetizers (zakuska) are served in almost as great a variety and are highly flavored. Caviar, salted herring, salted mushrooms, cucumbers, pickled beets and salmon are the most popular. Vegetables are prominent among the Italian antipasto and selections are very similar in the Greek oretika. Among those offered you will find green pickled peppers, pimiento halves, sliced beets, tomatoes, cucumber, pickled mushrooms, pickled cauliflower and celery hearts along with cheeses, and sliced salami or other meats.

The recipes that follow are extremely varied and give specific methods and seasonings. Nevertheless these recipes should in the last analysis serve only as a guide. They are presented with the suggestion that each be sampled and seasoned to taste as they are made. We believe they will stimulate your imagination and that you will want to elaborate on them and evolve your own favorites. With these hundreds of recipes as a base, you can evolve many thousands of variations with contrasts in colors, textures, designs, and seasonings. They include so many favorite flavors and foods that when the impromptu occasion arises anyone can find enough ingredients on the pantry shelf to make up a delectable array of dainties.

canape bases and butters

TOASTED CANAPE BASES

Cut rounds, squares or fancy shapes from thin bread slices with cooky or sandwich cutters. Place on broiler rack in preheated broiler oven. Place rack about 3 inches from flame. Toast bread on one side. Brush toasted side with melted butter or margarine. Spread appetizer mixture on untoasted side. Savory butters add flavor to canapé bases and many of them may be used, if applied liberally, without any additional canapé spread. A wide variety is given in this book.

SAUTEED BREAD BASES #1

Cut bread into desired shapes. Sauté on one side in a little butter or margarine in a heavy skillet over very low heat. Drain on absorbent paper. Spread plain side with desired canapé spreads.

SAUTEED BREAD BASES #2

Cut bread into desired shapes. Toast on one side as in Toasted Canapé Bases. Sauté untoasted side as in Sautéed Bread Bases #1. Drain. Spread untoasted side.

Note: You'll find that sautéed canapé bases are more desirable than ordinary toasted bread bases. They have far more flavor. All canapé bases should be spread as close to serving time as possible. Allowing them to stand too long will ruin them. If possible don't spread them more than ½ hour before serving time.

VARIETY CRACKER BASES

Use crisp savory crackers. Just brush with melted butter and delicately brown in a moderate oven (350° F.). For variations, sprinkle before toasting with caraway seed, celery salt, garlic salt, grated cheese or paprika.

SAVORY CRISP BREAD STICKS

Trim crusts from bread slices. Cut slices into strips. Brush with melted butter or margarine. Roll half the strips in grated Parmesan cheese and the balance in celery seed. Toast in moderate oven (350° F.) about 15 minutes.

MELBA TOAST

Cut stale bread into ¼-inch slices. Bake in slow oven (300° F.) until brown and dry (15 to 20 minutes).

TOAST STRIPS

Cut bread slices ⅓ inch thick. Remove crusts. Spread butter on both sides. Cut slices into ½-inch strips. Lightly brown under broiler.

PUFFY CRACKER BASES

Soak tiny soda crackers in ice water for 8 minutes. Drain on absorbent paper and remove to greased cooky sheet with a spatula. Brush with melted butter. Bake in very hot oven (450° F.) for 10 minutes. Reduce heat to moderate (350° F.) and allow to dry out for about 20 minutes. They should be crisp and delicately browned.

These cracker bases may be varied by sprinkling with grated cheese, caraway seed or finely chopped nuts before baking, or by mixing into the melted butter a little curry powder and paprika.

Many of the recipes in this book call for puff paste, plain pastry, or baking powder biscuits. The basic recipes offered here have been adjusted in size to conform to recipes such as Liver Sausage Turnovers, Sardine Surprises, Waffled Wafers, etc., which require pastry and biscuit mixes. For those special occasions when you really want to put forth some extraordinary effort, you'll find that tiny patty shells and other puff paste shapes filled with your favorite canapé spreads are ideal.

PLAIN PASTRY

1 cup all-purpose flour
½ teaspoon salt

½ cup shortening
Cold water

Mix and sift flour and salt. Cut in shortening with a pastry blender or two knives until mixture resembles small peas. Add cold water in small amounts, stirring lightly with a fork and tossing pieces of dough aside as soon as formed. Use only enough water to make particles hold together. Wrap dough in waxed paper and chill 10 to 15 minutes. Roll pastry out on a lightly floured board to ⅛ inch thickness and use in recipes calling for plain pastry. Baking times and temperatures are given in each recipe. The usual temperature for plain pastry is 450° F. and the time for most hors d'oeuvres baked in plain pastry is 15 to 20 minutes.

CHEESE STICKS

Prepare Plain Pastry. Roll out ⅛ inch thick. Sprinkle heavily with grated cheese and paprika, if desired. Fold in half, sprinkle again and roll out. Repeat twice. Cut into strips 3 to 4 inches long and ½ inch wide. Chill. Bake in very hot oven (450° F.) about 8 minutes.

PASTRY CANAPE BASES

Prepare Plain Pastry. Roll out ⅛ inch thick and cut into fancy shapes. Bake in very hot oven (450° F.) about 15 minutes. For variety, sprinkle before baking with allspice, cardamon, caraway, celery seed, coriander, curry powder, mace, mustard, paprika or grated cheese. Use with desired canapé spreads.

BAKING POWDER BISCUITS

2 cups sifted all-purpose flour
3 teaspoons baking powder
½ to 1 teaspoon salt

4 tablespoons shortening
⅔ to ¾ cup milk

Mix and sift flour, baking powder and salt. Cut or rub in shortening. Add milk to make a soft dough. Place on a floured board and knead lightly for not more than 30 seconds, using as little flour on board as possible. Roll out to ½ inch thickness and cut with biscuit cutters to make biscuits or use recipe for hot hors d'oeuvres as indicated in recipes such as Waffled Wafers, Quickie Meat Rolls, Quick Franks In Blanket, etc. For a more highly seasoned biscuit mix increase salt to 1 teaspoon. This recipe makes fourteen 2-inch biscuits. Bake biscuits in very hot oven (450° F.) 10 to 15 minutes, depending on the thickness or until they are golden brown. Serve immediately.

PUFF PASTE

1 cup butter
2 cups sifted all-purpose flour
¼ teaspoon salt

6 tablespoons ice cold water
(about)

Wash butter by placing it in a mixing bowl, holding it under cold running water and squeezing and pressing with hands until it is pliable and waxy. Reserve ¼ cup butter; form balance into a square and chill thoroughly before using. Mix and sift flour and salt twice; cut in the butter with pastry blender or two knives. Mix to a light dough with the water, adding a little at a time and only enough to moisten thoroughly. Form into a compact ball without overworking and set aside 20 minutes. Roll out on a lightly floured board into a rectangular shape about ¼ inch thick. Place washed chilled butter in center of lower half of sheet. Fold upper half over butter. Press edges firmly together. Roll out again until about ¼ inch thick. Fold together from opposite sides like a sheet to be fitted into an envelope. Again press the edges together. Wrap in waxed paper and chill about 25 minutes but not in contact with ice. Place on board again; repeat rolling and folding process altogether four times, chilling the last time for about an hour. Each rolling should be done in an opposite direction from the last so that the butter is combined and spread evenly. The dough may be wrapped in waxed paper and kept in the refrigerator for several days.

To bake Puff Paste: Shape and chill thoroughly. Arrange on baking sheets covered with 2 thicknesses of heavy brown paper. Bake in extremely hot oven (500° F.) and reduce heat 50° every 5 minutes down to moderate (350° F.). Turn as needed to brown evenly. Some pastry cooks like to bake puff paste at a uniform heat of 500° F. but in this case the paste must be covered with heavy waxed paper after 10 minutes baking.

Patty Shells: Roll puff paste ¼ inch thick. Cut into 3-inch rounds with floured cutter. Cut out centers from half of rounds with a smaller cutter. Moisten underside of each ring with cold water. Place 1 on each full round. Press down lightly. Bake smaller rounds to use as covers. Bake as directed for Puff Paste.

Bouchées: Follow method for Patty Shells, rolling pastry ⅛ inch thick and making cases smaller.

Vol-au-Vent: Work with about ¼ of pastry, keeping remainder chilled until needed. Roll paste ⅓ inch thick. Cut an oval with floured mold or knife. Brush outer edge with water. Add a rim of pastry about ¾ inch wide. Prick several places with fork, chill and bake. If desired, bake smaller ovals for covers, using the paste from center of outer rims. Watch carefully and cover with paper if it browns too quickly.

COCKTAIL CREPES

½ cup sifted all-purpose flour
½ teaspoon salt

2 egg yolks, beaten
1 cup water

Mix and sift flour and salt. Mix egg yolks and water. Combine the two mixtures and beat until smooth. Bake on a greased griddle or skillet. Cool and spread with desired canapé filling and roll. Yield: about 20.

TINY TIMBALE CASES

Very small timbale cases make attractive hors d'oeuvres when filled with anchovy paste, caviar, cream cheese or other desired spreads.

1 cup sifted all-purpose flour
½ teaspoon salt
½ teaspoon sugar

⅔ cup milk
1 egg, well beaten
1 tablespoon melted shortening

Mix and sift dry ingredients. Stir in milk and beaten egg. Add shortening and beat well. Place some of the batter in a cup. Dip the timbale iron on the end of its handle into deep fat. Heat the fat to 375° F. Drain out iron and dip into batter in cup. Allow batter to coat iron only ¾ of the way to top. Dip in hot fat and fry 1 to 2 minutes, or until golden brown. Remove from hot iron at once. Drain on absorbent paper. Fill as desired.

Cocktail Puff Shells

CANAPE PUFFS

½ cup water
¼ cup butter
⅛ teaspoon salt

½ cup sifted all-purpose flour
2 eggs

Place water, butter and salt in saucepan. Bring to brisk boil. Reduce heat and add flour all at once, stirring vigorously with a wooden spoon until mixture is thick and glossy. Remove from heat. Add eggs, one at a time, beating thoroughly after each addition. Continue beating until dough is thick and smooth and breaks off when spoon is raised. Spoon onto greased baking sheet in ¾-inch rounds, placing shapes 1½ inches apart. Bake in hot oven (400° F.) 15 minutes. (If preferred, dough may be stored in refrigerator several hours or overnight.) When cool, cut slit in side and fill with fillings such as fish flakes, sour cream, cheese and olive, etc. Chill in refrigerator until ready to serve. Yield: 2½ dozen.

Fried Puff Shells (Queen Fritters): Prepare the puff shell mixture above. Scrape mixture from tablespoon into deep hot fat (375° F.). Use 1 rounded tablespoon per puff. Fry until a nice crust has formed, turning frequently (about 12 minutes). Drain and cut off tops of shells. Fill with desired filling and replace tops. Yield: 6 large shells.

CHEESE FILLED PUFFS

Prepare the recipe for Canapé Puffs. When baked, cut a slit at sides and insert ½-inch cubes of sharp American cheese which have been sprinkled with cayenne. Put 1 cube in each puff. At serving time, reheat in a hot oven (400° F.) about 5 minutes.

SIMPLE CHEESE PUFFS

¼ *pound grated American*
cheese
¼ *cup butter*

½ *cup sifted all-purpose flour*
Dash of cayenne

Blend cheese and butter thoroughly. Work in the flour and cayenne. Chill 2 hours or longer. Roll into balls 1 inch in diameter. Bake in very hot oven (450° F.) 15 minutes. Yield: 30 puffs.

ANCHOVY STICKS OR RINGS

1 *cup sifted all-purpose flour*
⅓ *cup butter*

2 *tablespoons anchovy paste*
Cold water

Cut the butter into the flour with a pastry blender or two knives. Rub in the anchovy paste and add enough water to make a dough that will roll. Cut into sticks and bake in a very hot oven (450° F.) about 5 minutes. To form rings, fasten the ends of the sticks together or cut with a ring cutter, then bake.

CANAPE PIES

Canapé pies are popular for impromptu gatherings because they can be prepared quickly from supplies on the pantry shelf. To prepare a pie, cut a thin slice the length of a loaf of bread. For a special flavor use a round loaf of rye or pumpernickel. Spread the slice with a soft butter. Then starting in the center spread with separate rings of seasoned canapé spreads. Use spreads that contrast in colors and blend well in flavors. Separate each spread with rings of seasoned cream cheese. Apply the cream cheese with a pastry tube to give a nice decorative effect. Serve the pie, cut into small wedges, around a pile of olives. Specific, colorful examples follow.

RAINBOW CANAPE WHEEL

Cut thin slices of pumpernickel or steamed brown bread. Spread with softened butter. Place a slice of hard-cooked egg in the center. Spread red caviar around the egg slice in a narrow strip. Soften cream cheese with mayonnaise and color half of it green with vegetable coloring. Spread around caviar. Add a circle of black caviar, then a circle of white cream cheese. Edge with red caviar. Chill and serve cut into pie-shaped wedges.

PEGGY'S CANAPE PIE

Cut a large round loaf of rye bread in circular slices ¼ inch thick. Spread with soft butter. Place a teaspoon of caviar in the center. Surround with a ring of cream cheese, then with a ring of rolled anchovies, a ring of chopped ripe olives and another ring of cream cheese. Garnish the outer edge with halves of cooked or canned shrimp, whole stuffed green olives, and small pickled onions, alternating the foods. Chill and serve in pie-shaped wedges.

COCKTAIL "CAKE"

The cocktail "cake" may be made from a commercial bakery loaf if you use one of the small round loaves of white, rye or pumpernickel made by Swedish, Jewish, German, French or Italian bakeries. You may prefer, however, to bake your own loaf in a deep round pan using a prepared mix or half of a roll recipe. After baking, cool and remove crusts with a very sharp knife. Cut the loaf into 4 slices to form 4 "layers" of the cocktail "cake." Spread the individual layers with sticky sandwich fillings. For example, chicken salad alternating with vegetable salad, egg salad alternating with fish salad. Put the spread slices together to form original shape of loaf. Frost the loaf with softened cream cheese. Garnish as desired with sliced olives, pickles, radishes, etc. Chill thoroughly in refrigerator. To serve, place on a large round platter and surround with vegetable hors d'oeuvres. Cut into individual wedges as you would a cake.

CANAPE BUTTERS

Savory butters add flavor to canapés. If desired, some may be used alone without additional spreads. To prepare any of the following savory butters, mix the ingredients into ¼ cup of creamed butter. They keep well in the refrigerator if stored in a covered container. Larger quantities may be made by increasing the ingredients proportionately. If the butter is hard when you want to use it, cream it enough to soften, before spreading on canapés.

Anchovy Butter: Use 1 tablespoon anchovy paste or mashed anchovy fillets and ½ teaspoon lemon juice.

Caper Butter: Use 1 tablespoon finely minced capers.

Caviar Butter: Use 2 teaspoons caviar, ¼ teaspoon grated onion, and a few drops of lemon juice.

Cheese Butter: Use ¼ cup soft snappy cheese.

Chili Butter: Use 2 tablespoons chili sauce.

Chive Butter: Use 1 tablespoon finely minced chives and 1 teaspoon lemon juice.

Chutney Butter: Use 1 tablespoon chutney.

Crabmeat Butter: Use 3 tablespoons finely shredded crabmeat and ½ teaspoon lemon juice.

Curry Butter: Use ¼ teaspoon curry powder.

Egg Butter: Use 2 mashed hard-cooked eggs, ½ teaspoon lemon juice, a dash of Tabasco sauce, and salt and pepper to taste.

Garlic Butter: Use 1 small clove garlic, minced very fine.

Green Pepper Butter: Use 2 tablespoons grated green pepper, well-drained, and a few drops of lemon juice.

Green Savory Butter: Use 3 tablespoons spinach purée, 1 tablespoon anchovy paste, a dash of paprika, 1 teaspoon chopped capers, and salt to taste.

Herring Butter: Use 2 teaspoons ground smoked herring or herring paste, and a few drops of lemon juice.

Honey Butter: Use ¼ cup honey.

Horseradish Butter: Use 2 tablespoons drained horseradish.

Ketchup Butter: Use 2 to 3 tablespoons ketchup.

Lemon Butter: Use ½ teaspoon grated lemon rind and 1 tablespoon lemon juice. (Lime or orange rind and juices may be substituted for lemon.)

Liverwurst Butter: Use 2 tablespoons mashed liverwurst sausage and ½ teaspoon grated onion.

Lobster Butter: Use 2 tablespoons lobster paste, ½ teaspoon lemon juice, and a dash each of dry mustard and paprika.

Mint Butter: Use 2 tablespoons minced mint leaves and 1 teaspoon lemon juice.

Mustard Butter: Use 1 tablespoon prepared mustard.

Nut Butter: Use 2 tablespoons finely minced, salted nuts.

Olive Butter: Use ⅛ cup finely chopped green or stuffed olives and a few drops of onion juice.

Olive-Pimiento Butter: Use 1 pimiento, chopped fine, and ⅛ cup finely chopped stuffed olives.

Onion Butter: Use 1 teaspoon onion juice.

Paprika Butter: Use 2 teaspoons paprika and a few drops lemon juice.

Parmesan Butter: Use 2 tablespoons grated Parmesan cheese.

Parsley Butter: Use 2 tablespoons finely minced parsley and a few drops Worcestershire sauce.

Peanut Butter: Use ¼ cup peanut butter, 1 teaspoon honey, and salt to taste.

Pimiento Butter: Use 2 tablespoons mashed pimiento and 1 teaspoon finely chopped drained pickle.

Roquefort Butter: Use 1 tablespoon Roquefort cheese.

Salmon Butter: Use 1 tablespoon salmon paste or mashed smoked salmon (1 ounce) and 1 teaspoon lemon juice.

Sardine Butter: Use 2 tablespoons sardine paste or mashed sardines and ½ teaspoon each lemon juice and onion juice.

Shrimp Butter: Use 2 tablespoons ground cooked or canned shrimp and ¼ teaspoon each lemon juice and onion juice.

Tarragon Butter: Use 2 or 3 tarragon leaves, finely chopped, and a few drops tarragon vinegar.

Watercress Butter: Use 2 tablespoons finely chopped watercress, 1 teaspoon lemon juice, and a few drops Worcestershire sauce.

Worcestershire Sauce Butter: Use ¼ teaspoon Worcestershire sauce.

QUICK MAYONNAISE VARIATIONS

To prepare any of the following dressings, mix the ingredients into 1 cup of mayonnaise. These dressings are called for in various recipes throughout this book.

Green Mayonnaise: Color with green vegetable coloring or spinach purée. For additional variety when used as a dunking bowl, add 1 to 2 teaspoons each of chopped chives, parsley, tarragon, chervil, and dill.

Red Mayonnaise: Tint with red vegetable coloring, or pound a lobster coral, force it through a sieve and add to mayonnaise.

Russian Dressing: Add 1 chopped hard-cooked egg, ¼ cup chili sauce, and 2 tablespoons chopped green pepper.

Horseradish Mayonnaise: Add 3 tablespoons prepared horseradish.

Nippy Mayonnaise: Add 3 teaspoons prepared horseradish, 3 teaspoons prepared mustard, and 1 small chopped sweet pickle.

Savory Mayonnaise: Add ¼ teaspoon each of Worcestershire sauce, paprika, and dry mustard.

Roquefort Mayonnaise: Add 2 tablespoons crumbled Roquefort or blue cheese, a few drops of Worcestershire sauce, 1 tablespoon French dressing, and 1 tablespoon minced chives.

Ravigotte Mayonnaise: Mix and chop ½ cup watercress, ½ cup parsley, 2 teaspoons chives, 1 tablespoon capers, and 4 anchovies. Force mixture through a sieve and add to mayonnaise.

Tartar Sauce: Add 1 tablespoon each of chopped capers, olives, parsley, and pickles. Serve hot or cold.

dunking trays, bowls, vegetable hors d'oeuvres

DUNKING trays are among the most popular of drink accompaniments, and they can be relatively simple or very elaborate. Arrange one or two dunking bowls in the center of the tray. Around them place alternate layers of vegetable hors d'oeuvres such as celery, raw carrot cut in strips or very long slices curled in ice water, cauliflower broken and sliced in flowerets, asparagus tips, white and red radishes, green onion, tiny cherry or plum tomatoes, paper-thin slices of turnips, cucumber, and zucchini. You may want to extend the list; however, remember that the vegetables must be washed and iced thoroughly.

You may include cold boiled or hot fried shrimp, tiny fresh or smoked oysters, chunks of lobster or crabmeat. In addition to the suggestions for dunking and spread-your-own bowls that follow you may also want to choose one of the cocktail sauces or a salad dressing like green mayonnaise or Russian dressing. They are especially good with seafood or cubes of avocado. You'll find that a bowl of thick sour cream with chopped chives in it is especially welcome with vegetable hors d'oeuvres.

DUNKING BOWLS

Combine the enumerated ingredients, mix thoroughly and heap into a bowl.

CURRIED CHEESE DUNK

2 *cups cottage cheese*
6 *tablespoons mayonnaise*
4 *tablespoons cream*

3 *teaspoons curry powder*
1 *teaspoon salt*

VEGETABLE-CHEESE DUNK

2 *cups cottage cheese*
¼ *cup heavy cream*
¼ *cup grated raw carrot*

½ *cup finely cut green onions*
¼ *cup chopped green pepper*
6 *radishes, sliced very thin*

SOUR CREAM DUNK

2 *cups sour cream*
1 *cup finely chopped green pepper*
¼ *cup chopped chives*

¼ *cup chopped parsley*
¼ *cup thinly sliced radishes*
Salt and pepper to taste

PINK MAYONNAISE DUNK

1 *cup mayonnaise*
½ *cup chili sauce or ketchup*

Juice of 1 lemon
About 5 drops onion juice

CHIVES-CHEESE DUNK

2 *cups cottage cheese*
2 *tablespoons cream*
2 *teaspoons horseradish*

2 *tablespoons chopped chives*
1½ *teaspoons salt*
½ *teaspoon pepper*

ZIPPY EGG DUNK

4 *hard-cooked eggs, minced*
3 *strips crisp bacon, crumbled*
1 *teaspoon minced onion*
1 *teaspoon Worcestershire sauce*

1 *teaspoon horseradish*
Mayonnaise, enough to give nice spreading consistency

SARDINE DUNK

8-ounce package cream cheese
2 cans sardine fillets
3 tablespoons minced chives
½ cup minced parsley
Salt
Sweet cream

Soften cream cheese to room temperature. Mash sardines with the oil. Blend cheese, sardines, chives, and parsley. Add salt to taste and enough cream to thin mixture to dunking consistency.

SHRIMP AND COTTAGE CHEESE DUNK

½ pound fresh, cooked shrimp
or 1 5-ounce can shrimp
1 cup creamed cottage cheese
3 tablespoons chili sauce
½ teaspoon onion juice
½ teaspoon lemon juice
¼ teaspoon Worcestershire sauce
About 4 tablespoons milk

Chop cleaned shrimp fine. Combine with cottage cheese, seasonings, and enough milk to make a creamy mixture. Add salt if desired. Pile into bowl.

QUICK SOUR CREAM AND RED CAVIAR DUNK

Combine thick sour cream with red caviar and a few drops of onion juice, to taste. Serve with squares of pumpernickel or rye bread.

CLAM-CREAM CHEESE DUNK

1 garlic clove, cut in half
8-ounce package cream cheese
2 teaspoons lemon juice
1½ teaspoons Worcestershire sauce
½ teaspoon salt
Dash of freshly ground pepper
½ cup (7-ounce can) drained minced clams
4 tablespoons clam broth

Rub a small mixing bowl with cut garlic clove. Place all remaining ingredients in bowl. Blend well. For a thinner dip, add more broth.

GUACAMOLE (MEXICAN AVOCADO DUNK)

2 soft, ripe avocados, peeled and pitted
3 green onions, minced
2 peeled and chopped tomatoes
2 chopped canned chili peppers or 1 teaspoon chili powder
Salt and pepper to taste
1 tablespoon lemon juice

Put avocados through a sieve. Mix with onions, tomatoes, and peppers. Add salt and pepper to taste. Add lemon juice. Whip until fluffy.

CREAM CHEESE SPREAD-YOUR-OWN BOWLS

In each of the following cream cheese bowls, soften the cream cheese with the cream. Blend thoroughly with the other ingredients and heap into a bowl.

HORSERADISH-CREAM CHEESE BOWL

4 (3-ounce) packages cream cheese
½ cup light cream

3 teaspoons prepared horse-radish
Worcestershire sauce to taste
Minced onion to taste

DEVILED HAM-CREAM CHEESE BOWL

4 (3-ounce) packages cream cheese
½ cup light cream

2 tablespoons deviled ham
1 teaspoon finely chopped chives

AVOCADO-CREAM CHEESE BOWL

3 (3-ounce) packages cream
½ cup light cream
1 large avocado, peeled, pitted and mashed

1½ teaspoons lemon juice
1½ teaspoons onion juice
1 teaspoon salt

Avocado pulp and cream cheese should be about equal in amount.

ROQUEFORT-CREAM CHEESE BOWL

2 (3-ounce) packages cream cheese
½ cup light cream
8 ounces Roquefort or blue cheese

¼ cup finely minced onion
2 teaspoons lemon juice
¾ teaspoon salt

SHRIMP SPREAD-YOUR-OWN BOWL

½ pound cooked, cleaned shrimp
3-ounce package cream cheese
Cream as needed
2 tablespoons prepared horseradish

1 tablespoon chopped parsley
1 teaspoon lemon juice
1 teaspoon Worcestershire sauce
Dash of Tabasco sauce
Salt to taste

Put shrimp through grinder using medium blade. Mash cream cheese with enough cream to moisten thoroughly. Add seasonings and beat until creamy. Beat into shrimp. Heap into bowl. Chill.

AVOCADO SPREAD-YOUR-OWN BOWL

1 avocado
1 to 2 teaspoons minced onion
3 tablespoons mayonnaise

Juice of ½ lemon
Salt to taste
3 drops Tabasco sauce

Mash the peeled avocado pulp. Add other ingredients and blend well.

CARLTON CHEESE MOUND

½ pound sharp cheddar cheese
¼ pound Roquefort cheese
3-ounce package cream cheese

Finely chopped chives
Heavy cream
Paprika

Grate cheddar and Roquefort cheese or put through food chopper. Blend with cream cheese, chives, and heavy cream to moisten. Beat until fluffy. Mound on a plate. Sprinkle with paprika.

TOMATO-CREAM CHEESE BOWL

1 cut clove garlic
2 very ripe tomatoes
8-ounce package cream cheese

1 teaspoon Worcestershire sauce
1 teaspoon grated onion
½ teaspoon salt

Rub a chopping bowl with garlic. Chop tomatoes in same bowl until completely mashed. Add remaining ingredients. Beat until smooth. Serve with crackers and potato chips.

ALMOND CHEESE ROLLS

3-ounce package cream cheese
½ pound sharp American cheese
1 cup unblanched almonds
1 canned pimiento
3 teaspoons lemon juice

1½ teaspoons salt
1 teaspoon Worcestershire sauce
1 teaspoon scraped onion
Dash of cayenne
Paprika
Finely chopped almonds

Put cheese, almonds, and pimiento through food chopper using fine blade. Add lemon juice, salt, Worcestershire sauce, onion, and cayenne. Mix well. Shape into 2 rolls about 7 inches long. Roll 1 in paprika, the other in finely chopped almonds. Wrap in waxed paper. Chill thoroughly. To serve, let guests cut thin slices to place on thin crackers.

CAVIAR SERVICE

When serving caviar by itself, set the jar in a bed of cracked ice. Serve with accompaniments of sour cream, lemon juice, minced onion, and melba toast or dark rye bread. Use both black and red caviar. Imported caviar is expensive, therefore don't hesitate to follow the example of many prominent hostesses by using domestic varieties.

COCKTAIL SAUCES

A bowl of cocktail sauce is almost a necessity in the center of a dunking tray containing seafoods. Many people like a sharp cocktail sauce with vegetable hors d'oeuvres as well.

Standard Cocktail Sauce #1: Mix 1½ cups ketchup, 1 tablespoon horseradish, ¼ cup lemon juice, 1 teaspoon finely chopped celery, 1 tablespoon Worcestershire sauce, a few drops onion juice, a few drops Tabasco sauce, and ½ teaspoon salt. Chill thoroughly. Yield: about 1¾ cups.

Standard Cocktail Sauce # 2: Mix 1 cup ketchup, 4 teaspoons prepared horseradish, ¼ cup lemon juice, 1 teaspoon Worcestershire sauce, a dash of Tabasco sauce, and 1 teaspoon salt. Chill. Yield: about 1½ cups.

Cocktail Dressing: Mix ½ cup mayonnaise 1 tablespoon lemon juice, 1 tablespoon ketchup, 1 tablespoon horseradish, ¼ teaspoon paprika, 3 drops Worcestershire sauce, 2 drops Tabasco sauce, and salt to taste. Chill. Yield: about ¾ cup.

Piquant Cocktail Sauce: Mix ⅓ cup ketchup, 1 teaspoon onion juice, ½ teaspoon Tabasco sauce, and salt and pepper to taste. Chill. Yield: about ⅓ cup.

Celery Cocktail Sauce: Mix ¾ cup ketchup or chili sauce with 2 tablespoons lemon juice, 1 teaspoon Worcestershire sauce, ¼ cup chopped celery, and a dash each of salt and cayenne. Chill. Yield: about 1 cup.

Cucumber Cocktail Sauce: Mix ½ cup chili sauce with 1 teaspoon onion juice, 1 teaspoon lemon juice, ½ cup pared and grated cucumber, and a dash each of pepper, salt, and Tabasco sauce. Chill. Yield: about 1 cup.

Pickle Relish Cocktail Sauce: Mix ¾ cup chili sauce or ketchup with 5 tablespoons sweet pickle relish, 1 teaspoon prepared horseradish, and ½ teaspoon Worcestershire sauce. Chill. Yield: about 1 cup.

Vegetable Hors d'Oeuvres with Dip Sauce

VEGETABLE HORS D'OEUVRES

Asparagus Tips: Marinate small tips in French dressing. Sprinkle ends with paprika.

Beets, Plain or Pickled: Use tiny canned beets. They go well with a bowl of sour cream.

Carrot Strips: Wash and scrape young tender carrots. Cut in thin strips lengthwise. Wrap in damp cloth and chill.

Carrot Fans: Wash and scrape young tender carrots. Cut in quarters lengthwise. With a very sharp knife cut each quarter into thin lengthwise slices almost to the end. Spread on ice in a tray. Cover and chill.

Celery Curls: Slit celery on one end about 1½ inches down and at about ⅛-inch intervals. Stalks should be about 3 to 4 inches long. Chill in ice water.

Cauliflowerets: Break cauliflower into small flowerets. Crisp in ice water. Drain and sprinkle with paprika. Or, precook flowerets for just a few minutes, then marinate in sharp French dressing until serving time.

Cucumber Strips: Peel cucumber. Cut in half. Remove seeds. Cut solid part into narrow strips about 3 inches long. Cover with damp cloth. Chill well before serving. Sprinkle with paprika.

Cucumber Slices: Peel cucumber. Score it by running a 4-tined fork down the lengthwise surface of the cucumber. Cut into very thin slices. Chill in a tray of ice. Drain and sprinkle lightly with chopped parsley. When skin is tender, score without peeling and slice, thus adding a touch of color.

Radish Roses: Cut down thin strips of red peel of radishes almost through to stems to form petals. Place radishes in ice water. As they chill the peel will curl back like petals.

Radish Fans: Select firm and rather long radishes. With a very sharp thin knife, cut thin slices crosswise almost through radish. Chill in ice water. The slices spread, fan shaped, as they chill.

Whole Radishes: Select firm red or white radishes. Wash and scrub thoroughly. Cut off stems and root fibers. Wrap in damp cloth. Chill thoroughly in refrigerator.

Scallions: Trim washed green stalks, leaving about 3 inches. Trim onion if skin is loose or shriveled. Chill in ice water.

Marinated Onions: Skin and slice Bermuda onions. Soak in a brine made of 1 cup water to 1 tablespoon salt. Drain and soak in vinegar for 20 to 30 minutes. Drain again. Chill thoroughly.

Stuffed Eggs and Stuffed Celery

stuffed eggs and stuffed vegetables

STUFFED EGGS

With an endless variety of fillings, stuffed eggs are the most popular of all snacks to serve with cocktails. Hard-cook the eggs in water just below the boiling point for 12 to 15 minutes. If the eggs are taken directly from the refrigerator start them in cold or lukewarm water. Hot water may crack the shells. When done, chill in cold water to prevent darkening of the yolks and to make shelling easier. Cut the eggs in half lengthwise. If you want to, cut them crosswise and trim the bottoms so they won't roll over. Remove the yolks and put through a sieve or mash with a fork. Combine with seasonings and refill the whites of eggs. To give a more decorative effect use a pastry tube. Garnish with chopped parsley, chopped chives, paprika, tiny pearl onions, or slices of stuffed olive. The fillings that follow are for 6 eggs.

DEVILED EGGS

6 *hard-cooked eggs, shelled*
1 *tablespoon cream or mayonnaise*
1½ *teaspoons vinegar*
   Dash of pepper

¾ *teaspoon prepared mustard*
½ *teaspoon Worcestershire sauce (optional)*
¼ *teaspoon salt*

Remove yolks and mash with a fork. Add seasonings and beat until smooth and fluffy. Refill whites of eggs. Garnish.

Savory Deviled Eggs: Season to taste with additional seasonings such as onion juice, sardines, anchovies, cheese, pickles, olives or chives.

With Caviar: Dip the halves in caviar to cover filling. Sprinkle with a few drops lemon juice.

ANCHOVY STUFFED EGGS

6 *hard-cooked eggs, shelled*
2 *tablespoons anchovy paste*

1 *tablespoon minced chives*
1 *teaspoon lemon juice*

Mash egg yolks with a fork. Blend with other ingredients and refill whites of eggs. Garnish.

CAVIAR STUFFED EGGS #1

6 *hard-cooked eggs, shelled*   ¼ *teaspoon salt*
3 *tablespoons mayonnaise*   Pinch of pepper
2 *ounces caviar*

Mash yolks with a fork. Mix lightly with caviar, mayonnaise, and seasonings. Reserve a little caviar to decorate the top. Refill whites of eggs. Garnish tops with caviar.

CHEESE STUFFED EGGS

6 *hard-cooked eggs, shelled*   ⅓ *cup grated Swiss cheese*
2 *tablespoons butter, creamed*   Salt and pepper

Mash yolks with a fork. Blend with butter and cheese. Add seasonings to taste. Refill whites of eggs. Garnish.

CRABMEAT STUFFED EGGS

6 *hard-cooked eggs, shelled*   1 *tablespoon chopped green*
½ *cup flaked crabmeat*   *pepper*
½ *cup finely chopped celery*   ½ *teaspoon dry mustard*
                                    ⅓ *cup mayonnaise*

Mash yolks with a fork. Combine with other ingredients and refill whites of eggs. Garnish.

DRIED BEEF STUFFED EGGS

6 *hard-cooked eggs, shelled*   ¼ *teaspoon* Worcestershire
⅓ *cup shredded dried beef*   *sauce*
Juice of ½ small lemon   2½ *tablespoons salad dressing*

Frizzle dried beef until slightly crisp in butter in heavy skillet. Mash egg yolks with a fork. Add beef and other ingredients and combine well. Refill whites of eggs. Garnish with paprika or chopped parsley.

HAM STUFFED EGGS

6 *hard-cooked eggs, shelled*   About ½ *teaspoon salt*
¼ *cup ground ham*   Mayonnaise
1 *teaspoon dry mustard*

Mash yolks with a fork. Blend with other ingredients using enough mayonnaise to form into smooth paste. Refill whites of eggs. Garnish.

Deviled Eggs with Scalloped Edges

OTHER STUFFED EGG FILLINGS

1. Chopped celery mixed with mashed egg yolk, moistened with mayonnaise or salad dressing.

2. Crisp bacon mixed with mashed egg yolk and minced parsley, moistened with mayonnaise.

3. Sautéed chicken livers, chopped fine and mixed with mashed egg yolk.

4. Chopped mushrooms and chopped onions sautéed in butter and mixed with mashed egg yolk.

5. Mashed egg yolk mixed with finely chopped pickle, moistened with mayonnaise.

6. Mashed sardines, seasoned with salt and lemon juice, mixed with mashed egg yolk and moistened with mayonnaise.

CAVIAR STUFFED EGGS #2

Quarter hard-cooked eggs. Remove yolks. Fill whites with caviar seasoned with lemon and onion juices. Sprinkle grated yolk on top.

EGG SARDINE HORS D'OEUVRES

Cut hard-cooked eggs in halves, lengthwise. Season with salt, pepper, and paprika. Place a small well-drained sardine or rolled fillet of anchovy over each egg half. Arrange on a crisp lettuce leaf. Garnish with a bit of lemon.

STUFFED VEGETABLES

Pickled Beets: Hollow out tiny pickled beets. Chill and just before serving fill with caviar. Sprinkle lightly with lemon juice and grated onion. Top with a tiny bit of sour cream.

Stuffed Cucumber Slices: Cut cucumber in half crosswise. Pare and remove seeds leaving center hollow. Fill center with Roquefort or seasoned cream cheese spread. Wrap in waxed paper. Chill thoroughly. To serve, cut into ¼-inch slices. Garnish with small green caper.

Stuffed Pickles: Remove centers from dill pickles with a vegetable corer. Fill tightly with a snappy cheese spread, deviled ham, or liver sausage. Chill and cut crosswise into ½-inch slices.

Stuffed Radishes #1: Hollow out radishes with a sharp pointed knife. Crisp in ice water. Stuff with a mixture of caviar, minced parsley, mayonnaise, lemon juice, and onion juice, seasoned to taste.

Stuffed Radishes #2: Prepare radishes as in #1. Fill with an assortment of softened cheeses. In some cases it may be desirable to melt the cheese first and then allow it to cool before stuffing into the shells.

Celery Pinwheels: Cut base from celery bunch. Separate, wash and dry stalks. Fill each stalk with tangy cheese spread. Press stalks together in shape of original bunch and tie with string. Chill. To serve, cut into ¼ to ½-inch slices.

Stuffed Pepper Slices: Select long thin peppers in a variety of shades of green and red. Stuff so that all corners are filled with a seasoned cream cheese mixture. Chill 2 to 3 hours. To serve, cut with a very sharp knife into ¼-inch slices.

Tiny Stuffed Tomatoes: Select firm cherry or plum tomatoes. Cut out centers and stuff with a favorite fish, seafood, or meat mixture.

Tomato-Egg Boats: Cut medium-sized tomatoes in eights and cut out centers, leaving ½-inch thick piece. Chop 2 hard-cooked eggs fine; add ½ teaspoon salt, a little finely chopped celery, 1 tablespoon mayonnaise, and 1 teaspoon mustard-with-horseradish. Fill the tomato boats and garnish with a bit of parsley.

Artichoke Cups: Remove centers from canned artichoke hearts leaving ⅛ inch. Chop centers and add equal quantity of chopped pimiento and ½ quantity chopped browned almonds or peanuts. Fill centers.

Stuffed Brussels Sprouts: Drain cooked or canned Brussels sprouts. Cut out centers and stuff with favorite canapé spread to which may be added the chopped centers of sprouts.

Celery Pinwheels

Stuffed Carrots or Beets: Use new carrots and small beets. Cook until just tender. Remove centers with a vegetable corer and stuff with seasoned cottage cheese. Chill and serve in slices.

STUFFED CELERY

Wash tender celery stalks in cold water to crisp. Trim leaves. Cut large stalks in 2-inch lengths. Fill grooves with any of the following fillings, pressed through pastry tube or spread with knife.

Avocado: Mash avocado pulp. Sprinkle with lemon juice. Season to taste with salt and pepper. Moisten slightly with mayonnaise. Stuff and garnish with bits of pimiento.

Avocado-Flaked Fish: Put soft avocado through a sieve. Mix with flaked fish and chopped stuffed olives. Season with lemon juice. For a sharper flavor, use cayenne pepper or mustard.

Avocado-Roquefort. Mash peeled and pitted avocado. Combine with Roquefort or blue cheese and make a smooth paste, adding lemon juice and onion juice to taste. Stuff and garnish with bits of pimiento.

Cottage Cheese: Season cheese with salt and spread into grooves. Garnish with thin slices of radish with red edge showing.

Cream Cheese: Mix cheese with finely chopped nuts. Spread in celery grooves. Or mix cheese with finely chopped stuffed olives.

Deviled Ham: Combine deviled ham, cream cheese, and mayonnaise to taste. Season with prepared mustard and horseradish.

Egg: Chop hard-cooked eggs fine. Moisten with mayonnaise and season with salt and pepper. Stuff and dust with paprika or minced parsley.

Peanut Butter-Cheese: Blend equal amounts of peanut butter and pimiento cheese.

Roquefort #1: Combine Roquefort style cheese with a little butter or cream cheese. Season with grated onion.

Roquefort #2: Soften 2 ounces Roquefort cheese with 2 tablespoons (1 ounce) butter. Mix in ½ cup crushed pineapple. Spread and sprinkle with paprika.

Sardine: Cut lengths of celery to sardine size. Stuff celery with cream cheese seasoned with onion juice and minced parsley. Lay a small whole sardine on each piece. Garnish with strip of pimiento.

Seafood: Combine tuna fish or other flaked, cooked or canned seafood with a little lemon juice to flavor and mayonnaise to moisten.

STUFFED CELERY TREES

Clean and wash celery thoroughly. Select the well curved stalks and cut them into 2½-inch pieces. Fringe the tops and let stand in ice water. Remove and wipe well. Fill with your favorite celery stuffing. Put pieces together to form a round tree-like stalk and hold them together with a toothpick. When trimmed at the bottom they will stand up, fringe end to the top like a tree.

STUFFED DILL PICKLE SLICES

Remove centers from dill pickles with a vegetable corer. Stuff pickles with a snappy cheese spread, well-seasoned ground cooked meat, mock pâté de foie gras, deviled ham, or liver sausage. Chill thoroughly and cut them crosswise into 1/3-inch slices.

hors d'oeuvres on picks

PORCUPINE BALL

Use a large grapefruit, a big red apple, a solid head of cabbage (green or red), or one of the wooden or metal figures made to hold hors d'oeuvres on toothpicks. Any sort of toothpick may be used but the specially made colored cocktail picks are most attractive. On the ends of the picks place stuffed olives, little sweet pickles, rolled anchovy fillets, little cocktail sausages, or other tasty simple hors d'oeuvres or balls on picks. A large variety of suggestions are given in the following pages.

TASTY SIMPLE HORS D'OEUVRES

Anchovy Olives: Select very large olives. Remove pits carefully. Stuff with anchovy paste. Twist a whole anchovy fillet around each. Fasten with picks. Serve with lemon wedges.

Apples and Cheese: Core and cut firm red eating apples into ½-inch slices. Do not pare. Dip in orange juice to prevent darkening. Spread with any sharp cheese. Cut into wedges. Spear each wedge.

Artichoke Hearts #1: Marinate tiny canned artichoke hearts in highly seasoned French dressing to which a clove of garlic has been added. Drain well.

Artichoke Hearts #2: Drain canned artichoke hearts. Wash in salted water. Dry carefully. With a pastry tube pipe edge with cream cheese. Fill center with caviar.

Braunschweiger Olives: Mash Braunschweiger sausage. Form a spoonful at a time into a small patty. Place a small stuffed olive in center and roll into ball to cover olive. Roll the balls in chopped parsley or very finely chopped pecans or walnuts. If nuts are used and they do not stick, add a little butter to sausage when mashing it.

Button Mushrooms: Sauté mushrooms, then chill and marinate in lemon juice. Top each with a slice of stuffed olive.

Cheese Cubes: Marinate tiny cubes of American cheese in chili sauce.

Cheese and Pickled Onion: Place a ½-inch square of American cheese, a tiny slice of pickle, and a tiny pickled onion on each pick.

Frank Quickies: Cut frankfurters in half, lengthwise. Spread the cut surface of half the franks generously with a cheese spread. Top each spread half with an unspread half, pressing back into original shape. Scrape off excess cheese. Wrap in waxed paper. Chill. Cut into ½-inch pieces. Serve on picks.

Frankfurter Ovals: Cut frankfurters on a slant about ½-inch thick. Cover one end with a mixture made of ½ cup cottage cheese seasoned with 2 teaspoons each of mustard-horseradish and minced onion, and 1 teaspoon finely chopped parsley.

Garlic Olives: Rub a small bowl thoroughly with a cut clove of garlic. Put green or ripe olives in bowl. Cover with salad oil. Let stand ½ hour. Drain off oil.

Ham Cubes with Grapes: Spear ham cubes with seedless grapes.

Ham and Pickled Onion: Spear small ham cubes and small pickled onions (or small stuffed olives or cubes of dill or sweet pickle).

Kabob in Variety: Place alternately on pick: sautéed mushroom, tiny pickled onion, olive half, and cheese cube.

Melon and Meat Kabobs: Cut melon into cubes. Dip in lemon juice. Spear each cube with a cube of ham or canned spiced meat.

Olive and Onion Kabobs: Alternate small stuffed olive and small pickled onion on pick.

Oysters: Chill small oysters thoroughly. Marinate in sharp dressing.

Pretzel Stick Dumbbells: Form small balls from tasty cheese. Place a cheese ball at each end of a small pretzel stick.

Prunes: Steam small prunes until tender. Remove pits. Fill with a tangy cheese spread.

Salami: Spear bite-size cubes with small olives.

Sausage Pickups: Cut sausage into cubes. Dip in cream, then roll in finely chopped parsley.

Shrimp with Avocado and Cucumber: Marinate cubes of avocado and pieces of cooked or canned shrimp in French dressing. Spear with cucumber cubes.

Shrimp Curls: Place an ice-cold shrimp in a small leaf of lettuce or romaine. Top with mayonnaise. Roll and secure with a pick.

Shrimp and Pineapple: Spear a small whole shrimp and a cube of canned pineapple on a pick. Provide dunking sauce.

Smoked Salmon, Tongue, or Anchovy Pickles: Wrap thin slices of smoked salmon, cooked tongue, or anchovy fillets around small gherkins. Secure with picks.

Spiced Pineapple Cubes: Sauté pineapple chunks in a little butter or margarine. Sprinkle with brown sugar, spices, and a dash of vinegar. Stir gently until glazed.

Stuffed Cheese Olives: Cut very large stuffed olives in half lengthwise. Cut cheddar cheese into ½-inch squares about ¼ inch deep. Place 1 cheese square between 2 halves of olive and press firmly together.

Stuffed Olives in Anchovy Fillets: Roll each large stuffed olive in an anchovy fillet. Secure with pick.

Swiss and Dill Kabobs: Cut Swiss cheese into ½-inch cubes. Put between 2 thin slices of dill pickle and skewer with pick.

Vienna Sausage-Cheese Cube Kabobs: Spear short pieces of Vienna sausage and cubes of cheddar or Swiss cheese.

NUTMEATS FOR HORS D'OEUVRES

Pecan or Walnut Bonbons: Put perfect pecan or walnut halves together with any cream cheese spread or anchovy paste.

Curried Nutmeats: Toast nutmeats in oven; while toasting sprinkle liberally with curry powder and add a little melted butter or oil.

Garlic Nutmeats: Sprinkle nutmeats with garlic salt and melted butter. Toast in oven until crisp. Or, mash a garlic clove and let stand in butter ½ hour. Strain butter and use to season nutmeats while toasting them.

Zesty Pecans: Add salt and 1 tablespoon melted butter to 1 pound shelled pecans. Mix and toast in slow oven (300° F.) about ½ hour, stirring frequently. After 15 minutes, add 3 tablespoons Worcestershire sauce and a few dashes Tabasco sauce or cayenne pepper.

BALLS ON PICKS

Anchovy Balls: Mash 4 ounces anchovy paste with 2 hard-cooked eggs. Add ¼ cup finely chopped parsley. Season with a few grains cayenne and Worcestershire sauce to taste. Form into tiny balls. Chill thoroughly.

Blackberries: Form small balls of cream cheese. Roll in caviar and press gently into shape to resemble blackberries.

Braunschweiger Balls: Form Braunschweiger sausage into small balls and roll in shredded dried beef.

Burning Bush: Soften 1 package (3 ounces) cream cheese and season with ½ teaspoon minced onion. Form into balls. Roll in minced dried beef.

Camembert Balls: Cut off rind of Camembert cheese. Season cheese with salt and pepper to taste. Soften with butter. Form into tiny balls. Roll in stale rye bread crumbs. Chill thoroughly.

Celery-Cheese Balls: Mix 1 cup finely chopped celery, 1 package (3 ounces) cream cheese, salt and pepper to taste. Roll balls in minced parsley. Chill.

Chipped Beef Balls: Season cream cheese with Tabasco and Worcestershire sauce to taste. Form into small balls. Roll in finely minced dried beef.

Chive-Cheese Balls: Mix 2 packages (6 ounces) cream cheese with ⅓ cup chopped chives, ¾ teaspoon French mustard, salt and pepper to taste. Form into tiny balls. Chill.

Cottage Cheese Balls: Blend dry cottage cheese with just enough milk or cream to form a smooth paste. Season with salt, pepper, and grated onion. Form into balls. Roll in chopped parsley. Chill.

Cream Cheese Balls: Shape cream cheese into tiny balls. Sprinkle with paprika or roll in finely chopped nuts or olives. Chill.

Cucumber Balls: With a ball vegetable cutter, cut large cucumbers into balls. Marinate in dressing. Sprinkle with paprika.

Green Balls: Mix together ½ cup grated Swiss cheese, ½ cup minced cooked ham, ½ teaspoon prepared mustard, 1 egg yolk, ¼ teaspoon salt, and a dash of pepper. Form in balls and roll in minced chives or parsley.

Liver Sausage Balls: Mix in a bowl which has been rubbed with a cut clove of garlic 1 cup liver sausage, ¼ cup finely chopped celery, and 2 tablespoons finely chopped green pepper. Form into balls and roll in finely chopped dill pickle.

Peanut Butter Balls: Mix with grated raw carrot or ketchup and form into balls.

Roquefort-Cream Cheese Balls: Mix together Roquefort or blue cheese and cream cheese. Form into balls. Roll in chopped nuts. Chill.

Strawberries: Form cream cheese to resemble strawberries in shape. Roll in paprika. Stick pieces of parsley in the ends.

PICKLED COCKTAIL MUSHROOMS

2 (4-ounce) cans button
  mushrooms
1 cup white wine or cider
  vinegar
1 tablespoon sugar
1 teaspoon salt
1 shredded bay leaf
3 cloves
3 peppercorns
1 clove garlic, sliced
1 slice lemon

Combine vinegar, seasonings, and mushroom liquor. Boil 3 to 4 minutes. Add mushrooms. Turn into a jar and let stand overnight. Letting them stand from 1 to 2 weeks will improve the flavor. Serve whole on toothpicks or chop and use as a canapé spread.

GLAZED SHRIMP HORS D'OEUVRES #1

1 *cup canned tomatoes*
6 *tablespoons water*
2 *tablespoons chopped celery*
1 *carrot, sliced*
1 *tablespoon chopped green pepper*
1 *whole clove*
¼ *teaspoon salt*
⅛ *teaspoon pepper*
¾ *tablespoon plain gelatin*
1½ *teaspoons lemon juice*
1 *pound fresh prepared shrimp, chilled*

Put tomatoes and 4 tablespoons water in saucepan. Add vegetables and seasoning and bring to boiling point on high heat. Reduce heat and cook 15 minutes; strain. Soften gelatin in 2 tablespoons cold water 5 minutes. Add to hot tomato juice and stir until gelatin is dissolved. Stir in lemon juice. Chill in refrigerator until of syrupy consistency. Dip cold shrimp in gelatin mixture. Drain on cake rack and chill. Repeat several times to build up heavy coating of aspic on shrimp. To serve, place a glazed shrimp on a potato chip.

Glazed Shrimp Hors D'Oeuvres #2: Soak 2 teaspoons plain gelatin in ¼ cup cold water. Dissolve over boiling water. Add to 1 cup French dressing. Dip whole cooked or canned cleaned shrimp into glaze. Chill until glaze is firm.

CHEESE CARROTS #1

1 *teaspoon plain gelatin*
2 *tablespoons cold water*
½ *cup smoked cheese spread*
¼ *teaspoon* Worcestershire *sauce*
2 *medium-sized carrots, grated*
Parsley

Soften gelatin in cold water 5 minutes. Melt over hot water. Cool slightly. Blend with cheese and Worcestershire sauce. Place in refrigerator until of pliable consistency. Divide into 1 teaspoon portions. Shape into cones. Roll in grated carrots and stick sprig of parsley in large end to represent carrot top. Yield: about 30.

Cheese Carrots #2: To ½ cup soft, sharp-flavored cheese, add 1 tablespoon butter or margarine and ¼ teaspoon Worcestershire sauce. Form into shape of little carrots. Roll in fresh grated carrot. Make a small hole in the big end and insert a tiny piece of parsley for "leaves." Chill.

Herring Appetizer

HOMEMADE PICKLED HERRING

6 matjes herring	¼ cup mixed pickling spices
6 milts from herring	1 cup vinegar
6 large onions, sliced	½ lemon, sliced (optional)

Soak herring in water overnight. Clean, skin and bone, if desired. On a wooden board thoroughly pound the milt. Slice herring into 1-inch slices or leave whole. Place in jar in alternate layers with onion and lemon slices. Pour over vinegar mixed with spices and milt. Cover and keep in cool place three days. Will keep a week or longer. Serve cold.

Pickled herring with sour cream: In above recipe add ½ pint sour cream at the last.

HERRING IN WINE SAUCE

Clean herring and remove fins, tail, and head. Leave skin on. Cut into 1-inch pieces. Prepare marinade of equal parts vinegar, wine, and brown sugar. Add well mashed milt and a bay leaf for each herring. Place herring in glass jar and cover with marinade. Let stand several hours before serving.

SCANDINAVIAN PICKLED HERRING

2 fat salted Iceland herring	½ cup sugar
1 medium-sized onion, finely chopped	3 bay leaves
	¼ teaspoon white pepper
1 cup white vinegar	1 teaspoon whole allspice

Clean herring and soak in cold water overnight. Cut in halves, bone and skin. Cut into ½-inch strips. Arrange herring and onion in layers in serving dish. Mix vinegar, sugar, bay leaf, pepper, and allspice; add to herring. Let stand overnight. Serve chilled.

wedges, rolls, cornucopias

BOLOGNA WEDGES

Put 2 or 3 thin slices of bologna together with a very thin layer of softened spicy cream cheese between each slice. Wrap in waxed paper. Chill thoroughly. To serve, cut into cubes or small wedges. Spear each with a pick.

Variations: Ham, tongue, or any desired luncheon meat may be substituted for bologna. For the filling use finely chopped hard-cooked egg mixed with mayonnaise and chopped pickle instead of cream cheese. Spear each wedge with a small pickled onion, if desired.

HAM AND SWISS CHEESE WEDGES

Have ham and Swiss cheese cut into very thin slices. Cream butter with horseradish-mustard and curry powder to taste. Spread a slice of ham with seasoned butter. Cover with slice of cheese. Spread with butter and continue in this way until stack is ½ inch thick. Wrap tightly in waxed paper. Chill thoroughly. To serve, cut into cubes or small wedges. Place 1 cube and pickled onion on each toothpick.

ROQUEFORT-MEAT WEDGES

⅓ cup Roquefort or blue cheese
2 tablespoons cream

1 tablespoon horseradish
12 thin slices bologna, salami, or tongue

Blend cheese, cream, and horseradish. Spread meats with mixture. Make two 6-slice stacks. Do not spread top slices. Wrap in waxed paper. Chill thoroughly. To serve, cut into small wedges. Stick each with a pick.

VEAL AND CHEESE WEDGES

½ can veal loaf
3-ounce package cream cheese
½ teaspoon grated onion

Dash of cayenne or Tabasco sauce
½ teaspoon milk or cream
Salt to taste

Cut veal loaf into very thin slices. Cream the cheese, onion, cayenne or Tabasco with milk or cream until smooth. Add salt to taste.

Spread 3 slices of veal with cheese mixture. Stack and top with an unspread slice. Repeat until all ingredients have been used up. Wrap each stack in waxed paper. Chill thoroughly. To serve, cut into bite-size wedges or squares and serve on picks.

BOLOGNA-CHEESE RIBBONS

4 tablespoons cream cheese
1/4 teaspoon finely minced onion
1/8 teaspoon salt

1 teaspoon horseradish
3 1/16 inch slices large bologna
2 1/8-inch slices cheddar cheese

Blend together first 4 ingredients. Alternate slices of bologna with cheddar cheese, putting cream cheese mixture between slices; chill. When cheese is firm, cut into strips approximately 1/2 inch by 1 1/2 inches. Yield: about 16.

MEAT CORNUCOPIAS

These simple but tasty and decorative hors d'oeuvres can be made from a variety of ready-to-eat meats with varied fillings. Use thinly sliced boiled or baked ham, bologna, cervelat, or salami spread with a filling of highly seasoned cream cheese. Roll up cornucopia fashion and secure each with a pick. Garnish each with a tiny sprig of parsley or watercress, or a bit of pimiento. Other favorite combinations include chicken or turkey breast with chopped sweet pickle and dried beef with cream cheese. Other specific suggestions follow.

HAM CORNUCOPIAS

Slice cold baked or boiled ham very thin. Trim neatly into oblongs about 2 1/2 by 3 inches. Then roll lengthwise into small cornucopias and fasten each with a toothpick. Whip cream until stiff. Fold in horseradish to taste. Fill cornucopias with mixture and garnish with sprig of parsley inserted in open end of cornucopia.

MELON AND HAM CORNUCOPIAS

Wrap small chilled wedges of melon with very thin slices of ham. Fasten with picks. Use Italian prosciutto ham and honeydew melon.

CANAPE SALAD ROLLS

Remove crusts from thin slices of bread. Use several kinds: white, whole wheat, and rye. Spread each slice with 2 tablespoons of a finely chopped salad sandwich mixture. Roll up jelly-roll fashion. Wrap in waxed paper. Chill until serving time. Slice to serve.

CHICKEN ROLLS

Soften cream cheese with brandy. Season with salt. Spread thin slices of chicken. Roll up and fasten with toothpicks.

SALAMI CORNUCOPIAS

Spread thinly sliced salami with mustard. Roll and fasten with tooth-picks. Serve plain or place a small pickle or a stuffed olive in the center as a filling, or roll each around a few stalks of watercress.

SMOKED SALMON AND CHEESE ROLLS

Spread thin slices of smoked salmon with cream cheese seasoned with horseradish, salt, and black pepper. Roll up. Fasten with picks.

SMOKED SALMON-CAVIAR CORNUCOPIAS

Roll very thin slices of smoked salmon into cornucopias. Fasten with toothpicks. Fill each with caviar seasoned with lemon juice, or caviar mixed with riced hard-cooked eggs seasoned with lemon juice and paprika.

PUFF PASTE-CAVIAR CORNUCOPIAS

Roll puff paste very thin. Cut into small squares. Fold over caviar seasoned with lemon juice. Pinch edges together. Fry in deep hot fat.

BOLOGNA ROLLS

2 *ounces cheddar cheese*	6 *slices large bologna*
2 *teaspoons softened butter*	4 *large stuffed olives, cut into*
1 *large stuffed olive, chopped fine*	*lengthwise strips*

Cream the cheese and butter together. Stir in chopped olive. Spread each round of bologna with 2½ teaspoons of cheese mixture. Cut rounds crosswise into 4 triangular parts. Beginning at point of tri-angle, roll and secure with toothpick. Garnish ends of roll with slice of olive. Chill. Yield: 24.

SMITHFIELD HAM ROLLS

Spread thin slices of Smithfield ham with cottage cheese mixed with piccalilli. Roll up. Fasten with picks.

HAM AND OLIVE PINWHEELS

3 *slices boiled ham*	2 *tablespoons olive-pimento*
About 12 small stuffed olives	*cheese spread*

Spread each slice of ham with 2 teaspoons cheese spread. Cut into ¾-inch strips. Place an olive at end of each strip and roll. Secure with toothpick and chill. When cheese is firm, remove toothpicks and cut each roll in half to form 2 pinwheels. Serve with cut side up. Yield: about 24.

Serve Yourself Canapé Spread Tray

ASPARAGUS ROLLS #1

Cut fresh bread in very thin slices and remove crusts. Spread with mustard or mayonnaise. Roll each slice around an asparagus tip. Fasten with toothpicks. Place in shallow pan and cover with damp cloth. Chill thoroughly. Remove toothpicks before serving.

Asparagus Rolls #2: Season mayonnaise with dry mustard to taste. Spread on small slices of tongue. Roll each slice around an asparagus tip. Secure with a toothpick.

HAM ROLLS

Spread thin evenly shaped slices of boiled or baked ham with a mixture of prepared mustard and mayonnaise. Cut as many thin strips of bread as there are rolls to be made. Place a bread strip on the end of each ham slice and roll ham over it very tightly. Dip sprigs of parsley or watercress in French dressing and insert 1 or 2 sprigs in each roll. Fasten the rolls with picks and keep in cold place until serving time.

DRIED BEEF WHIRLIGIGS

Dried beef slices	¼ *teaspoon finely chopped onion*
3-ounce package cream cheese	1 *tablespoon blue cheese*
⅛ *teaspoon finely chopped garlic*	½ *teaspoon Worcestershire sauce*

Place 2 slices of dried beef together, overlapping slightly. Beat the cream cheese with remaining ingredients and spread on beef slices. Roll up jelly-roll fashion. Chill, then cut diagonally with a very sharp knife into ¼-inch slices. Serve on picks. Yield: about 36.

canape spreads

CHEESE CANAPE SPREADS

Camembert or Liederkranz Spread: Blend Camembert or Liederkranz cheese with half as much cream cheese.

Cottage Cheese Spread: Mix 1 cup cottage cheese with 4 tablespoons melted butter and ½ teaspoon each of onion juice and lemon juice. Add salt, pepper, and paprika to taste. Garnish the spread canapé bases with slices of stuffed olive or strips of pimiento or bell pepper.

Cheese-Wine-Olive Spread: Combine aged American or cheddar cheese with enough sherry wine to make a smooth spread. Add half as much chopped stuffed olives. Mix well.

Cheese-Olive Spread #1: Put 2 parts American cheese and 1 part stuffed or pitted olives through the meat grinder using a fine knife. Mix together well.

Cheese-Olive Spread #2: Combine ¼ cup grated soft, sharp cheese, ¼ cup butter, and add ¼ cup finely chopped green or stuffed olives. Season to taste with salt and pepper.

Cheese-Pickle Spread: Combine 1 cup grated American cheese and ½ cup well-drained chopped dill pickle. Moisten with 1 tablespoon ketchup and 2 tablespoons mayonnaise.

Roquefort-Watercress Spread: Soften 8 ounces Roquefort or other blue cheese and blend thoroughly with ¼ cup finely minced watercress. Season with salt and pepper to taste and add 1 teaspoon Worcestershire sauce.

Roquefort Spread: Combine ¼ cup Roquefort or blue cheese with 2 tablespoons cream cheese, and 1 tablespoon mayonnaise. Season with a few drops of Worcestershire sauce.

Roquefort-Chives Spread: Mix Roquefort cheese with enough French dressing to moisten. Season with chopped chives.

CREAM CHEESE CANAPE SPREADS

Cheese-Watercress Spread: Cream 1 package (3 ounces) cream cheese. Dry and chop 1 cup watercress. Blend together with 1 teaspoon Worcestershire sauce and ¼ teaspoon salt.

Chili-Cheese Spread: Combine 1 package (3 ounces) cream cheese or ½ cup grated American cheese with enough chili sauce to moisten.

Orange-Cream Cheese Spread: Mix 1 package (3 ounces) cream cheese, grated rind of 1 orange, ¼ teaspoon salt, and ⅛ teaspoon paprika. Spread on buttered bases and top with chopped toasted pecan meats.

Cheese-Onion Spread: Soften cream cheese with cream. Add a few drops onion juice or minced onion. Season with salt and pepper. Garnish with paprika or minced parsley.

Cream Cheese-Pickle Spread: Mix finely chopped pickles with cream cheese. Garnish with slices of stuffed olives.

Cheese-Sour Cream Spread: Blend cream cheese with sour cream. Season with salt and pepper.

Garlic-Cream Cheese Spread: Rub a salad bowl with a cut clove of garlic. Moisten cream cheese with a bit of cream and work in the bowl until cheese is softened and has absorbed some of the garlic flavor. Garnish with finely minced parsley.

Cheese-Green Pepper Spread: Blend 1 package (3 ounces) cream cheese with 4 tablespoons minced green pepper, 2 tablespoons minced onion, 1 teaspoon French dressing, and a few grains of cayenne.

Cheese-Nut Spread: Blend cream cheese with chopped nuts and sweeten to taste with confectioners' sugar.

Cheese-Caviar Spread: Moisten cream cheese with cream. Spread on small crackers. Dot with caviar.

COCKTAIL CHEESE BALL

2 3-ounce *packages cream cheese*	1 *tablespoon minced onion*
1½ *ounces Roquefort cheese*	1 *tablespoon minced stuffed olives*
1 *jar (5 ounces) smoked cheese spread*	2 *tablespoons minced parsley*
1 *teaspoon Worcestershire sauce*	½ *cup finely chopped walnuts*

Combine all ingredients except parsley and nuts. Blend thoroughly. Chill overnight. Shape into ball. Roll in parsley and nuts. Serve surrounded with potato chips and crackers.

CHEESE LOG

3-ounce package cream cheese
3 ounces soft butter
1 teaspoon capers
1 teaspoon paprika
½ teaspoon caraway seed
½ teaspoon anchovy paste
1 tablespoon minced onion

Blend all ingredients. Shape into roll. Wrap in waxed paper. Chill thoroughly. Let your guests cut and spread it on crackers, melba toast, or thinly sliced bread.

COCKTAIL CHEESE MOLD

2 3-ounce packages cream cheese
¼ cup soft butter
½ teaspoon caraway seed
1 tablespoon anchovy paste
1 teaspoon paprika
1 tablespoon chopped chives
½ teaspoon salt
1 teaspoon capers

Cream the cheese and butter together until fluffy. Add remaining ingredients and mix well. Pack into small mold. Chill several hours. Unmold on tray or plate. Serve with potato chips and crackers.

FISH AND SEAFOOD CANAPE SPREADS

Anchovy-Cheese Spread: Combine 1 part anchovy paste with 2 parts cream cheese. Spread and garnish with minced egg yolk.

Anchovy-Egg Spread: Mash and blend 4 hard-cooked egg yolks and 4 anchovies. Moisten to spreading consistency with mayonnaise. Season with grated onion and black pepper. Spread and garnish with chopped egg white.

Caviar Spread #1: Flavor caviar with onion juice and lemon juice. Spread and decorate with tiny pearl onions.

Caviar Spread #2: Mash yolks of 3 hard-cooked eggs. Blend with ⅓ cup creamed butter and ⅓ cup caviar.

Chopped Herring Spread: Wash, clean, bone, and chop salted herring which has been soaked in cold water for several hours. For each herring use 1 onion, 1 sour apple, 1 slice of toast soaked in vinegar or lemon juice. Chop all together very fine and add 1 teaspoon salad oil, a dash each of cinnamon and pepper. Serve garnished with finely chopped hard-cooked egg.

Crabmeat or Lobster Spread: Make a paste of canned or cooked seafood. Moisten with mayonnaise. Season with lemon juice and grated onion.

Crabmeat or Lobster and Deviled Egg Spread: Drain, bone, and wash contents of 1 can (6 ounces) seafood. Mash with 2 hard-cooked eggs, ½ teaspoon mustard, 2 tablespoons mayonnaise, 1 tablespoon lemon juice, and about 1 teaspoon curry powder.

Kippered Herring Spread: Combine 1 cup mashed kippered herring with 1 chopped hard-cooked egg and ¼ cup minced cucumber. Moisten with mayonnaise and season with 2 drops lemon juice.

Sardine Spread #1: Mash and blend together 3 sardines and 1 package (3 ounces) cream cheese. Season with lemon juice to taste.

Sardine Spread #2: Drain oil from 1 can sardines. Mash sardines and season with ½ tablespoon lemon juice, a few drops of Worcestershire sauce, salt and pepper to taste. Add enough butter to form a smooth paste.

Sardine Spread #3: Drain oil from 1 can sardines. Mash sardines with fork. Add 1 tablespoon mayonnaise, 1 tablespoon lemon juice, and ¼ teaspoon Tabasco sauce. Mix to a smooth paste.

Sardine and Hard-Cooked Egg Spread: Combine mashed sardines with mashed hard-cooked egg yolk. Season to taste with lemon juice. Add enough butter to form a smooth paste. Spread on toasted canapé bases. Garnish with riced white of egg. Sprinkle with chopped parsley.

Shrimp Spread: Combine ½ cup cut-up cleaned cooked or canned shrimp, 1 package (3 ounces) cream cheese, and 1½ teaspoons anchovy paste.

Shrimp and Pecan Spread: Grind and mix thoroughly equal parts smoked shrimp and pecan meats.

Smoked Salmon-Egg Spread: Chop or grind ½ pound smoked salmon. Add and blend 1 tablespoon olive oil, dash of paprika, and ½ teaspoon lemon juice. Mince yolks and whites of 2 hard-cooked eggs. Spread salmon mixture on canapé bases. Sprinkle with yolks, then with whites in circles.

Smoked Salmon and Mayonnaise Spread: Chop smoked salmon and combine with chopped hard-cooked eggs. Add mayonnaise and paprika.

Tuna or Salmon Spread: Make a paste from cooked or canned salmon or tuna. Moisten with mayonnaise and add lemon juice to taste. Spread and decorate with minced parsley.

Sturgeon-Cheese Spread: Combine 1 cup flaked kippered sturgeon (or herring), 1½ cups grated cheddar cheese, and ½ medium-sized

Bermuda onion, grated. Spread and garnish with slices of stuffed olives.

QUICK AND EASY FLAKED FISH CANAPE SPREADS

Cook, cool and flake fish fillets or use canned flaked fish. Then:

1. Mix equal quantities of flaked fish and chopped pearl onions, mix with mayonnaise and chili sauce. Serve on whole wheat crackers.

2. Mix equal quantities of flaked fish and chopped mustard pickle. Serve on crackers or toast strips.

3. Moisten flaked fish with cream and horseradish. Serve on crackers or toast strips, garnished with green pepper.

FRUIT AND VEGETABLE CANAPE SPREADS

Avocado Spread: Pare avocados and mash pulp with a fork. Season with lemon or lime juice and salt. Spread on canapé base and garnish with minced parsley.

Avocado-Egg Spread: Mash and blend equal parts of avocado pulp and hard-cooked egg yolk. Season with lemon juice and salt to taste.

Avocado-Olive Spread: Mix 1 cup mashed avocado pulp with ¼ cup finely chopped ripe or green olives. Season with lemon or lime juice. Spread on canapé base. Garnish with paprika, curled anchovies, pimiento strips, or red radish rounds.

Avocado-Onion Spread: Season mashed avocado pulp with minced onion, salt, and a dash of Tabasco sauce. Place a slice of tomato on canapé base and cover with spread.

Mushroom Spread: Wash and chop or grind mushrooms fine. Fry gently in butter for 5 minutes. Cool and season to taste with lemon juice, salt, and pepper.

Onion-Egg Spread: Chop 1 large onion fine. Add about 4 tablespoons melted chicken fat, 1 hard-cooked egg, chopped fine, and salt to taste.

Pickled Beet and Egg Spread: Combine equal parts of finely minced pickled beets and minced hard-cooked eggs. Season to taste.

MUSHROOM CANAPE SPREAD #2

4-ounce can mushrooms (use pieces and stems)
4 tablespoons butter
¼ cup heavy cream

Onion juice to taste
Salt and pepper to taste
¾ cup English cheddar cheese

Drain mushrooms. Sauté in butter. Add cream, seasonings, and cheese. Mash to a paste. Spread toast rounds or squares with a softened butter, then spread with mushroom mixture. Sprinkle with paprika.

EGGPLANT BIARRITZ

1 medium-sized eggplant
2 medium-sized onions, minced
1 green pepper, minced
¼ cup olive oil (about)
¼ teaspoon oregano

1 can (2½ cups) tomatoes
1 large clove garlic, chopped fine
1 teaspoon salt (about)
⅛ teaspoon pepper

Cut eggplant in half. Boil in water to cover until tender (about 20 minutes). Sauté onions and green pepper in oil until brown. Add garlic. Peel eggplant and mash pulp and seeds with a fork. Add to onions with tomatoes and seasonings. Simmer on a very low flame 20 to 30 minutes. Let cool, if desired. Serve hot or cold on squares of pumpernickel or rye bread.

EGGPLANT CAVIAR

1 eggplant
2 small onions, minced
2 cloves, minced
1 clove garlic, minced

1 ripe tomato, peeled and minced
Salt and pepper
Vinegar
Olive oil

Broil the whole eggplant over direct flame or in a broiler for 15 to 20 minutes. Remove the inside pulp and mix with the onions, cloves, and garlic. Add the tomato and season to taste with salt, pepper, vinegar, and oil. Serve on greens, garnished with quartered tomatoes and black olives or use as spread on rye or pumpernickel bread.

MEAT CANAPE SPREADS

Chicken-Ham-Olive Spread: Combine ½ cup chopped cooked chicken, ½ cup chopped cooked ham, and ¼ cup chopped green olives. Moisten with mayonnaise.

Chicken Liver Spread: Combine ½ cup chopped cooked chicken livers with 1 or 2 hard-cooked eggs, finely chopped, and 1 teaspoon finely chopped onion. Season to taste with salt and pepper. Moisten with butter or chicken fat.

Chicken or Turkey Spread: Chop or grind cooked chicken or turkey. Moisten with mayonnaise. Add finely chopped celery. Season to taste. Garnish with watercress.

Chopped Liver and Egg Spread: Grind or chop very fine, ½ pound fried chicken livers, 1 hard-cooked egg, 1 small stalk celery, and 1 small onion. Moisten with melted chicken fat or butter. Add salt and pepper to taste. Mix to a smooth paste.

Chopped Liver and Mushroom Spread: Chop fine ½ pound fried chicken or calves' livers. Sauté ½ cup fresh mushrooms for 5 minutes in 3 tablespoons of chicken fat or butter. Chop fine and add both mushrooms and the fat in which they were fried to the liver. Season to taste with salt, pepper, and onion juice.

Deviled Ham Spread #1: Combine ¼ cup deviled ham, 1 tablespoon finely chopped celery, and 1 chopped hard-cooked egg. Combine ¼ teaspoon curry powder and ½ teaspoon olive oil. Add to ham mixture and moisten with mayonnaise. Add salt to taste.

Deviled Ham Spread #2: Blend equal parts of deviled ham and creamed butter. Season with mustard to taste.

Deviled Ham and Cheese Spread: Combine 6 ounces deviled ham with ¼ cup pimiento cheese spread and 2 tablespoons chopped sweet pickle. Moisten with mayonnaise.

Dried Beef-Cheese-Almond Spread: Combine 1 cup chopped dried beef and ½ cup each of pineapple cheese and chopped toasted almonds. Season with 2 tablespoons lemon juice.

Ham-Cheese Spread: Combine 1 cup finely chopped cooked ham, ¼ cup grated American cheese, ½ teaspoon finely chopped onion, and 1 teaspoon chili sauce.

Liverwurst Spread: Mash ½ cup liverwurst to a paste. Season with 2 tablespoons horseradish and ½ teaspoon prepared mustard.

Liverwurst and Bacon Spread: Chop cold crisp bacon very fine. Combine 1 part bacon with 3 parts liverwurst. Season with salt, pepper, Worcestershire sauce and Tabasco sauce to taste.

Minced Ham Spread: Moisten finely ground cooked ham with mayonnaise. Add a little chopped dill pickle or sweet pickle relish.

Pate de Foie Gras Spread: Mix 3 tablespoons of pâté de foie gras, ¼ cup cream, and salt and pepper to taste. Force the mixture through a sieve.

Mock Pate de Foie Gras Spread: Fry 1 ounce salt pork until crisp. Grind with 8 ounces cooked chicken livers. Season with lemon juice, salt, and pepper. Moisten with mayonnaise.

Roast Beef or Veal Spreads: Moisten finely ground meat with mixture of horseradish and mayonnaise. Season to taste.

Tongue, Corned Beef, Bologna, or Salami Spreads: Moisten finely ground cooked meat with mayonnaise. Add a little finely chopped sweet pickle and pimiento. Season to taste.

BRAUNSCHWEIGER PINEAPPLE CENTERPIECE

Use 1½ to 2 pounds cold, firm Braunschweiger sausage. Remove covering and mold it into shape of a fresh pineapple. Brush with a little lemon juice or soft butter. Cover surface with slices of stuffed olive to resemble "eyes" of pineapple. Top with 3 or 4 green onions or leaves from fresh pineapple. Serve surrounded with crackers and potato chips.

LIEDERKRANZ CANAPE SPREAD

4 ounces soft Liederkranz cheese	½ teaspoon prepared mustard
½ cup soft butter	¼ teaspoon Worcestershire sauce
½ teaspoon salt	3 tablespoons minced green pepper
¼ teaspoon pepper	per
⅛ teaspoon paprika	2 tablespoons minced onion

Cream the cheese until smooth and fluffy. Gradually blend in butter. Blend in remaining ingredients. Serve with thin slices of rye or pumpernickel bread.

DRIED BEEF AVOCADO WHIP

1 ripe avocado	Juice of ½ lemon
¼ teaspoon salt	⅓ cup frizzled dried beef

Slice avocado in half lengthwise. Remove seed and scoop out pulp carefully so that shells may be used as natural containers for the whipped spread. Mash the pulp and add salt, lemon juice, and frizzled beef. (To frizzle beef, brown in butter in heavy skillet until crisp.) Mix well and heap into shells.

CHICKEN LIVERS AND GIZZARDS SPREAD

4 chicken gizzards	3 tablespoons chicken fat
1 medium onion, minced	2 hard-cooked eggs
8 chicken livers	1 teaspoon parsley, minced
	Salt and pepper

nmer gizzards until tender. Fry chopped onion in chicken fat
_.til lightly brown; add and saute livers and cooked gizzards. Chop
eggs, gizzards, livers, and onions; add seasoning, parsley, and some
chicken fat. Force this through a sieve and serve cold.

miscellaneous cold canapes

THREE COLOR CAVIAR CANAPES

Use black and red caviar. Spread diamond or round canapé bases
with cream cheese seasoned with onion juice. Divide the canapé
down the middle with a ridge of cream cheese, minced parsley, or
minced chives. Put red caviar on 1 side and black caviar on other
side. If desired, border canapés with grated hard-cooked egg yolk or
white, or with minced parsley.

POLKA DOT CANAPES

Shape cream cheese into small balls. Chill thoroughly. Roll in caviar
until well dotted. Cover rounds of toast with mayonnaise. Place 1
ball on each toasted round.

CAVIAR TOAST SQUARES

Spread caviar on toast squares. Pipe with edging of chopped egg.
Garnish center with sieved egg yolk and chopped onion.

CAVIAR-EGG ROUNDS

Spread sides of toasted round bases with mayonnaise. Roll sides in
sieved egg yolk. Spread top with caviar. Place thin ring slice of
cooked egg white over caviar.

CAVIAR CANAPE FINGERS

Cut bread into narrow strips. Toast in oven until thoroughly dry. Spread with softened butter, then with a thin layer of caviar. Divide the canapé diagonally down the middle with a narrow ridge of piccalilli or finely chopped pickle. Garnish one end with sieved hard-cooked egg yolk, the other end with sieved hard-cooked egg white. For added color, garnish with thin strips of pimiento.

Variations: Use anchovy or sardine paste instead of caviar.

DANEN CANAPES

Toast round of bread on one side. Spread untoasted side with mayonnaise. Add thin slices of tomato, then slices of hard-cooked egg. Sprinkle lightly with salt. Garnish with a slice or two of olive.

RYE BREAD CANAPES

Combine yolks of 2 hard-cooked eggs, ½ teaspoon dry mustard, 1 teaspoon mayonnaise, and 1½ tablespoons deviled ham. Mix until smooth. Spread on rounds of rye bread. Top with ring slices of hard-cooked egg white. Sprinkle with paprika.

HALF-AND-HALF CANAPES

2 3-ounce packages cream cheese	Few leaves sage, shredded
1 tablespoon chopped onion	1 medium-sized jar red caviar
1 tablespoon chopped parsley	Mayonnaise
	Toasted canapé bases

Mix cream cheese with onion, parsley, and sage. Cover half of each toast round with cream cheese mixture. Cover other half with caviar. With a pastry tube place a garnish of mayonnaise between the caviar and cheese and around the edges.

MANHATTAN CANAPES

12 strips of toast	1 teaspoon onion juice
¼ cup butter	1 teaspoon lemon juice
2 tablespoons capers	1 hard-cooked egg
1 tablespoon minced parsley	2 ounces caviar

Cream butter and mix it with the capers, parsley, onion juice, and lemon juice. Spread on toast strips. In the center place a slice of hard-cooked egg and a small round of caviar.

JEFF'S HALF-MOONS

6 *slices bread*
3 *tablespoons mayonnaise*
2 *hard-cooked eggs*

1 *tablespoon minced onion*
1 *ounce caviar*

Cut bread into half-moons. Spread with mayonnaise. Sprinkle with chopped egg whites and onion. Cover with mounds of caviar mixed with chopped egg yolks.

JOSHUA'S SMILE

Cut bread into crescents. Toast crescents on one side. Edge the untoasted side with strips of pimiento. Next to the pimiento place a row of very tiny pickled onions. Fill center with black caviar slightly flavored with lemon juice.

CRAB CANAPES

1 *cup flaked crabmeat*
2 *hard-cooked eggs, chopped*
1 *teaspoon lemon juice*
3 *tablespoons mayonnaise*
½ *teaspoon Worcestershire sauce*

Dash of Tabasco sauce
Salt and pepper
Ripe olives or capers
Cream cheese

Mix crabmeat with chopped egg and seasonings. Cut bread with diamond-shaped cutter; toast and spread with soft butter and crab mixture. Decorate with cream cheese (blend ⅓ cup cream cheese with 2 tablespoons mayonnaise, and ¼ teaspoon Worcestershire sauce) and put through pastry bag. Garnish. Yield: 24 canapés.

CRAB FLAKE SQUARES

Cover toast squares with Russian dressing. Spread with crab flakes. Spread chopped radishes around edges.

SARDINE FINGERS

1 *can sardines*
3 *tablespoons butter*
½ *teaspoon prepared horseradish*

6 *stuffed olives*
1-inch *toast strips*

Remove skin and bones from sardines and rub to a paste with the sardine oil, and butter. Add horseradish. Blend well and spread on toast strips. Slice olives thin and arrange in overlapping row down center of fingers.

SARDINE CANAPES

1 *can sardines*
¼ *cup minced olives*
1 *hard-cooked egg, minced*

1 *tablespoon mayonnaise*
Toasted canapé bases

Blend the ingredients thoroughly and spread on bases which have been toasted on one side.

TRIPLE DECKER CANAPES

Cut crusts from 2 slices whole wheat bread and 1 slice white bread. Spread with softened butter or a savory canapé butter. Cover 1 slice of whole wheat bread with a canapé spread. Cover with white slice, buttered side down. Spread white slice with softened butter and then spread with a second kind of canapé spread. Cover with the other slice of whole wheat bread. Trim evenly. Wrap in waxed paper. Chill thoroughly. To serve, cut in lengthwise slices ¼-inch thick, then cut crosswise to make 2 canapés from each ¼-inch slice. Yield: about 15 canapés.

ROQUEFORT CHEESE CANAPES

8 *slices bread*
3 *ounces Roquefort cheese*

½ *teaspoon Worcestershire*
   sauce
½ *teaspoon French dressing*

Cut bread in heart shapes and sauté in butter. Combine cheese, sauce and dressing and spread on sautéed bread bases. Garnish with little pieces of green and red pepper.

PARMESAN-TOMATO CANAPES

Place thin slices of tomato on toasted canapé bases. Sprinkle with grated Parmesan cheese and then with chopped parsley.

YELLOW CHEESE CANAPES

Spread soft yellow cheese on round canapé bases. Decorate with minced parsley or sliced stuffed olives.

CHEESE STRIPS

Spread long strips of toast with a cream cheese spread. Place a long thin slice of green gherkin on top. Sprinkle edges with paprika.

CRADLE OF THE DEEP

Place a shrimp in the center of a crisp cracker, spread with savory butter. Encircle with cream cheese rippled from a decorating tube.

EGG-OLIVE CANAPES

4 hard-cooked eggs, shelled
12 cheese wafers
4 tablespoons ground boiled ham

4 tablespoons minced olives
2 tablespoons mayonnaise
3 stuffed olives

Cut the hard-cooked eggs in ½-inch slices. Remove the yolks and place the white rings on round cheese wafers. Make a paste of egg yolks, ham, olives, and mayonnaise and fill the cavities of the egg white rings. Top each with a slice of stuffed olive.

DEEP SEA CANAPES

Make a paste by mashing kippered herring with lemon juice, and moistening with mayonnaise. Spread on toasted bread cut in diamond shape. Garnish edges with mayonnaise to which sifted egg yolks have been added. Decorate each canapé diagonally with tiny strips of herring.

WHOLE SHRIMP CANAPES

Spread untoasted side of canapé bases with mayonnaise. Place a whole cooked shrimp on each. Garnish with minced parsley.

SMOKED FISH CANAPES

Arrange thin strips of smoked salmon and smoked herring on bases. Decorate edge with chopped egg yolk. Sprinkle with minced parsley.

AVOCADO CANAPES

1 medium-sized avocado
1 tablespoon onion juice
1 tablespoon lemon juice
¼ teaspoon salt
Dash of Tabasco sauce

2 tablespoons mayonnaise
Tomato slices
Toast rounds
Stuffed olives

Pare and pit the avocado. Mash pulp with a fork; add onion juice, lemon juice, salt, and Tabasco sauce. Moisten with mayonnaise and spread on toast rounds. Top each with a thin slice of tomato. Put a small mound of avocado mixture in the center. Garnish with sliced olives.

AVOCADO AND SHRIMP CANAPES

Peel and mash a small avocado. Season with 1 teaspoon lemon juice, 1 teaspoon minced onion, and a dash of salt. Spread on crackers and top each with a whole shrimp.

CUCUMBER-SHRIMP CANAPES

Flute a firm, unpeeled cucumber by drawing lines down the side with a fork, making parallel grooves. Cut into thin slices. Marinate whole, cleaned, cooked shrimp in French dressing for 1 hour. Drain well. Place a slice of cucumber on each round, thin cracker. Put a shrimp on top. Garnish with chopped parsley.

LOBSTER CANAPES

3 tablespoons lobster paste
3 tablespoons butter
6 small rounds of toast

2 hard-cooked eggs
3 stuffed olives

Cream together the lobster paste and butter. Spread evenly on toast rounds. Arrange thick slices of hard-cooked egg in center. Cut olives in halves and press a half into the center of egg slices, cut side up.

HARD-COOKED EGG AND LOBSTER CANAPES

Cut hard-cooked eggs in halves lengthwise. Remove yolks and part of whites to make cases a little larger. Fill cases with coarsely chopped lobster meat moistened with tartar sauce. Invert on sautéed oval-shaped pieces of bread. Pipe green butter over egg. Garnish with a tip of watercress.

ANCHOVY CURLS

Place anchovy curls or fillets on toast fingers. Dip edges in mayonnaise, then in sieved egg yolks. Garnish with strips of pimiento.

ANCHOVY AND KETCHUP CANAPES

Cut bread into rounds and spread with ketchup. Place an anchovy fillet in the center. Make a rim of cream cheese around the edge.

ANCHOVY ROUNDS

Spread rounds of melba toast with cream cheese. Cover with slice of hard-cooked egg. Top each with rolled anchovy fillet.

ANCHOVY AND CUCUMBER CANAPES

Spread bread canapé bases with Anchovy Butter. Chop cucumber rather fine and marinate in a little French dressing (2 tablespoons to 1 medium-sized cucumber). Place a layer on the canapé bases. Place a stuffed olive in the center of each.

SMOKED SALMON CANAPES #1

Trim crusts from thinly sliced bread. Cut in strips. Toast on one side. Spread untoasted side with Lemon Butter. Brush edges with mayonnaise and dip in chopped parsley. Place a wafer-thin slice of smoked salmon on each. Garnish with chopped hard-cooked egg white and chopped parsley.

SMOKED SALMON CANAPES #2

Chop 2 hard-cooked egg whites very fine. Mix with ½ teaspoon grated onion, salt and pepper to taste, and mayonnaise for spreading consistency. Spread on buttered toast. Place sliced olive in center and strips of salmon at each end.

SMOKED SALMON CANAPES #3

Split small hard rolls. Spread with cream cheese. Top with thinly sliced smoked salmon. Cut into bite-size wedges.

SMOKED SALMON CANAPES #4

Spread pumpernickel or dark rye bread with sweet butter. Cut into fingers. Cover with thin slices of smoked salmon. Sprinkle with minced parsley. Serve with lemon wedges. If desired, season with olive oil and freshly ground black pepper.

MARINATED HERRING CANAPES

Place small slices of Bermuda or Spanish onion on squares of rye or pumpernickel bread. Top each with small squares of marinated herring.

SMOKED FISH TIDBITS

Arrange smoked eel, sturgeon, trout, or whitefish on buttered dark rye bread. Sprinkle with lemon juice. Top with onion ring.

SALAMI CANAPES

½ pound hard salami	Bread, sliced thin
3 hard-cooked eggs	Parsley
½ cup salad dressing	Pimiento

Put salami and hard-cooked eggs through food chopper 2 or 3 times. Blend with salad dressing. Trim crust from bread and cut into small squares. Toast on one side. Spread untoasted side with salami mixture. Sprinkle with chopped parsley and garnish with pimiento strips.

ANYA'S CANAPES

Cut toast in triangle shape. Spread with Anchovy Butter. Decorate one edge with finely minced egg white, the second edge with finely minced egg yolk, the third edge with minced green gherkins. Place a stuffed olive in the center.

FRANKFURTER AND BEAN CANAPES

Mash baked beans and spread on toasted canapé bases. Garnish with slices of frankfurters and stuffed olives.

OLIVE CANAPES

Sauté ¼ inch thick rounds of bread in olive oil until a delicate brown. Stuff ripe olives with pâté de foie gras and cut in halves lengthwise. Spread the rounds of toast with Parsley Butter. Place an olive on top and top with a dab of mayonnaise.

CUCUMBER-CHEESE-SARDINE CANAPES

Soak thin slices of cucumber in salted ice water to crisp. Cut canapé bases to size of cucumber and spread with cream cheese. Top each with a cucumber slice. Top cucumber with chopped sardines mixed with mayonnaise and lemon juice. Garnish with a bit of pimiento.

TOMATO WHEEL CANAPES

Remove seed sections from small slices of tomatoes. Place on buttered toast rounds. Fill alternate sections with chopped hard-cooked egg and black caviar.

TOMATO-CHEESE CANAPES

Mix 1 (3-ounce) package cream cheese with 2 teaspoons tomato paste. Spread on toast bases. Garnish with pimiento strips. Sprinkle with chopped parsley.

PEANUT BUTTER AND CHOPPED PICKLE CANAPES

Mix equal amounts of peanut butter and chopped pickle. Spread on crisp thin wafers.

PUMPERNICKEL CANAPES

Combine 1 tablespoon prepared horseradish, ¼ teaspoon dry mustard, 2 tablespoons butter, and a dash of paprika. Mix until smooth. Spread mixture on rounds of pumpernickel. Lay 2 small strips of anchovy on each.

SAVORY OYSTER CANAPES

Use round canapé bases toasted on one side. Spread untoasted side with Mustard Butter. Dip chilled raw oysters in mayonnaise and press one into each round. Garnish with sieved hard-cooked egg yolk mixed with minced chives.

REDSKINS

Chop crisp bacon and mix with mayonnaise. Spread on toast rounds. Cover each with thin slice of tomato. Garnish with chopped parsley.

GUAVA-CHEESE CANAPES

Spread cream cheese over canapé bases, then spread with guava jelly. Sprinkle chopped nuts over top.

SAUERKRAUT CANAPES

1 *cup well-drained sauerkraut*	*Rounds of rye bread*
¾ *cup mayonnaise*	*Stuffed olives*

Chop sauerkraut very fine and mix with ¼ cup mayonnaise. Spread on rye bread rounds which have already been spread with remaining mayonnaise. Garnish with sliced olives.

NEW YEAR'S DAY CANAPES

Use a bell-shaped cooky cutter and cut bread into bell shapes. Toast or sauté the bases as suggested for other canapé bases. Spread with cream cheese or any light-colored canapé spread such as tuna fish or chicken. Dot with bits of pimiento and chopped parsley.

INDEPENDENCE DAY CANAPES

Spread small rounds of toast with butter. Arrange on each tiny bundles of small strips of pimientos to resemble tiny red firecrackers. Place cream cheese in a pastry tube and make small lines to resemble fuses for the firecrackers.

ST. VALENTINE'S DAY CANAPES

Use a heart-shaped cooky cutter and cut bread into heart shapes. Toast or sauté the bases as suggested for other canapé bases. Spread with a desired cheese spread. Top each with smaller hearts cut from canned pimiento. Garnish the edges of the pimiento with cream cheese rippled from a pastry tube.

HALLOWEEN CANAPES

Use a cooky cutter in the shape of a pumpkin (or make card cutout). Cut bread into shapes and toast or sauté as suggested for other canapé bases. Spread with cream cheese which has been tinted with vegetable coloring to resemble a pumpkin. Form the eyes, nose, and mouth with bits of pimiento or white cream cheese.

THANKSGIVING DAY CANAPES

Use a cooky cutter in the shape of a tall pilgrim's hat (or make card cutout) and cut bread into hat shapes. Toast or sauté the bases as suggested for other canapé bases. Spread with black caviar and then form a line near the bottom with riced egg white or finely minced onion to resemble the band of the hat.

CHRISTMAS CANAPES

Use a cooky cutter shaped like a Christmas tree or one shaped like a wreath. Cut bread into desired shapes. Toast or sauté the bases as suggested for other canapé bases. Spread with cream cheese which has been tinted green with vegetable coloring. Dot with white cream cheese and very fine bits of pimiento to resemble decorations on tree or wreath.

SHAMROCK CANAPES

Tint cream cheese with green vegetable coloring. Cut canapé bases in the shape of shamrocks and spread with the cream cheese. Garnish with slices of stuffed olive. Or use white seasoned cream cheese on shamrock-shaped pieces of toast. Garnish with chopped parsley or chopped green pepper.

DECORATION DAY CANAPES

Spread rectangles of toast with butter. Form an American flag by covering the upper left corner with cream cheese tinted blue with vegetable coloring and dotting this with bits of white cream cheese for the stars. Form the stripes by alternating tiny strips of pimiento and white cream cheese forced through a pastry tube.

hot kabobs

A FEW of the many and varied combinations which could be termed kabobs are given below. Some hostesses like the idea of a "broil-your-own" kabob party. For such a party you would have to have on hand a supply of metal skewers and/or some sturdy twigs whittled to a sharp point. The kabobs are held over coals, small cans of lighted Sterno, or little spirit lamps (the little glass ones with wicks used by chemists) and they are rotated slowly until the food is "done to a turn." A nice effect is obtained by placing small lamps in the centers of hollowed-out heads of cabbage with the lamps hidden and only the flames showing. Any of the tender meats, seafoods, and many combinations suggested for the broiler may be selected as long as you bear in mind that they must be foods that cook quickly. Suggestions include tiny sausages or cubes of sausage, cubes of ham, tender steak, lamb, kidney, shrimp, oysters, whole button mushrooms, tiny onions, and so forth. Let your imagination rule the choice of additional fruits and vegetables to alternate with the tender meats on the skewers. Be sure to stick a cork or an olive on each metal skewer to protect your guests' fingers.

MUSHROOM AND FRANK KABOBS

Place small canned mushrooms and 1-inch pieces of frankfurter on picks. Brush with melted butter. Broil.

BROILED HAM AND PINEAPPLE KABOBS

Place chunks of pineapple and cubes of ham on picks. Brush with corn syrup. Broil until golden brown.

HOT COCKTAIL SAUSAGES

Broil or sauté cocktail-size sausages. If larger ones are used, cut into 1-inch lengths. Spear each with a pick.

BROILED FRUIT BITS

Roll in small bacon strips, 1-inch squares of watermelon, peach, pear, or any spiced fruit. Fasten with a pick and broil.

PEARL ONION KABOBS

Wrap pearl onions in small strips of bacon. Fasten with picks. Broil until bacon is crisp.

BACONETTES

Spread small slices of uncooked bacon with peanut butter. Roll tightly. Fasten with picks. Broil until bacon is done. Replace picks if they are burnt.

HOT BACON ROLLS IN VARIETY

Wrap small strips of bacon around combinations of any of the following: ham cubes, stuffed olives, tiny pickles, cooked shrimp, stuffed prunes, cocktail frankfurters or other sausage, or small button mushrooms. Fasten with picks. Broil until bacon is done.

BROILED CHICKEN LIVERS

Cut chicken livers into serving size pieces. Broil and sprinkle with onion juice to taste, or sauté in chicken fat and season to taste. Spear each with a pick.

BACON SCALLOPS

Parboil scallops in their own liquor for 3 minutes. Drain and dry with paper towels. Cut scallops into bite-size pieces. Wrap each in a piece of bacon. Fasten with a pick. Broil or bake in a hot oven until bacon is crisp. Serve hot with a bowl of cocktail sauce.

SHRIMP KABOB

Alternate on a skewer whole shrimp, tomato wedges, okra, and bacon. Broil until done.

HOT SHRIMP AND PINEAPPLE KABOBS

Marinate cooked, cleaned shrimp in soy sauce. Spear a small whole shrimp and a cube of canned pineapple on each pick. Bake or broil until hot.

CERVELAT KABOBS

Cervelat
Small boiled onions

Canned button mushrooms
Melted butter

Cut the cervelat into small thick cubes. Thread alternating cubes of cervelat, small boiled onions, and small button mushrooms on skewers. Brush with melted butter. Broil until hot and slightly browned. These make hearty hors d'oeuvres. If the cervelat is cut into larger size cubes this combination may be used for a quick lunch or dinner dish with ½ pound cervelat, 5 onions, and 10 mushrooms serving 55.

SHISH KEBAB FOR HORS D'OEUVRES

¼ cup olive oil
1 teaspoon salt
¼ teaspoon pepper
2 tablespoons wine (optional)
2 pounds lean lamb, cut into
  small cubes
3 small firm tomatoes, cut into
  wedges

3 small onions, cut into thick
  slices
Small whole mushrooms
1 large green pepper, cut into
  small squares
Cubed eggplant

Combine olive oil, pepper, salt, and wine. Spread over meat and vegetables. Let stand in cool place 2 to 3 hours. Place meat and vegetables alternately on skewers. If desired, rub skewers first with cut clove of garlic. Broil slowly under moderate heat until tender, turning to brown all sides.

CHICKEN LIVERS EN BROCHETTE

Cut livers in bite-size pieces. Cut sliced bacon in 1-inch pieces. Fill skewers with alternate pieces of chicken liver, bacon, and small button mushrooms. Dip in melted butter and roll in bread crumbs. Broil under moderate heat until browned on all sides. Season with salt and pepper.

HAWAIIAN TERIYAKI

1 pound tender beefsteak
¼ cup soy sauce
1 tablespoon sugar

1 clove garlic, minced
1 teaspoon fresh ginger, minced

Slice meat across grain into thin strips. Place on bamboo sticks. (They can be bought in Chinese stores.) Mix soy, sugar, garlic, and ginger. Soak meat in sauce 30 minutes or longer, turning to marinate evenly. Broil 5 minutes on each side. Serve hot.

cheeses

CHEESE TRAYS

Cheese trays offer limitless possibilities for variety both in the choice of cheeses and the foods accompanying them. Cheeses are world-wide favorites for snacks because cheese is one of the friendliest of foods, mixing well in many ways. In making up a tray, provide an assortment of cheeses together with a variety of breads and crackers as well as some of the suggested fruits. And remember that some of your guests like butter with their cheese.

CHEESE GUIDE

American Cheddar: Colored or natural. Firm to crumbly in texture. Mild to sharp in flavor. A favorite to serve on snack trays, with crackers, fruit, cobblers, pies, in sandwiches, creamy sauces, and in omelets.

Bel Paese: Light yellow. Mellow flavor. Soft to solid consistency. Delicious with plain crackers or with fruit for dessert.

Blue: Includes French Roquefort and Bleu, America and Danish Blue, English Stilton, and Italian Gorgonzola. All are marbled with blue-green mold, have a mild to sharp, sort of pungent salty flavor. Use for canapé spreads and snacks or crumbled in crunchy salads and in salad dressings. Particularly delicious with fresh pears or toasted unsalted crackers and sherry.

Brick: Creamy white. Has small eyes and an elastic texture. Mild to sharp flavor. Use on cheese trays, with crackers, and in sandwiches.

Brie: Soft, creamy interior with light russet-brown crust. Pronounced odor. Sharp flavor. Spread it, crust and all, on crackers, dark wholegrain breads, on French bread, or on slices of unpeeled apple.

Camembert: Soft, creamy, yellowish interior with a thin, whitish crust. Rich, mild flavor. To serve, soften it at room temperature. At its peak its interior will be like thick cream. World-wide favorite dessert cheese. Spread it, crust and all, on slices of unpeeled apple, on crackers plain or toasted, and on French bread.

Chantelle: Robust American cheese with a shiny red coat, a semisoft, creamy yellow interior. Mellow flavor. Use on cheese trays, for snacks, sandwiches, and for dessert. Serve wedges with apples, pears, or pineapple.

Cottage: White, mild, uncured. There are two types: Pot type is the plain curd of skimmed milk; cottage type has cream added. Use plain in salads or spreads, or mixed with chives, nutmeats, pickle relish, diced fruit, etc. The dry type is frequently called for in certain recipes.

Cream: White, delicately flavored and fresh as cream. Soft texture. Thin with cream to top fruit salads and desserts or for spreads. Particularly good as a sandwich filling with date and nut breads. Cube it for fruit salads. Season and form into balls for hors d'oeuvres.

Edam or Gouda: Round cheeses with flattened ends and red coatings. Mild flavor which is sometimes salty and nut-like. Gouda weighs less than a pound. Edam weighs 2 to 4 pounds. Use as a hub for a snack or dessert tray. They are pretty to look at and the mild flavor blends well with tart apples, grapes, and tangerines.

Gjetost: Dark brown. Smooth textured. Full sweet flavor. Slice thin and serve with crackers or raisin bread.

Liederkranz: Golden yellow with a hearty, robust flavor. Odor somewhat resembles Limburger. Soft, creamy spreading consistency. Serve with toast, crackers, rye, and pumpernickel breads. The thin crust should be eaten for fullest enjoyment.

Limburger: Soft textured. Characteristic odor and flavor. Despite the fact that there is so much jesting about it Limburger is among the most delicious of cheese flavors. Serve the same way as Liederkranz.

Münster: Orange-colored rind with light-yellow interior full of tiny holes. Often flavored with anise or caraway seed. Has a semi-hard texture. Serve with vegetable relish tray. Good with scallions, cucumbers, carrot sticks, radishes, etc. Excellent with pumpernickel bread or date-nut bread.

Parmesan: Rich yellow color. Mild to full flavor. Texture is firm to hard—usually the latter. Grate to serve on spaghetti, soups like minestrone and onion, on salads and casseroles.

Pineapple: Named for its shape. Yellow to orange color. Molded from American cheese and has similar flavor. Use as centerpiece in a tray. Hollow out cone-shaped piece in center; cut in cubes and return to shell. Serve with cocktail picks.

Port Salut: Delicate in flavor. It has a moderately soft interior but it slices well. Serve with plain bland crackers or all by itself. Good either way.

Provolone: A smoky-tasting cheese that comes in several shapes. It is commonly seen hanging in ball shapes or long cylindrical forms in Italian grocery stores. Excellent with rye or whole-wheat crackers.

Swiss-Emmenthal: Pale yellow hard cheese with round rather large holes. Has a nut-like sweet flavor. Slice thin to serve on platters with other foods. Use with rye breads or serve in small sticks with salad plates. Gruyère, another Swiss cheese, can be bought in small packaged wedges as well as in bulk. The flavor is mild.

Processed Cheeses: They come in a number of flavors which include American (white and yellow), Brick, Pimiento, Olive-Pimiento, Limburger, Swiss, Caraway, etc. They have smooth, creamy textures. They spread easily and slice well when chilled. They melt smoothly and quickly. Use for snack and dessert trays, for cheese sauce, in soufflés, and other cheese cookery.

Cheese-Flavored Spreads: They include a variety of cheese spreads and cheese blends with a soft spreading consistency.

Smoked Cheeses: Processed cheese foods that are hickory-smoked or have smoke-flavored solids added. Serve sliced or cubed as an appetizer or snack. Some spread easily.

hot cheese canapes and hors d'oeuvres

THE judicious use of cheese in many forms makes for a fascinating array of hot tidbits. Most of them take a little effort and watching after your guests have arrived. That work, however, may be cut down to a minimum if you remember that many may be prepared in advance and stored in the refrigerator until you are ready to give them the final touch. Moderate heat gives the best results in cheese cookery unless otherwise indicated as in recipes where biscuit dough or pastry is used.

APPETIZER PUFFS

Soften one 8-ounce package of cream cheese at room temperature and cream it until it is soft. Add 1 teaspoon grated onion, ½ teaspoon baking powder, 1 egg yolk, and salt and pepper to taste. Blend all ingredients thoroughly. Toast 18 small bread rounds. Spread two 2½-ounce cans of deviled meat on the bread rounds. Place a heaping spoonful of the cream cheese mixture on top of the deviled meat. Place in a moderate oven (375° F.) until heated through, lightly browned, and puffy, about 8 to 10 minutes.

HAM AND CHEESE PUFFS

1 cup ground cooked ham
3 tablespoons minced green
pepper
1 tablespoon prepared mustard
¼ teaspoon Worcestershire
sauce
½ cup thick white sauce

1 package (3 ounces) cream
cheese
1 beaten egg yolk
1 teaspoon grated onion
¼ teaspoon baking powder
18 2-inch toast rounds

Combine ham, green pepper, mustard, and Worcestershire sauce. Stir in white sauce and mix well. Combine cheese, egg yolk, onion, and baking powder. Spread toast rounds with ham mixture. Top with cheese mixture. Broil under moderate heat until topping puffs and browns. Serve hot.

QUICK CHEESE PIZZA #1

6 English muffins
3 ripe tomatoes or 1¼ cups
drained stewed tomatoes
24 anchovy fillets
or dash of rosemary

12 thin slices of cheese
Olive oil
Salt and pepper

Break muffins apart. Toast until slightly crispy. Thinly slice tomatoes and place 1 slice or 2 tablespoons stewed tomatoes on each muffin half. Add either 2 anchovy fillets or dash of rosemary. Add another layer of fresh tomato or stewed tomatoes and top with slice of cheese. Sprinkle with olive oil, salt, and pepper. Place under broiler and broil until cheese melts.

Quick Cheese Pizza #2: Break the muffins apart. Spread with mayonnaise. Top with tomato slices. Sprinkle with grated Parmesan cheese. Add 2 or 3 anchovy fillets to each. Broil until muffins are toasted.

DELUXE CHEESE DREAMS

½ pound sharp cheese, grated
3-ounce package cream cheese
2 tablespoons butter, melted
1 egg, beaten

1 tablespoon cream
1 whole loaf white bread
(unsliced)

Combine grated cheese with softened cream cheese, melted butter, and beaten egg, adding cream to moisten. Slice bread lengthwise or crosswise of loaf, as preferred. Spread lengthwise slices with the cheese mixture. Roll up like jelly roll and slice ⅜ inch thick. Spread thin crosswise slices with the mixture and roll from corner to corner, fastening with toothpick. (Sliced bread may be cut in rounds or other shapes and spread with cheese mixture, if desired.) Toast under broiler until golden brown. Serve hot. Yield: 2½ to 3 dozen.

QUICK CHEESE STRAWS

1 *cup prepared biscuit flour* 1 *cup grated American cheese*
Ice water

Add just enough water to the flour to make the dough stick together. Roll out to ¼-inch thickness. Spread with cheese. Fold dough over cheese and roll again. Repeat until cheese is all folded in. Chill. Roll thin and cut into strips. Bake in hot oven (400° F.) 15 minutes. Yield: about 4 dozen strips, 4 inches long.

CHEESE STICKS

Cut bread into thin strips, lengthwise. Spread with butter. Sprinkle with grated cheese and season with salt and cayenne. Bake until delicately browned in moderate oven (350° F.). Sprinkle with finely minced ripe olives and serve.

HOT CHEESED CHICKEN CANAPES

Whip a small jar of nippy cheese spread until creamy. Add an equal amount of boned canned chicken or turkey. Season with Worcestershire sauce. Mix lightly but do not mash. Spread on cocktail crackers. Place on baking sheet. Bake in very hot oven (450° F.) or broil until cheese melts, about 5 minutes. Serve hot.

Quick Cheese Pizza Snacks

PIZZA

1 package hot roll mix
½ cup minced onion
1 tablespoon olive oil
1 can (8 ounces) tomato sauce
1 can (6 ounces) tomato paste
1 teaspoon salt
¼ teaspoon oregano
⅛ teaspoon garlic salt

⅛ teaspoon pepper
Olive oil or salad oil
½ pound Italian or other white cheese
¼ cup finely-cut parsley
2 to 3 tablespoons grated Parmesan cheese, if desired

Prepare dough and let rise as directed in basic recipe on hot roll mix package. Sauté ½ cup minced onion in 1 tablespoon olive oil until golden brown. Combine and add tomato sauce, tomato paste, salt, oregano, garlic salt, and pepper. Divide dough into 4 parts. Flatten each piece and pat into bottoms of four 9- or 10-inch piepans. (If desired, dough may be divided in half, rolled to two 12x8x2-inch rectangles and placed on ungreased baking sheets.) Brush with olive oil or salad oil. Slice thin or grate ½ pound Italian or other white cheese. Arrange half of cheese on dough. Cover with the tomato sauce. Top with remaining cheese and additional topping as desired. See suggestions below. Sprinkle with ¼ cup finely-cut parsley and 2 to 3 tablespoons grated Parmesan cheese, if desired. Bake immediately in very hot oven (450° F.) 15 to 20 minutes. Serve hot.

Pizza Variations:

Mushroom Pizza: Place 1 cup mushrooms, chopped or sliced, over dough.

Anchovy Pizza: Place 12 to 14 anchovies (whole or pieces) over dough.

Italian Sausage Pizza: Arrange 1 cup pepperoni or other Italian sausage, diced or sliced thin, over dough.

Salami Pizza: Arrange 1 cup salami, cut into thin strips, over dough.

Pork Sausage Pizza: Place 1 cup cooked pork sausage over dough.

HOT CHEESED FRANK CANAPES

Simmer frankfurters until thoroughly heated. Drain and remove casings. Put through food chopper, using medium blade. Season to taste with prepared mustard. Add a little piccalilli and enough mayonnaise to give spreading consistency. Spread on toasted bread bases. Sprinkle with grated cheddar cheese. Just before serving, heat under moderate broiler until cheese melts. Serve hot. If desired, the frankfurter mixture may be used as a cold spread.

PARMESAN TOAST

Moisten Parmesan cheese with cream. Spread on toast or crackers. Bake in moderate oven until cheese melts.

SIMPLE TOASTED CHEESE CANAPES

Have soft American cheese at room temperature. Spread 1 teaspoon on each toasted canapé base. Broil until cheese is bubbly.

SAUTEED SANDWICH BITS

Use nippy spreads and make simple sandwiches. Cut into 1-inch squares. Sauté in butter.

HOT WAFFLED TEASERS

Place a very thin slice of Swiss cheese or ham or both between thinly sliced buttered bread. Spread lightly with horseradish mustard. Make sandwiches very small. Toast in waffle iron.

SIMPLE CHEESE DREAMS

Put a slice of American cheese between 2 thin slices of bread. Cut into small triangles. Broil under a moderate flame to toast both sides.

OPEN-FACED CHEESE DREAMS

Beat 2 egg whites with ⅛ teaspoon salt until very stiff. Fold in 1 cup grated American cheese seasoned with 1 teaspoon Worcestershire sauce. Toast small rounds or squares of bread on one side. Spread untoasted side with cheese-egg mixture. Top with a tiny piece of bacon. Broil under moderate flame until cheese is lightly browned and puffed.

ROQUEFORT PUFFS

Beat 1 egg white until stiff. Cream 2 ounces Roquefort cheese spread and fold into egg white. Heap on crackers or bread rounds. Bake in slow oven (300° F.) until browned (about 15 minutes). Garnish with paprika. Yield: eight 2-inch puffs.

POTATO CHIPS AU GRATIN

Sprinkle potato chips with grated American cheese. Broil only enough to melt cheese.

CHEESED TUNA FISH CANAPES

Mix flaked tuna fish with mayonnaise. Add chopped stuffed olives. Season with Worcestershire sauce. Spread on toast rounds. Sprinkle with grated cheese. Broil only until cheese melts. Serve hot.

CHEESED BOLOGNA CUPS

Spread thin slices of bologna with a nippy cheese spread. Place in moderate oven (350° F.) until cheese melts and edges of bologna curl to form cups.

CHEESED SQUARES

Cut white bread into 1-inch squares. Dip in mixture of 1 beaten egg and 2 tablespoons melted butter. Roll in finely grated dry American cheese. Bake on a cooky sheet in moderate over (350° F.) until cheese melts and squares are brown.

CHEESED OYSTER CANAPES

Toast rounds of bread on one side. Spread untoasted side with Anchovy Butter. Cook oysters in white wine until edges curl, about 1 minute. Place an oyster on each round. Cover with Roquefort cheese which has been creamed with sweet butter and seasoned with pepper. Sprinkle with paprika. Broil until bubbly and lightly browned.

HOT CHEESED MUSHROOM HORS D'OEUVRES

Fill cavities of fresh mushroom caps with small pieces of sharp cheddar cheese. Dot with butter. Broil slowly until cheese melts and mushrooms are cooked through. Spear each with a cocktail pick. Serve at once.

HOT CHEESED MUSHROOM CANAPES

1 cup sliced fresh mushrooms or ½ cup sliced canned mushrooms	4 hard-cooked eggs, finely chopped
2 tablespoons minced onion	Salt and pepper
½ cup butter or margarine	1 slightly beaten egg
2 tablespoons minced parsley	Canapé bases toasted on 1 side
	Grated cheese

Sauté mushrooms and onion in melted butter or margarine. Add hard-cooked eggs, parsley, and salt and pepper to taste. Add beaten egg and cook only until thick. Spread on untoasted sides of canapé bases. Sprinkle with grated cheese. Broil until cheese melts. Serve hot.

CANADIAN BACON-CHEESE GRILLS

Have Canadian bacon cut into slices ⅛ inch thick. Cut the slices into quarters. Place ½ teaspoon softened American cheese in the center of each small cracker. Cover with a quarter slice of Canadian bacon. Broil until bacon is hot and crisp at edges.

HOT CHEESE-BACON CANAPES #1

1 egg yolk, well beaten
½ cup grated nippy cheese
1 tablespoon cream
Salt and pepper
1-inch strips of bacon

Combine egg yolk, cheese, and cream. Season to taste. Toast bread squares or rounds on one side and spread mixture on untoasted side. Top each with a bacon strip. Bake in moderate oven (350° F.) until bacon is crisp.

HOT CHEESE AND BACON CANAPES #2

2 cups grated cheese
¼ cup crisp minced bacon
1 tablespoon Worcestershire sauce
Few grains cayenne
Toasted canapé bases

Mix cheese with bacon, Worcestershire sauce, and cayenne. Spread untoasted side of canapé bases. Broil under moderate heat until cheese melts.

HOT HAM AND CHEESE CANAPES #1

Cover toasted canapé bases with baked ham slices cut to same size and shape as canapé bases. Dot with bits of pimiento and chopped olive or pickle. Sprinkle heavily with grated Swiss cheese. Broil under moderate heat until cheese melts.

HOT HAM AND CHEESE CANAPES #2

Spread small toast bases with Garlic Butter. Cover with a thin slice of ham, then with a thin slice of cheese. Place on baking sheet. Bake until cheese melts. Sprinkle with paprika. Serve hot.

HOT CREAM CHEESE ROLLS

Trim crusts from unsliced loaf of bread with a very sharp knife. Cut into extremely thin slices. If necessary, flatten slices with rolling pin. Spread with softened butter, then with cream cheese. Roll up and place on baking sheet with open end at bottom. Toast under moderate broiler heat until delicately browned. Serve hot.

Variations: Snappy cheese spreads or other fillings may be substituted for cream cheese.

BACON AND CHEESE ROLLS

Place thin slices of cheese on thin slices of bread. Roll up and wrap in bacon strips. Broil slowly until bacon is done.

PICKLE-CHEESE CANAPES

Top untoasted sides of canapé rounds with slices of pickle. Sprinkle liberally with grated cheese. Bake in moderate oven (350° F.) until cheese melts.

BUBBLY CHEESED CANAPES #1

Mix softened butter or margarine with seasoned chopped crabmeat, lobster, shrimp, or hard-cooked egg. Spread on toast canapé bases. Top with grated cheese. Broil until bubbly. Serve hot.

BUBBLY CHEESED CANAPES #2

Season grated cheese with mustard or Worcestershire sauce or a little of each. Spread on toasted canapé bases or plain bread. Broil until cheese is bubbly. Serve at once.

CHEESED CRABMEAT CANAPES

Moisten crabmeat with mayonnaise. Spread on untoasted side of bread bases. Cover thickly with grated cheese. Broil under moderate heat until cheese melts.

SAVORY CHEESE CANAPES

Spread toast fingers or squares with Mustard Butter. Spread with a mixture of equal parts of minced parsley and finely chopped olives. Top each with a thin slice of American cheese. Broil under moderate heat until cheese melts. Sprinkle with paprika and serve hot.

HOT ASPARAGUS TIP CANAPES

Heat tiny canned asparagus tips in melted butter until hot throughout. Place on toast fingers. Sprinkle heavily with grated American cheese. Broil under moderate heat until cheese melts.

INDIAN CANAPES

Spread toasted or sautéed rounds of bread with a mixture of equal parts of chutney sauce and boiled ham put through the food chopper, or deviled ham. Sprinkle with grated Parmesan cheese or other well-flavored cheese. Brown in a hot oven (400° F.). Serve hot or cold garnished with parsley.

CHEESEWICH

Cut day-old bread in ¼-inch slices. Slice American cheese thin. Make sandwiches, seasoning with salt, paprika, and a light covering of pre-pared English mustard. Press sandwiches gently together and trim off crusts. Cut sandwiches in quarters or triangle shape. Melt some butter in frying pan. Over very low heat fry sandwiches until lightly browned, taking care in turning them that they do not separate. Serve hot.

HOT CHEESE-ONION CANAPES

Use double quantity of the Plain Pastry recipe. Roll out into thin sheet and cut strips 4 inches long and ½ inch wide. Sprinkle with ½ cup grated cheese, ½ cup chopped onion, and salt and pepper to taste. Roll as for jelly roll and fasten with toothpicks. Place on baking sheet, cut side down. Bake in very hot oven (450° F.) 15 minutes, or until done.

PIMIENTO-CHEESE CANAPE

6 *large canned pimientos*	¼ *pound sliced sharp American*
Salt and pepper	*cheese*
Cayenne	*Flour*
	Buttered toast rounds

Sprinkle inner surface of pimientos with salt, pepper, and cayenne to taste. Cut the cheese slices into rectangles the same size as the pimientos. Place cheese rectangles on pimientos and roll up. Skewer with toothpicks and roll in flour. Sauté in hot butter for 3 minutes, or until the cheese melts. Serve hot on the toast rounds.

HOT CHEESE BALLS #1

2 *teaspoons flour*	2 *teaspoons minced pimiento*
Dash of paprika	1 *egg white, beaten*
½ *teaspoon salt*	¼ *cup crushed salted peanuts*
1 *cup grated American cheese*	

Mix flour, paprika, and salt with grated cheese. Add pimiento. Fold into egg white, beaten until stiff, but not dry. Form into small balls and roll in peanuts. Fry in deep hot fat (375° F.) until lightly browned. Serve hot.

FOUR-IN-ONE CANAPES

Cut a package of 8 slices of pasteurized process American cheese in half and then into quarters. Place the 32 squares of cheese on assorted crackers arranged on a baking sheet. Place in moderate oven or under low broiler heat until cheese is melted. Garnish each cheese square with an olive slice, an anchovy curl, or a cocktail onion. Arrange the hors d'oeuvres on a round tray and garnish the center with olives.

HOT CHEESE BALLS #2

1½ cups grated cheese
1 tablespoon flour
¼ teaspoon salt

Few grains cayenne
3 egg whites, stiffly beaten
¾ cup fine cracker crumbs

Mix cheese, flour, salt, and cayenne. Add to stiffly beaten egg whites. Chill in refrigerator until hard. Form into small balls. Roll in crumbs and fry in deep fat (370° F.) until browned. Drain on absorbent paper. Serve hot on picks.

HOT CHEESE BALLS #3

1 pound American cheese
½ teaspoon dry mustard
Dash of Tabasco sauce
¼ teaspoon salt
2 teaspoons Worcestershire sauce

1 tablespoon flour
4 egg whites
1 tablespoon water
Dry breadcrumbs

Put cheese through meat grinder, then mash with a spoon to form a paste. Add seasonings and flour, and last, 3 stiffly beaten egg whites. Form into ½-inch balls. Chill thoroughly. Just before cooking, roll in breadcrumbs, then in remaining egg white which has been beaten and mixed with water. Fry in deep fat (375° F.) until golden brown. Drain on absorbent paper. Serve hot on picks.

BAKED HOT CHEESE BALLS #4

2 cups grated sharp cheddar cheese
½ cup butter
1 cup flour

⅛ teaspoon salt
¼ teaspoon paprika
¼ teaspoon dry mustard

Blend cheese and butter. Add flour, salt, paprika, and mustard. Form into tiny balls. Place on greased baking sheet. Bake in moderate oven (350° F.) about 10 minutes.

COTTAGE CHEESE BALLS

Mix 1½ pounds cottage cheese, 4 tablespoons melted butter, 4 tablespoons caraway seed, 1 egg, and 1 tablespoon sugar. Blend thoroughly. Form into small balls. Place on baking sheet. Bake in moderate oven (350° F.) 12 to 15 minutes. Serve hot on picks.

TURKISH CHEESE APPETIZERS (BEUREKS)

Cut ½ pound Gruyère cheese into small pieces. Put into a saucepan with ¼ cup thick white sauce. Stir until cheese is melted and mixture is thick. Spread on a platter to cool. Chill if necessary. Shape into small sausage-like shapes. Wrap each in a thin piece of plain pastry and fry in deep hot fat (385° F.) until golden brown. Drain. Serve hot or cold.

ARMENIAN CHEESE BOURAG

2 cups sifted all-purpose flour	½ cup milk (about)
¼ teaspoon salt	½ pound sharp cheese, grated
3 teaspoons baking powder	3 tablespoons minced parsley
3 tablespoons butter	¼ teaspoon salt

Mix and sift flour, salt, and baking powder. Cut in butter with a pastry blender or 2 knives and mix to a dough with milk. Roll out very thin on a floured board and cut into 2-inch squares. Mix remaining ingredients together. Put squares together by pairs with tablespoon of cheese mixture between. Press edges well together and fry until brown in deep hot fat (360° to 370° F.). Drain and serve.

HOT CHEESE AND CLAM CANAPES

3-ounce package cream cheese	Toasted canapé bases
1 small can minced clams	Salt and pepper

Use bread cut ½ inch thick and toasted on one side. Drain clams and mix with cream cheese, adding salt and pepper to taste. Spread on untoasted side of canapé bases. Broil until delicately browned. Yield: about 12 canapés.

HOT TOMATO AND ANCHOVY CANAPES

2 tablespoons butter	8 tomato slices
2 tablespoons anchovy paste	3 tablespoons grated American
8 toast rounds	cheese

Mix butter and anchovy paste. Spread on toast rounds. Place a thin slice of tomato on top of each. Sprinkle with grated cheese. Place under moderate broiler until cheese is melted. Serve at once very hot, garnished with chopped parsley.

HOT CHEESED SARDINE CANAPES

Rub mixing bowl with a cut clove of garlic. Mash sardines to a paste, seasoning with lemon juice and prepared mustard. Spread on toasted rye bread rounds. Sprinkle lightly with grated cheese. Brown in hot oven (400° F.).

FRANKFURTER-CHEESE-BACON HORS D'OEUVRES

Slit frankfurters in half lengthwise. Fill each sandwich-fashion with a ¼-inch stick of sharp cheese. Secure with toothpicks placed at ¾-inch intervals along frankfurters. Slice between picks to make bite-size servings. Wrap each with a piece of bacon. Secure with toothpick. Broil until bacon is crisp. Serve hot.

WELSH RABBIT CANAPES

1 *cup freshly grated American cheese*	*Dash of cayenne*
½ *cup finely chopped ham*	¼ *teaspoon Worcestershire sauce*
2 *tablespoons light cream*	*Toasted bread bases*
1 *teaspoon prepared mustard*	*Grated American cheese*

Combine cheese, ham, cream, and seasonings. Heat in top of double boiler until cheese melts. Spread warm mixture on bases. Sprinkle with grated cheese. Broil lightly. Serve hot.

FRANK TOP-NOTCHERS

Slit franks lengthwise down the middle without cutting all the way through. Insert a stick of cheese. Cut into 1-inch pieces and wrap each piece in bacon. A pick holds all in place. Broil to heat and crisp the bacon. Keep hot on a grill or in pan set over hot water.

Frank Top-Notchers

hot fish and seafood canapes and hors d'oeuvres

In THE chapter on the Dunking Trays a suggestion was made that shrimp, fried, boiled, or canned, as well as chunks of lobster and crab-meat should be speared on picks for "dunking." In this section along with other canapés and hors d'oeuvres you'll find recipes for other fish and seafood that may be used in this manner. While, strictly speaking, broiled whole lobster or whole soft-shell crabs should not be considered as hors d'oeuvres, nevertheless we have included them for those users of this book who may be partial to them.

HOW TO SPLIT A LOBSTER FOR BROILING

Remove claws from live lobster. Place lobster on its back. Insert the point of a sharp knife into the lobster at the head and cut the shell open from head to tail. Remove the sac behind the head and the dark vein along the back. Crack both sides of each big claw.

Cut through the back shell

Remove the stomach and intestinal vein

HOW TO BROIL SPLIT LOBSTER

Season split lobster with salt and pepper and brush with butter. Put the lobster, split side up, on the broiler and lay the claws around. Broil in preheated broiler for 15 to 18 minutes, having the pan far enough from the heat so the lobster will not scorch. Serve with melted butter and quarters of lemon.

HOW TO BOIL LOBSTERS

Plunge live lobsters into boiling salted water. If desired, season each 2 quarts water with 2 tablespoons salt, 1 sliced onion, 1 sliced carrot, 1 cup vinegar, 10 peppercorns, 2 bay leaves, and a bouquet garni (made by tying together 2 sprigs of parsley, 1 stalk of celery, 1 clove of garlic, and a little thyme). Let lobsters boil for 20 to 25 minutes if to be served immediately. For serving cold, cook 15 minutes and leave in water to cool. Before serving, split lobster, remove the sac behind the head and the dark vein along the back, and crack the claws. To remove the claw meat in one piece from the boiled lobster, cut off the claw at the first joint and break off the small pincer. Lay the big part down on a board and hit it with the cutting side of a large knife about 1 inch from the joint. Turn it over and do the same on the other side. Pick up the claw in your left hand and pull the end with your right. It will separate, and the claw meat will come out in one piece. The remainder of the claw meat below the joint can then be removed easily.

BAKED LOBSTER

Prepare lobster as for broiling. Dot meat with butter. Sprinkle with salt, pepper, and buttered breadcrumbs. Place on rack in roasting pan. Cover and bake in hot oven (425° F.) 30 to 35 minutes, basting once with melted butter. Use one medium-sized lobster per serving.

LOBSTER NEWBURG

2 cups cooked or canned lobster	¾ cup thin cream
3 tablespoons butter	3 egg yolks, slightly beaten
2 tablespoons flour	½ teaspoon salt
¼ cup sherry wine	Few grains of cayenne

Cook lobster (4 pounds lobster in the shell gives 2 cups meat) in butter for 3 minutes. Sprinkle in flour and stir well. Stir in sherry and cook 2 minutes. Combine egg yolks and cream; add slowly to lobster and cook over very low heat, stirring constantly until it thickens. Overcooking will curdle sauce. Remove from heat and season with salt and cayenne. Serve on toast or in patty shells. Serves 6.

Shrimp Newburg: Use 2 cups cooked or canned shrimp.

Scallops Newburg: Cook 1½ pints of scallops in their own liquor and strain.

Crab Newburg: Use 2 cups flaked canned crabmeat.

Mixed Seafood Newburg: Use 1 cup each of shrimp and scallops.

HOT LOBSTER CANAPES

½ pound cooked or canned lobster meat, chopped
1 cup medium white sauce
½ pound mushrooms, sliced and sautéed
1 tablespoon minced green pepper
1 tablespoon chopped pimiento
1 teaspoon Worcestershire sauce
2 tablespoons sherry wine
½ teaspoon salt (about)
20 small toast diamonds or rounds
½ cup grated American or Swiss cheese
3 tablespoons butter

Mix lobster, white sauce, mushrooms, pepper, pimiento, Worcestershire sauce, and sherry. Add salt to taste. Heat and pile on toast. Sprinkle with cheese and bits of butter. Broil under moderate heat until cheese is bubbly. Yield: 20 canapés.

Variations: Substitute cooked or canned crabmeat or shrimp for lobster.

HOT LOBSTER AND BACON CANAPES

Use canned or freshly cooked lobster meat. Season with salt and paprika. Brown in melted butter in which a little minced onion is cooked. Roll when brown in slices of uncooked bacon. Fasten with toothpicks. Broil until bacon is crisp. Serve on toast squares or rounds with coating of tartar sauce. Garnish with pimiento strips.

BOILED FRESH SHRIMP

To 1 quart boiling water, add 1 tablespoon white vinegar, 1 teaspoon salt, dash of pepper, 1 bay leaf, 1 whole onion, and 1 whole carrot. Cook 10 minutes. Drop in shrimp. Lower heat and simmer 5 minutes until shrimp are pink and tender. Let shrimp cool in cooking water, then drain and peel.

Note: In preparing all shrimp, fresh, boiled, or canned, the black vein along the back is removed with a sharply pointed knife, then the shrimp are rinsed under cold water.

FRIED SHRIMP FOR HORS D'OEUVRES

1 pound raw shrimp, peeled and cleaned
1 well beaten egg
1 teaspoon salt
About ¼ teaspoon black pepper
1 teaspoon chopped parsley
1 tablespoon prepared mustard
1 teaspoon dried basil
1 mashed clove garlic
1 teaspoon chopped chives

Mix shrimp with other ingredients. Let stand overnight. Sauté in butter or fry in deep fat (365° F.). Serve hot on picks.

SOUTHERN FRIED SHRIMP

2 cups cooked cleaned shrimp	1 egg, well beaten
¼ cup flour	1 tablespoon cold water
Black pepper	½ cup cracker meal

Roll shrimp in flour, then sprinkle with pepper. Dip each shrimp in beaten egg combined with water, then dip in cracker meal. Fry in deep fat (390° F.) until golden brown. Drain on absorbent paper.

BATTER-FRIED SHRIMP

½ cup sifted flour	1 slightly beaten egg
½ teaspoon baking powder	⅓ cup milk
½ teaspoon salt	2 or 3 drops Tabasco sauce
¼ teaspoon black pepper	2 pounds cleaned shrimp

Mix and sift flour, baking powder, salt, and pepper. Mix egg and milk. Add to dry ingredients and beat smooth. Add Tabasco. Dip shrimp in batter. Fry in deep fat (375° F.) until golden. Serve hot.

HOT SHRIMP HORS D'OEUVRES

Melt ¼ cup butter in a heavy skillet. Add 6 tablespoons lemon juice. When mixture bubbles add 3 pounds cooked, cleaned shrimp. Keep hot on very low heat. Serve with Standard Cocktail Sauce #1 as a dunk.

HOT SHRIMP CANAPES

Wrap cleaned, cooked or canned shrimp in small slices of bacon. Fasten with picks. Brown slowly in frying pan, or grill in the broiler, or bake in hot oven (400° F.) until bacon is done. Replace burnt picks with fresh ones.

HOW TO COOK HARD-SHELL CRABS

Plunge live crabs head first into boiling salted water, using 1 teaspoon salt per quart water. Boil in covered kettle until shell is red and meat white (20 to 25 minutes). Fold back tapering points on each side of back shell and remove spongy material underneath. Remove apron, small pointed piece at lower part of shell. Serve in shell or remove the meat for other dishes. Allow 1 hard-shell crab or ½ cup meat per serving.

HOW TO COOK SOFT-SHELL CRABS

They are usually sold ready for cooking, with soft spongy exposed portions and viscera at front removed. Wash and sprinkle with salt and pepper. Dip in slightly beaten egg and roll in crumbs. Fry in deep fat (365° F.) until well browned. Drain on absorbent paper. Serve at once. The entire crab, including shell, is edible.

HOT CRABMEAT HORS D'OEUVRES

1 tablespoon chopped onion
1 tablespoon melted cooking fat
2½ tablespoons flour
½ cup cream
1 cup crabmeat
½ teaspoon Worcestershire sauce
Salt and pepper
½ cup dry breadcrumbs

Sauté onion in hot fat until tender. Stir in flour and gradually add cream. Cook, stirring constantly, until mixture thickens. Carefully remove all bony particles from crabmeat and add to the sauce with Worcestershire sauce and salt and pepper to taste. Mix well and cool. When cool enough to handle drop by teaspoonfuls into breadcrumbs and roll into small balls. Fry in deep fat (385° F.) for 2 minutes or until brown, or, if preferred, place in a shallow greased pan and broil under moderate heat, turning to brown all sides. Serve hot or cold on picks. Yield: about 40 hors d'oeuvres.

SEA DEVIL

Combine crabmeat with a thick cream sauce. Season with salt, pepper, and a little curry powder. Spread on small pieces of toast. Sprinkle with grated cheese. Dot with butter. Put under broiler to toast lightly. Serve very hot.

HOT CRABMEAT CANAPES

12 ounces crabmeat
Salt and pepper
3 tablespoons butter
1 small onion, minced fine
2 tablespoons flour
1 cup broth or water
2 ounces grated Parmesan cheese
2 ounces grated Swiss cheese
Toast squares

Season crabmeat with salt and pepper to taste. Melt 2 tablespoons butter in a saucepan. Add onion and sauté gently until cooked. Add 1 tablespoon flour and stir constantly for 2 minutes. Add broth or water and crabmeat and let cook slowly 15 minutes, stirring occasionally. Turn mixture into a bowl and let cool. Place 1 tablespoon butter in a pan and blend in 1 tablespoon flour; add the cheese, mix well and turn out to cool. Spread the toast squares with the crabmeat mixture. Roll the cheese into tiny balls and place one in the center of each canapé. Place under broiler until lightly browned, about 5 minutes.

SOUTHERN DEVILED CRABS

8 *hard-shell crabs, boiled*	*Salt and pepper*
4 *slices bread, crumbled*	*Milk*
¼ *cup butter*	*Dash of Tabasco sauce*
1 *tablespoon* Worcestershire *sauce*	*Buttered crumbs*

Remove meat from crab shells and wash shells carefully. Combine meat, crumbled bread, butter, Worcestershire sauce, salt and pepper to taste. Moisten with a little milk seasoned with Tabasco sauce. The mixture should be soft. Pack loosely into shells. Top with buttered crumbs. Bake in moderate oven (350° F.) until delicately browned.

FRIED OYSTERS OR SCALLOPS

Drain oysters or scallops. Dry carefully between towels. Roll in flour seasoned with salt and pepper, then in beaten egg diluted with 1 tablespoon water. Roll in dry bread or cracker crumbs. Fry in deep fat (375° F.) until golden brown. Drain on absorbent paper. Serve on hot toast rounds spread with tartar sauce.

SCALLOPS ON HORSEBACK

1 *pound scallops*	1 *green pepper*
3 *tablespoons butter*	*Salt and pepper*
8 *slices of bacon*	1 *large raw potato*

Place scallops in a saucepan with the butter and cook for 5 minutes. Cut bacon into 2-inch pieces. Cut pepper into 1-inch squares. Arrange bacon, scallops, and green pepper alternately on toothpicks. Sprinkle scallops with salt and pepper. Stick the toothpicks upright into a large raw potato. Bake in hot oven (400° F.) 20 minutes, or until bacon is crisp and scallops are browned.

SAUTEED SCALLOPS

1 *pound scallops*	¼ *teaspoon salt*
¼ *cup butter or margarine*	⅛ *teaspoon pepper*
¼ *cup flour*	

Wipe scallops with a damp paper towel. Roll in flour seasoned with salt and pepper. Melt butter in skillet. Add scallops and cook only 5 minutes over high flame, turning constantly to brown evenly. Serve at once on picks. If large sea scallops are used, cut in small pieces.

Clams Casino

CLAMS CASINO

Open clams carefully to retain juice. Remove upper shell, leaving clams in deeper half. Sprinkle each with few drops of lemon juice, a bit of finely minced green pepper, and chopped onion. Season with salt and pepper. Put 3 bits of bacon on each. Set in pan and bake in very hot oven (450° F.) or under broiler until bacon crisps.

FRIED CLAM CAKES

2 cups sifted flour	1 cup milk
1 teaspoon baking powder	½ cup clam liquor
½ teaspoon salt	1 pint fresh clams
2 eggs, well beaten	Deep fat for frying

Mix and sift flour, baking powder, and salt. Add well beaten eggs, milk and clam liquor slowly; stir well and add clams which have been ground quite fine in a food chopper. Drop by spoonfuls into deep fat (375° F.). When nicely browned, remove from kettle and drain. Serve hot.

COCKTAIL FISH BALLS #1

1 cup salt codfish	½ tablespoon butter
2½ cups potatoes	⅛ teaspoon pepper
1 egg, well beaten	

Wash fish in cold water. Pick in very small pieces or cut, using scissors. Wash, pare, and soak potatoes, cutting in pieces of uniform size before measuring. Cook fish and potatoes in boiling water to cover until potatoes are nearly soft. Drain thoroughly through strainer and return to kettle in which they were cooked. Shake over heat until thoroughly dry. Mash thoroughly and add butter, egg, and pepper. Beat with fork 2 minutes. Add salt if necessary. Take up by spoonfuls and sauté in butter or fry 1 minute in deep fat (385° F.) until brown. Drain on paper. Serve hot with toothpicks.

COCKTAIL FISH BALLS #2

Shape canned codfish cake mixture into small balls or cones the size of marbles and roll in flour. Fry in deep fat (375° F.) until brown. Insert cocktail pick and serve hot on hors d'oeuvres tray with ketchup.

HOT OYSTER BALLS

1 *pint oysters*	*Dash of Tabasco or cayenne*
1 *teaspoon grated onion*	*Pinch of mace*
1 *teaspoon minced parsley*	2 *eggs*
1 *cup soft breadcrumbs*	2 *tablespoons butter*
About ¼ *teaspoon salt*	*Corn meal or fine dry bread-*
About ¼ *teaspoon pepper*	*crumbs*

Pour boiling water over drained oysters. Drain well and chop fine. Add onion, parsley, and soft breadcrumbs. Season to taste and mix to stiff paste with 1 beaten egg and the butter. Form into small balls. Roll in beaten egg, then in corn meal or dry crumbs. Fry in deep fat (360° F.) until browned. Drain on absorbent paper. Serve hot on picks.

BROILED BREADED OYSTERS

Roll fresh oysters in mixture of half bread and half cracker crumbs. Press flat with hands. Broil 2 minutes on each side. Salt lightly and brush with melted butter. Serve on buttered hot toast rounds.

ANGELS ON HORSEBACK

Wrap small oysters in 3-inch strips of bacon. Fasten with picks. Broil in oven until bacon is crisp. Remove picks and place on ovals of toasted bread spread with tartar sauce.

HOT OYSTER CANAPES #1

Place small oysters on small rounds of toast. Sprinkle with salt, pepper, and lemon juice, then with grated cheese. If desired, add a tiny piece of bacon. Broil just until cheese melts. Serve immediately.

HOT OYSTER CANAPES #2

36 oysters
2 tablespoons Hollandaise sauce
Buttered toast squares
2 tablespoons minced parsley
2 tablespoons butter

Blanch oysters and chop very fine. Mix with sauce and spread over buttered toast squares. Sprinkle with parsley. Dot with butter. Broil under moderate heat for a few minutes. Serve very hot.

HOT OYSTER AND MUSHROOM CANAPES

Peel large mushrooms and remove stems. Dip in melted butter or olive oil. Put a fresh oyster in each. Season to taste with salt, pepper, paprika, and celery salt, if desired. Broil under moderate heat. Serve on hot toasted canapé bases or in the oyster shells.

DEVILED ROE CANAPES

Mix 1 tablespoon melted butter, ⅓ teaspoon mustard, 1¼ teaspoons Worcester sauce, and salt to taste. Drain 4 pieces canned fish roe and roll in this mixture. Mash the roe and spread on toast squares. Place in hot oven (425° F.) for 5 minutes. Serve with lemon wedges.

BACON WITH SHAD ROE

Wrap small wedges of canned shad roe in small pieces of bacon. Fry until crisp. Spear each with a pick.

HOT TUNA CANAPES

Combine 1 can (6 to 7 ounces) drained, flaked tuna with ¼ cup mayonnaise and 1 tablespoon each ketchup and vinegar. Add salt, cayenne, and Worcestershire sauce to taste. Pile on toast bases or crackers. Broil under moderate heat. Garnish with chopped parsley, pimiento, or green pepper. Serve hot.

TOASTED SARDINE ROLLS

Drain oil from sardines, mash and mix with horseradish and lemon juice to taste. Spread on thin squares of very fresh bread. Roll up. Fasten with toothpicks. Brush with melted butter. Toast in hot oven (400° F.) until delicately browned. Serve at once.

PARMESAN-SARDINE CANAPES

Drain and bone skinless sardines. Mash and season with finely minced celery, ketchup, minced onion, and pepper. Add enough mayonnaise to make a paste of spreading consistency. Spread lightly on thin slices of ice-box rye bread. Sprinkle with Parmesan cheese. Broil until well heated throughout.

WHOLE BROILED SARDINE CANAPES

Mix 2 tablespoons soft butter with 1 teaspoon dry mustard and a few drops Worcestershire sauce. Drain large sardines and brush with mixture. Dip in cracker crumbs. Broil quickly. Serve on toast strips and sprinkle with lemon juice. Garnish with minced parsley .

biscuit and pastry
hors d'oeuvres

ALMOST all of the hors d'oeuvres that follow lend themselves to infinite variations in fillings. As a starter we suggest that you try the Cornish Pasties or Piroshke à la Russe with a nicely seasoned meat filling—but make lots of them. You'll find all other canapés and hors d'oeuvres practically ignored until these are "all gone."

CORNISH PASTIES

¼ pound mutton or beef, diced
3 small potatoes, peeled and diced
1 small onion, minced
Salt and pepper

2 cups sifted all-purpose flour
1 teaspoon baking powder
6 tablespoons shortening
Cold water

Mix meat, potatoes, and onion. Season to taste with salt and pepper. Mix and sift flour, baking powder, and a dash of salt. Rub in shortening. Add enough cold water to make a stiff dough. Roll out on floured board in a square about ⅛ inch thick. Cut into small squares. Place a spoonful of mixture on each. Wet edges with cold water. Draw opposite edges together and press well together with thumb and finger to seal in filling. Place on greased pan. Bake in hot oven (400° F.) until browned, about 30 minutes. Serve hot.

PIROSHKE A LA RUSSE

1½ cups sifted all-purpose flour
¼ teaspoon baking powder
½ teaspoon salt
¼ teaspoon pepper

½ cup shortening
1 egg
¼ cup cold water (about)

Mix and sift dry ingredients. Cut in shortening. Add egg and gradually add enough water to keep dough together. Roll out on a floured board to ⅛-inch thickness. Cut into 3-inch rounds or squares. Place a spoonful of filling in center of each. Pinch edges together well to seal in filling. Brush with melted shortening or egg yolk diluted with equal amount of water. They will form triangles from squares and half-moons from rounds. Bake in moderate oven (375° F.) on greased pans for 20 minutes or until brown. Serve hot.

Variations: Piroshke may be made in any desired size from yeast dough, well kneaded, or any pie crust dough. If yeast dough is used be sure to let them rise for 1 to 1½ hours after they have been filled.

PIROSHKE FILLINGS

Meat Filling: Brown 1 minced onion in hot fat or salad oil. Add 1 pound lean ground beef or veal. Season to taste. Brown slightly.

Rice and Mushroom Filling: Brown 1 minced onion in hot fat or salad oil. Add ½ cup chopped canned or fresh mushrooms or ¼ cup chopped dried mushrooms which have been soaked in cold salted water. Add 1 cup cooked rice and season to taste. Mix thoroughly.

Beef and Onion Filling: Fry 1 pound chopped lean beef and 2 sliced onions lightly in hot fat. Remove and add 3 hard-cooked eggs, 1 teaspoon fennel or dill, salt and pepper to taste. Mix well.

Other Fillings: Use highly seasoned chopped cooked liver, poultry, or fish and seafood fillings. Cooked buckwheat groats and highly seasoned chopped cooked lung are popular with people of Eastern European origin.

HOT TASTY TURNOVERS

Prepare Plain Pastry and roll out on a floured board to ⅛-inch thickness. Cut into small rounds or squares and fill with seasoned meat or fish fillings. Fold over to form half moons from the rounds or triangles from the squares. Prick the top of pastry to allow escape of steam. Brush with milk. Place on ungreased baking sheet. Store in refrigerator until ready to use. Bake in very hot oven (450° F.) 15 to 20 minutes. Serve immediately.

LIVER SAUSAGE TURNOVERS

Plain Pastry
    3 ounces liver sausage
1½ teaspoons prepared horse-
    radish
½ teaspoon grated onion
¾ teaspoon mustard

Blend all ingredients together. Cut rolled pastry dough into 2-inch squares. On each square place 1 teaspoon sausage mixture. Fold over to form triangles. Press edges together with fork. Prick top of pastry to allow escape of steam. Brush with milk. Place on ungreased baking sheet. Store in refrigerator until ready to use. Bake in very hot oven (450° F.) 15 to 20 minutes. Serve immediately. Yield: about 24.

SARDINE SURPRISES

Prepare Plain Pastry and roll pastry thin. Cut into squares the length of sardines. Cut each square diagonally to form triangles. Have small sardines drained on absorbent paper. Lay a sardine on each piece of pastry. Sprinkle with lemon juice. Fold point of triangle opposite diagonal over sardine. Press tightly to opposite side. Place on ungreased baking street. Store in refrigerator until ready to use. Bake in very hot oven (450° F.) 15 to 20 minutes. Yield: about 24.

OLIVE PASTRY SNACKS

Prepare Plain Pastry. Roll out ⅛ inch thick on a slightly floured board. Cut into 2-inch squares. Place a medium-sized stuffed olive in each square and fold pastry around it. Roll lightly between the palms of hands to form balls. Bake on ungreased cooky sheet in very hot oven (450° F.) until crisp and delicately browned, about 15 minutes. These snacks may be prepared in advance and kept in refrigerator until ready to be baked.

PIGS IN A BLANKET

Prepare Plain Pastry. Roll out ⅛ inch thick on a slightly floured board. Cut into small squares. Roll a small cocktail sausage in each square. Bake in very hot oven (450° F.) until pastry is nicely browned, about 15 minutes. Serve hot.

Biscuit Teasers

BISCUIT TEASERS

Prepare the recipe for Baking Powder Biscuits, increasing salt to 1 teaspoon and using only enough milk to form a soft dough. Roll out to ¼-inch thickness. Cut into rounds about 1 inch in diameter with a small biscuit cutter. Slice tiny cocktail sausages or other highly seasoned sausages very thin. Cover a biscuit with sausage slices, then with another biscuit, more sausage and another biscuit. Press together at one side. Set "sandwiches" on end in small muffin pans. Bake in very hot oven (450° F.) 12 to 15 minutes. Serve hot.

TINY FILLED BISCUITS

Prepare the Baking Powder Biscuit recipe. Make tiny hot baking powder biscuits. Split and spread half with a favorite cheese spread, with deviled ham and pickle relish, minced sautéed mushrooms, finely chopped chicken and olive spread, or a favorite seafood spread. Cover with other half. Serve hot.

Waffled Wafers

WAFFLED WAFERS

Prepare the recipe for Baking Powder Biscuits. Cut into 2-inch rounds. Cover half the biscuits with a sandwich spread and cover each with another biscuit. Place a "sandwich" in each section of a hot waffle iron. Bake until well browned, about 3½ minutes. Serve hot.

QUICKIE MEAT ROLLS

Use a prepared biscuit mix or prepare the recipe for Baking Powder Biscuits. Roll dough out thin. Spread with liverwurst. Roll up jelly-roll fashion, or wrap Vienna sausage halves in the thinly rolled dough, letting the edges show. Bake in very hot oven (450° F.) about 10 minutes.

QUICK FRANKS IN BLANKET

Use a prepared biscuit mix or prepare the recipe for Baking Powder Biscuits. Roll dough out ⅜ inch thick. Cut into small rectangles to fit cocktail frankfurters. Place a frankfurter on each alternate rectangle. Wet the edges of the dough and cover each frank with a biscuit rectangle. Pinch edges together to seal. Place on baking sheet and bake in very hot oven (450° F.) 10 to 12 minutes.

SAUSAGE ROLLS

Form finely ground sausage meat into a long thin roll. Wrap in Plain Pastry. Cut into ¾-inch slices. Place on baking sheet. Bake in very hot oven (450° F.) until crisp and delicately browned. Serve hot.

BISCUIT SANDWICHES

⅔ cup sifted all-purpose flour   2 tablespoons butter
½ teaspoon salt   2 to 3 tablespoons milk
 6 tablespoons grated American   Deviled ham
   cheese

Mix and sift flour with salt. Cut or rub in the cheese and butter. Add milk to form dough. Roll out ⅛ inch thick. Cut into tiny rounds. Spread deviled ham on alternate rounds. Cover with unspread rounds. Pinch edges together. Bake in very hot oven (450° F.) 12 to 15 minutes. For variety, you may want to try other favorite fillings in place of deviled ham.

BEEF BITES

⅓ cup mayonnaise   1 tablespoon cold water
 1 cup sifted all-purpose flour   ½ pound lean ground meat,
                                          seasoned to taste

Add mayonnaise to flour and stir with a fork. Add water and stir until dough begins to form. Roll out to long strip about 4 inches wide and ¼ inch thick. Press the seasoned meat into a rope shape and place on top of rolled dough. Moisten edge of dough and bring together around meat. Cut in 1-inch slices. Bake in very hot oven (450° F.) 15 to 20 minutes. Serve hot or cold.

ANCHOVY TURNOVERS

3-ounce package cream cheese   1 cup sifted all-purpose flour
½ cup butter or margarine   Anchovy paste

Blend cheese and butter. Mix with flour. Chill. Roll very thin and cut with 2-inch cooky cutter. Spread with anchovy paste. Fold over and bake in hot oven (400° F.) 10 minutes. Serve hot. Yield: about 48.

TINY SAUSAGE RISSOULES

Make Puff Paste and roll out ⅛-inch thick. Cut into rounds. Place a tiny cooked sausage in center. Fold pastry over. Press edges together with tines of fork or a pastry marker. Prick top. Brush tops lightly with a mixture of 1 egg yolk beaten with 1 teaspoon cold water. Bake in very hot oven (450° F.) 10 minutes. To vary, substitute small sardines or rolled anchovy fillets for sausage. Serve hot.

HUSH PUPPIES

2 cups corn meal
1 tablespoon flour
1 teaspoon baking powder
½ teaspoon baking soda
1 teaspoon salt

3 tablespoons finely chopped onions
1 egg, well beaten
1 cup buttermilk

Mix and sift dry ingredients. Add onion, well beaten egg, and buttermilk. Drop by the spoonful into hot fat. Fry until golden brown. Drain on absorbent paper.

PASTRY SNAILS

Prepare Plain Pastry. Roll into very thin oblongs. Spread with any of the fillings given below. Roll up jelly-roll fashion and cut into ½-inch slices. Place on greased cooky sheet. Bake in hot oven (425° F.) until crisp and delicately browned, 10 to 15 minutes.

FILLINGS FOR PASTRY SNAILS

Deviled Ham: Spread with deviled ham. Season with mustard and salt. Sprinkle with grated cheese, then with a little paprika.

Cream Cheese: Soften cream cheese with just a little cream. Season with salt and paprika.

American Cheese: Spread with grated American cheese seasoned to taste.

Roquefort Cheese: Crumble Roquefort or blue cheese and blend with equal amount cream cheese which has been softened with just a bit of cream.

Cottage Cheese: Season cottage cheese with salt and pepper to taste and a little paprika, if desired.

Anchovy-Cheese: Soften cream cheese and blend with equal amount of anchovy paste or anchovy fillets mashed to a paste.

Other Fillings: You may want to experiment with many of the fillings suggested for canapé spreads such as the cheese, fish, and seafood fillings.

KNISHES

2 cups sifted all-purpose flour
1 teaspoon baking powder
½ teaspoon salt

2 tablespoons water
1 tablespoon vegetable oil
2 eggs, well beaten

Mix and sift flour, baking powder, and salt. Form a well in center and add water, oil, and eggs. Mix and form into a smooth dough. Roll out on a lightly floured board to ⅛-inch thickness. Cut into rounds or squares or if desired leave whole. Fill with desired filling. Moisten edges and fold over the filling. Press edges firmly together. Bake in a pan greased with hot vegetable oil in a moderate oven (350° F.) until brown and crisp. If the dough is left in a whole sheet, fill and roll up like a jelly roll. The fillings given here are only suggestions. In fact the methods for making knishes and the fillings are limited only by the imagination of the cook.

CHICKEN FILLING FOR KNISHES

2 cups chopped cooked chicken About 1 cup chicken gravy
½ cup breadcrumbs Salt and pepper

Combine all ingredients. Season to taste.

MEAT FILLING FOR KNISHES

2 cups cooked ground meat ½ teaspoon salt
½ cup mashed potatoes ¼ teaspoon pepper
2 tablespoons melted fat 1 egg, beaten
1 small onion, minced Paprika (optional)

Combine all ingredients. Mix well.

LIVER FILLING FOR KNISHES

1 onion, minced ½ cup cooked buckwheat groats
1 tablespoon chicken fat or rice
½ pound cooked liver Salt and pepper
¼ pound cooked lung 1 egg
½ pound cooked beef

Fry minced onion in chicken fat until lightly browned. Put liver, lung, and beef through food chopper. Combine with remaining ingredients.

CHEESE KNISHES

DOUGH:
4 cups sifted all-purpose flour
2 teaspoons baking powder
½ teaspoon salt
2 eggs, well beaten
1 tablespoon melted butter
1 cup thick sour cream

FILLING:
1 pound dry cottage cheese
½ cup thick sour cream
2 tablespoons bread or matzo crumbs
2 tablespoons melted butter
2 tablespoons sugar
2 tablespoons raisins
2 eggs, well beaten

Mix and sift flour, baking powder, and salt. Add eggs, butter, and sour cream. Knead into a soft dough, adding a little milk if necessary. Roll out on floured board to ¼-inch thickness. Cut into small rounds or squares. Fill with cheese filling made by combining the ingredients in the order given. Moisten edges; fold over and pinch edges firmly together. Place in a greased baking pan. Bake in moderate oven (350° F.) until brown on top.

miscellaneous hot canapes and hors d'oeuvres

CHICKEN LIVER-WATER CHESTNUT
HORS D'OEUVRES #1

Slice canned water chestnuts in 3 parts. Cut chicken livers into slices slightly larger than chestnut slices. Make sandwiches of 2 slices of liver and 1 slice of chestnut. Wrap each in bacon strips. Secure with toothpicks. Fry in deep hot fat.

CHICKEN LIVER-WATER CHESTNUT
HORS D'OEUVRES #2

Half-cook strips of bacon. Cut chicken livers in quarters and sauté in butter for 1 minute. Season with salt and pepper. Put each quarter of liver on a slice of water chestnut. Wrap each with a half-cooked bacon slice. Fasten with toothpicks. Broil until bacon is crisp. Serve hot.

BAKED CHICKEN LIVERS #1

Rinse chicken livers in cold water. Cut each in half. Spread with a mixture of equal parts finely chopped olives and prepared mustard. Wrap each piece in a small slice of bacon. Fasten with picks. Roll in fine breadcrumbs. Bake in hot oven (400° F.) 10 to 15 minutes. Serve hot.

BAKED CHICKEN LIVERS #2

Half-cook bacon strips. Cut chicken livers in halves and sauté in butter for 1 minute. Season with salt and pepper and a little minced onion. Wrap with bacon strips. Bake or broil. Serve hot.

FRENCH-FRIED CHICKEN LIVERS (Chinese Style)

Cut chicken livers into small strips. Dip in soy sauce, then in a very light batter made of egg and flour. Fry in deep hot fat (270° F.).

CHICKEN BALLS

Mince 2½ cups cooked chicken. Add ½ teaspoon minced onion, ¼ teaspoon salt, and 2 tablespoons mayonnaise. Form into small balls. Roll balls in flour and dip in melted butter or margarine. Brown quickly in hot oven (400° F.). Serve hot.

PETITE HAMBURGER CANAPES

Season ½ pound lean ground beef with 1 teaspoon minced onion, ½ teaspoon salt, ⅛ teaspoon pepper, and a dash of Worcestershire sauce. Mix thoroughly. Spread on toasted canapé bases. Broil until done. Yield: about 24 (2-inch) canapés.

HOT CHILI-BEEF CANAPES

1 *pound ground beef*	¼ *cup ketchup*
1 *tablespoon chili powder*	12 *slices toast, buttered and*
1 *teaspoon salt*	*crusts cut off*
Dash of Tabasco sauce	*Chili sauce*

Stir and heat meat, chili powder, salt, Tabasco, and ketchup in skillet until red color disappears and mixture becomes spreadable. Spread on hot buttered toast. At serving time, cut toast into 8 triangles or 9 squares. Bake in very hot oven (450° F.) 10 minutes. To serve, garnish with a dash of chili sauce.

HOT CHICKEN GIBLET CANAPES

Cover squares or rounds of toast with chopped chicken giblets seasoned to taste. Sprinkle generously with grated Parmesan cheese. Broil under moderate heat until cheese melts.

HAMBURGERS IN BLANKETS

Form seasoned ground beef into small sausage-like shapes. Wrap each in a small thin slice of bacon. Broil under moderate heat until done. Serve very hot on a small canapé base with a slice of mild onion.

Tiny Meat Balls

TINY HOT MEAT BALLS #1

½ *pound ground round steak*
¼ *cup evaporated milk*
½ *teaspoon salt*
⅛ *teaspoon pepper*
1 *teaspoon Angostura bitters*
Breadcrumbs

Mix meat, milk, salt, pepper, and bitters. Roll into small balls. Coat lightly with breadcrumbs. Brown in bacon fat in a hot skillet. Drain on paper. Serve hot on picks.

TINY HOT MEAT BALLS #2

1 *pound ground round steak*
1 *cup fine dry breadcrumbs*
2 *tablespoons minced onion*
2 *tablespoons minced green pepper*
1 *teaspoon salt*
⅛ *teaspoon black pepper*
Dash of cayenne
Milk to moisten slightly
1 *egg, slightly beaten*

Combine all ingredients. Shape into tiny balls. Brown on all sides in butter. Add a little hot water, bouillon, or meat stock to balls and keep hot in chafing dish or top of double boiler while being served. Serve with picks.

FRIED RICE BALLS

Form ½-inch balls from a snappy cheese. Spread lightly with prepared mustard. Roll each ball in salted cooked rice. Use rice that sticks together rather than rice that is fluffy or steamed. Roll balls in hands to make them firm and compact. Fry in deep hot fat until lightly browned. Serve hot on picks.

Variations: Use cooked cleaned shrimp, stuffed olives, or anchovy paste balls instead of cheese.

SMALL SWEDISH MEAT BALLS

1 pound lean beef	¼ teaspoon pepper
½ pound lean pork	1 clove garlic, mashed fine
1 pound veal	⅛ teaspoon nutmeg
4 slices bread	⅛ teaspoon allspice
¾ cup milk	2 eggs, slightly beaten
1 onion, finely chopped	Fat for frying
2 teaspoons salt	2 cups beef bouillon

Have meats ground together 2 or 3 times. Crumble bread and add milk. Stir to paste-like consistency. Add to meat in a mixing bowl. Add seasonings and eggs. Mix until well blended. Form into 1 -inch balls. Set on waxed paper and let dry for half an hour. Brown meat balls in ½-inch of hot fat in heavy skillet. Place browned balls in single layer in large shallow baking pan. Add hot bouillon and bake in moderate oven (350° F.) until bouillon is absorbed, about 30 minutes. Serve hot on picks without gravy or sauce.

Variation: Remove browned balls from skillet. Pour off all but 3 tablespoons of fat. Stir in 4 tablespoons flour. Add enough water to make desired consistency of gravy. Boil 3 minutes. Put in top of double boiler. Add meat balls. Keep warm until served.

Small Swedish Meat Balls

PORK SAUSAGE BALLS #1

1 pound pork sausage meat
¼ cup minced onion
⅓ cup water
¼ cup lemon juice
2 tablespoons vinegar

2 teaspoons Worcestershire sauce
2 tablespoons sugar
½ teaspoon salt
1 teaspoon prepared mustard
Dash of cayenne or Tabasco sauce

Form sausage meat into small balls. Brown slowly on all sides. Remove balls and drain off all but 1 tablespoon fat. Brown onion lightly, stirring frequently. Add remaining ingredients. Simmer until thickened, 15 to 20 minutes. Pour sauce into a chafing dish or top of double boiler. Stick each ball with a pick and stand up in sauce.

PORK SAUSAGE BALLS #2

Shape seasoned pork sausage meat into tiny balls. Heat slowly in a skillet until balls are evenly browned and thoroughly cooked. Serve on picks with slices of stuffed olive.

SAUERKRAUT BALLS

½ pound lean ham
½ pound lean pork
½ pound corned beef
1 medium-sized onion
1 teaspoon minced parsley
3 tablespoons shortening
2 cups flour
1 teaspoon salt

1 teaspoon dry mustard
2 cups milk
2 pounds sauerkraut, cooked and drained
Flour
2 eggs, slightly beaten
Dry breadcrumbs

Put ham, pork, corned beef, and onion through food chopper, using medium blade. Add parsley and blend well. Sauté in shortening until browned. Add flour, salt, mustard, and milk. Blend thoroughly. Cook, stirring constantly, until thick. Add sauerkraut and put entire mixture through food chopper. Mix thoroughly. Cook in skillet, stirring constantly, until thick. Cool. Form into balls the size of a walnut. Roll balls in flour. Dip in beaten egg. Roll in crumbs. Fry in deep fat (370° F.) until browned. Serve hot on picks.

HOT BRAUNSCHWEIGER CANAPES

Toast bread canapé bases on one side. Spread untoasted side with Mustard Butter. Cover thickly with mashed Braunschweiger which has been seasoned with a little grated onion. Broil under moderate heat until hot and puffy, 8 to 10 minutes. Garnish with stuffed olive slices before serving.

KIDNEY SPOON CAKES

Wash 1 pound kidney and put through food chopper. Add 1 teaspoon salt and 2 eggs; beat until well mixed. Drop into hot fat by spoonfuls. Brown thoroughly on one side. Turn and brown second side until crisp. Serve hot.

HOT NUTTY CANAPES

Cut slices of rye bread into finger-length sandwiches. Spread with prepared mustard, then with a mixture of ½ cup ground ham mixed with 1 tablespoon chili sauce and ¼ cup thinly sliced Brazil nuts. Toast and serve hot.

THREE LITTLE PIGS

Cut link pork sausage into 1-inch segments. Remove crusts from slices of bread. Cut each slice in 3 strips. Toast one side. Butter other side. Sprinkle generously with ground sage and cayenne pepper. Fry sausage segments on one side, and putting this side next to the butter, place 3 of the pieces on each strip of bread. Toast in oven and serve hot.

FRANKFURTER ROLLS

Wrap tiny cocktail frankfurters in thin slices of white bread (crust removed). Spread with grated cheese seasoned with cayenne. Fasten with toothpicks. Place on baking sheet. Bake in hot oven (400° F.) until cheese melts.

TINY STUFFED FRANKFURTERS

Cut small crosswise slits in cocktail-size frankfurters and spread mustard in the slits. Insert tiny slices of onion. Broil under moderate heat turning to brown on all sides. Baste with a savory butter while broiling. Serve hot.

VIENNA PICKUPS

Trim crusts from slices of bread. Roll the bread around Vienna sausage. Seal the edges with mayonnaise. Fasten with pick. Bake or broil until lightly brown.

BACON PINWHEELS

Trim the crusts from a fresh loaf of white bread and cut ¼-inch lengthwise slices. Spread each slice with cream cheese which has softened at room temperature. Roll up each slice like a jelly roll. Cut each roll in half crosswise, and wrap a slice of bacon around each pinwheel, fastening it with a toothpick. Place the pinwheels on a broiler rack, and toast them under moderate broiler heat, turning often until the bacon is cooked. Arrange the pinwheels on a chop plate and serve with stuffed olives.

HOT SCRAMBLED EGG CANAPES

2 eggs, slightly beaten
3 tablespoons chopped ham,
    cervelat, salami, or other
    sausage
1 teaspoon minced parsley

Salt and pepper
Butter or margarine
Toasted bread bases
Grated cheese

Combine eggs with ham or sausage and parsley. Season to taste and cook in butter or margarine over low heat until thick but not dry. Mix with fork while cooking. Spread on toasted bread bases. Sprinkle with cheese. Just before serving, broil under moderate heat until cheese melts. Serve hot.

HOT MUSHROOM CANAPES

1 cup chopped mushrooms
2 tablespoons butter
½ cup ground cooked ham
1 tablespoon pepper relish

1 tablespoon salad dressing
Bread, sliced thin
Stuffed olives
Pimiento

Sauté mushrooms in butter 5 minutes. Add ham and cook 3 minutes. Stir in pepper relish and salad dressing. Spread on toast rounds. Bake in very hot oven (450° F.) 3 to 5 minutes. Garnish with sliced olives and pimiento strips. Yield: 30 canapés.

CURRIED BUTTON MUSHROOMS

Sauté whole small mushrooms in butter. Season with salt and curry powder. Serve hot on picks.

HOT STUFFED MUSHROOM CANAPES #1

Spread toast rounds with Pimiento Butter. Top with sautéed mushroom cap filled with ground meat or fish mixed with relish and salad dressing. Bake in very hot oven (450° F.) about 5 minutes.

HOT STUFFED MUSHROOM CANAPES #2

12 large mushrooms
1 small onion, minced
3 tablespoons butter or
    margarine
¾ cup minced ham or drained
    spinach purée

Salt and pepper
Salad oil
Grated cheese
Toast rounds

Wash mushrooms quickly. Remove stems. Chop stems and sauté with onion in butter about 3 minutes. Add ham or spinach purée and season to taste with salt and pepper. Dip the whole mushrooms in oil and place in baking dish. Fill with mixture. Sprinkle with grated cheese. Bake in moderate oven (350° F.) about 15 minutes. Serve on toast rounds. Yield: 12 canapés.

HOT STUFFED MUSHROOM CANAPES #3

Use caps of large mushrooms. Sauté and stuff with a mixture of fine buttered breadcrumbs, sautéed minced mushroom stems, minced onion, and seasonings to taste. Sprinkle with grated cheese. Broil until cheese melts. Serve hot on small toasted canapé bases.

SAUTEED ARTICHOKE HEARTS

Drain canned hearts well. Sauté in butter until lightly browned. Sprinkle with salt, pepper, lemon juice, and minced parsley.

ARTICHOKE HEARTS—CRISP FRIED

1 package frozen artichoke hearts	½ cup flour
1 egg	½ teaspoon baking powder
½ cup milk	Salt and pepper to taste

Thaw artichokes thoroughly and quarter if so desired. Make batter with egg, milk, flour, baking powder, and add salt and pepper to suit taste. Dip artichokes in batter and fry to golden brown. Serves 4.

Artichoke Hearts—Crisp Fried

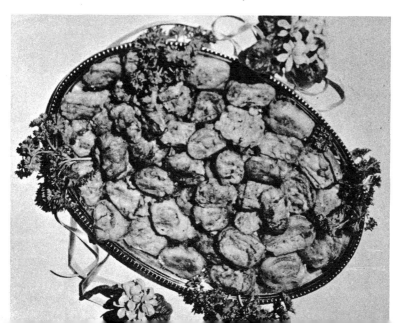

BAKED STUFFED PRUNES

Steam large prunes until tender but firm. Remove pits and fill each with a small pitted or stuffed olive. Wrap each prune in a thin slice of bacon. Arrange on rack in baking pan with end of bacon under prune to hold it in place. Bake in hot oven (400° F.) about 10 minutes or until bacon is crisp. Serve on small squares or rounds of lightly toasted bread.

BROILED STUFFED PRUNES

Steam large prunes until almost tender. Carefully remove pits and stuff cavities with American, Roquefort, or Swiss cheese. Wrap each in small strips of very thin bacon. Secure with picks. Broil under moderate heat until bacon is crisp. Replace burnt picks with clean ones.

HOT WATERMELON PICKLES

Wrap cubes of watermelon pickle in half-cooked strips of bacon. Secure with picks. Bake in moderate oven (350° F.) until hot.

HOT SALAMI AND EGG CANAPES

1 *cup ground, hard salami*	1 *onion, minced*
4 *to 6 eggs*	*Salt and pepper*

Beat all ingredients together until frothy. Drop by spoonfuls into a well greased hot skillet. Serve on canapé bases spread with mustard.

HOT SALAMI CUPS WITH CHUTNEY

Arrange thin slices of salami on a baking sheet. Place a little chutney in the center of each slice. Broil until edges curl up and filling is hot.

TOASTED PEANUT BUTTER CANAPES

½ *cup peanut butter*	¼ *teaspoon pepper*
1 *cup milk*	1 *egg, slightly beaten*
½ *teaspoon salt*	12 *slices bread*

Cream together peanut butter and milk. Add salt and pepper, then add slightly beaten egg. Remove crusts from bread slices and cut into narrow strips. Dip in the mixture and sauté in butter.

HOT RED PEPPER CANAPES

2 *hard-cooked eggs, minced*	2 *tablespoons grated sharp*
1 *tablespoon canned red*	*American cheese*
pepper, minced	*Melted butter*
¼ *teaspoon salt*	6 *rounds rye bread*
⅛ *teaspoon dry mustard*	

Mix together the eggs, red pepper, salt, mustard, cheese, and enough melted butter to make a paste. Fry the bread rounds in deep hot fat (390° F.). Drain and cool. Spread them evenly with the paste and place in an extremely hot oven (500° F.) for 3 minutes. Garnish with watercress and serve hot.

SARDINE-CHEESE CANAPES

Brush oblong toast canapé bases with sardine oil. Top with a sardine. Sprinkle with grated Parmesan cheese. Broil until lightly browned.

BACON-TOMATO CANAPES

Cover rounds of buttered toast with thick slices of tomato. Season tomato slices with salt, paprika, and brown sugar. Cover with small thin bacon strips. Broil until bacon is crisp.

APPETITE TEMPTERS

Small bread rounds   1 smoky pasteurized process
Salad dressing   cheese food link, sliced
Sliced dill pickles

Spread each round of bread with salad dressing. Cover with a slice of pickle, then with a slice of cheese food. Place under low broiler heat until the cheese food is melted.

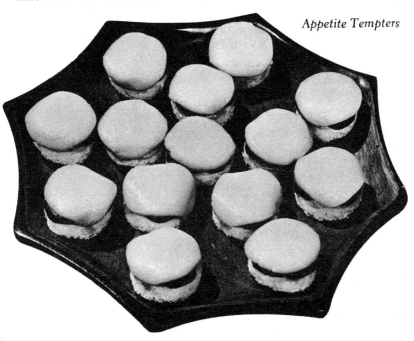

Appetite Tempters

HOT ANCHOVY CANAPES

Arrange flat anchovy fillets on buttered toast strips. Sprinkle liberally with grated Parmesan cheese. Broil under moderate heat until cheese melts.

HOT BOLOGNA ROLLS

Cut thin slices of bologna. Spread with mixture of cream cheese, chopped pickles, chopped chives, and chopped olives. Roll slices and fasten each with toothpicks. Dip in salad dressing seasoned with ketchup and Worcestershire sauce. Broil a few minutes. Serve hot.

HOT BACON-AVOCADO CANAPES

Mash avocado pulp with fork. Season with salt, paprika, and lemon juice to taste. Spread on toast strips. Sprinkle with chopped bacon. Broil until crisp.

HOT PEANUT BUTTER AND BACON CANAPES #1

Mix peanut butter with diced, crisp bacon. Toast rounds or squares of bread on one side. Spread untoasted side with mixture. Place under broiler just long enough to heat slightly.

HOT PEANUT BUTTER AND BACON CANAPES #2

Spread untoasted side of canapé bases with peanut butter. Cover with small thin strips of bacon. Toast in broiler until bacon is crisp.

HOT DEVILED CRACKERS

¼ cup butter	Dash of Worcestershire sauce
2 teaspoons dry mustard	½ teaspoon paprika

Cream butter until soft. Mix thoroughly with other ingredients. Spread on thin crackers. Bake in moderate over (350° F.) until delicately brown.

BRAZIL AND HAM TOASTIES

Trim thin slices of white bread to make 3-inch squares. Spread squares with deviled ham and sprinkle with chopped Brazil nuts. Press nuts into ham. Add, if desired, a slight sprinkling of grated onion. Bring together 2 opposite corners of squares of bread. Fasten with toothpicks to form cornucopias. Brush outside of bread lightly with melted butter. Toast in broiler or hot oven. Serve hot.

Eggs Goldilocks

EGGS GOLDILOCKS

Cut 4 hard-cooked eggs in half lengthwise. Remove the yolks, mash and combine with 4 tablespoons mayonnaise. Season to taste with salt and pepper. Fill the whites. Remove the crusts from 4 slices of bread. Cut in half diagonally and toast. Arrange the toast points on a chop plate and top each with a stuffed egg half. Melt ½ pound of pasteurized process cheese food in the top of a double boiler. Gradually add 1/3 cup milk, stirring constantly until the sauce is smooth. Pour the cheese sauce over the eggs. Garnish with parsley and serve at once.

Cheese Pixies

CHEESE PIXIES

6 large apple slices (½-inch thick) 6 slices Cheddar cheese
4 tablespoons butter 6 slices bacon
6 rusk or toast rounds

Sauté thick apple rings in 2 tablespoons butter until lightly browned on both sides. Butter top side of each rusk with remaining butter. Put apple ring on top of each. Top with slice of cheese and broil until cheese melts. Meanwhile make bacon curls in skillet, rolling each with fork and cooking until lightly browned. Top each Pixie with bacon curl. Serve immediately. Serves 6.

TINY FRITTERS

Tiny fritters always make interesting party fare; however we suggest that the sweet varieties should be avoided when serving cocktails. The binding batter and cover batter that are included here may be used for a vast variety of tiny fritters.

FRITTER BINDING BATTER

1¾ cups sifted all-purpose flour 2 eggs, slightly beaten
3 teaspoons baking powder 1 cup milk
1 tablespoon sugar 1 tablespoon melted shortening
½ teaspoon salt

Sift dry ingredients. Omit sugar unless batter is to be used for fruit. Combine beaten eggs, milk and melted shortening. Mix liquid and dry ingredients and stir until smooth. Add 1 to 2 cups chopped vegetables, cooked or canned, or chopped fruit, well drained, or 1 to 2 cups drained corn. Drop from a spoon into deep fat (365° to 370° F.). Turn as soon as fritter comes to surface. Remove from fat when well browned on both sides. Drain on absorbent paper.

FRITTER COVER BATTER

1 egg, slightly beaten	1 cup sifted all-purpose flour
1 cup milk, water or fruit juice	½ teaspoon sugar
1 tablespoon melted shortening	¼ teaspoon salt

Combine egg, milk and shortening. Add gradually to mixed and sifted dry ingredients. Mix until smooth. Dip fruit into cover batter and fry in deep fat (365°–370° F.). Remove when light brown on both sides. Drain on absorbent paper. This cover batter may be used for apple, banana, pineapple slices, or orange sections. Serve fruit fritters sprinkled with confectioners' sugar. It may also be used for seafoods or meats, but omit sugar from batter.

Variation 1: For a thicker batter decrease milk to ⅔ cup and add 1 teaspoon baking powder to flour with sugar and salt. Use with berries or very juicy fruits.

Variation 2: Vary by adding ¼ teaspoon cinnamon, nutmeg, grated rind of lemon or orange.

TINY CHEESE FRITTERS

1¼ cups sifted all-purpose flour	⅔ cup milk
¼ teaspoon salt	1 egg, well beaten
2 teaspoons baking powder	¾ cup grated cheese

Mix and sift flour, salt, and baking powder. Mix together the milk and egg; combine the two mixtures. Add grated cheese and beat 3 minutes vigorously or until smooth. Drop by spoonfuls into deep fat (360° to 370° F.). Fry until brown and drain on paper. Serve hot.

CHEESE AND EGG FRITTERS

2 tablespoons butter	1 teaspoon minced chives
6 eggs, well beaten	½ teaspoon salt
1 tablespoon cream	⅛ teaspoon pepper
½ cup grated cheese	1 cup diced bread
1 teaspoon minced parsley	

Brown diced bread in butter and set aside. Melt 2 tablespoons butter in a saucepan. Mix together the eggs, cream, cheese, parsley, chives, salt and pepper, add the browned bread and add mixture to melted butter. Stir and cook until thick and smooth, about 8 minutes. Spread mixture out on a platter and let cool. Cut in inch squares and fry until browned in deep fat (360° to 370° F.). Drain on paper. Serve plain or with any desired tomato or tartar sauce.

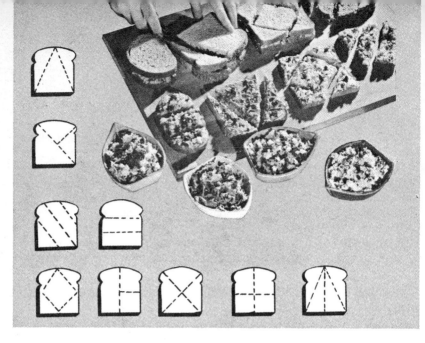

*Vary not only the bread and fillings but also
the way you cut the sandwiches.*

sandwiches

HINTS FOR MAKING SANDWICHES

Bread: Use a variety of breads and rolls including white, whole wheat, rye, raisin, nut, brown bread, gingerbread, soft buns, and crisp poppy seed rolls. To facilitate slicing and spreading of ordinary sandwiches use day-old bread. For rolled sandwiches use very fresh bread. For very thin, dainty sandwiches buy unsliced bread and cut with a razor-sharp knife into slices not more than ¼ inch thick. If many sandwiches are to be made sharpen knife frequently. For sandwiches without crust, cut the crust from the loaf before slicing. For fancy sandwiches to be cut with cooky cutter, slice the bread lengthwise.

Butter: Cream butter before applying it. Never melt butter. To facilitate creaming let butter stand at room temperature for about an hour. Butter, if it is well spread, helps to keep a moist filling from making the bread soggy. For savory sandwiches use savory butters or soften butter with mayonnaise. For sweet sandwiches soften butter with a little cream or whipped cream.

Arrangement for make-your-own sandwich tray.

Fillings: Use a variety of fillings for contrast in color, flavor, shape, and texture. Vegetables, such as cucumber, sliced tomato, and lettuce, should be prepared and added just before serving. Sliced fillings such as meat and cheese should be cut very thin and arranged to fit the sandwich. Use salad dressings to thin out and hold together chopped, flaked, or ground fillings. To add color to fillings, use chopped pimiento, pepper, parsley, olives, or pickle.

To Keep Sandwiches: Avoid making sandwiches with moist fillings in advance, or the bread may become soggy. If sandwiches are made in advance, wrap in waxed paper or slightly dampened cloth. To keep sandwiches for an hour or longer, wrap first in waxed paper, then in a damp cloth and place in refrigerator. To prevent an interchange of flavors, when different sandwiches are made, wrap each separately in waxed paper. Ribbon, checkerboard, loaf, and other sandwiches, which have to be chilled or even frozen in the refrigerator, should always be well wrapped in waxed paper in order to preserve the flavor and prevent them from drying out.

PARTY SANDWICHES

Party glamor is added to the snack tray by a patterned arrangement of the sandwiches. Many of these tiny finger sandwiches can be prepared beforehand, chilled in the refrigerator and brought to the serving table freshly sliced and tempting.

CHECKERBOARD SANDWICHES

Cut an unsliced white bread and an unsliced graham or whole wheat bread in 3 slices lengthwise, ½ inch thick. Remove crusts. Spread a slice of white bread with creamed butter or softened cream cheese and place a slice of graham on it. Spread this with creamed mixture. Place on it a slice of white bread, making graham bread the middle layer. Repeat this process beginning this time with a slice of graham so that a slice of white bread is the middle layer. Trim each pile evenly, and cut each pile in three 1-inch strips. Spread these strips with creamed mixture and put together in such a way that a white block will alternate with a graham one, forming a checkerboard at ends. There will be two checkered loaves. Wrap each loaf in waxed paper and place in refrigerator. When ready to serve, slice about ¼ inch thick.

PINWHEEL SANDWICHES

Remove all crust from white and whole wheat loaves of bread. Spread cut ends lengthwise with creamed butter or other soft filling, using contrasting colors for each. Cut a very thin slice from each loaf and put the two together. Spread top slice with filling and roll as for jelly roll. Fasten with toothpicks. Wrap in waxed paper, then in a damp cloth and place in refrigerator for about one hour. Just before serving, slice in ¼-inch slices. Sprinkle cut sandwiches with paprika, or garnish with finely minced parsley, stuffed olives cut in thin slices, or small wedges of green sweet pickle.

RIBBON SANDWICHES

Spread creamed butter or other soft filling between whole wheat and white bread slices. Spread creamed butter or soft filling between each two sandwiches, alternating white and whole wheat bread. Press firmly together. Wrap in waxed paper and then with damp towel. Place in refrigerator under a light weight. Chill thoroughly. Remove crust and cut in thin slices.

LAYER SANDWICHES

Remove crust from a whole loaf of sandwich bread and slice the loaf lengthwise in ½-inch slices. A different filling may be used between each two slices or the same may be used throughout. Colored cream cheese makes the finished sandwich look like a piece of layer cake. Jam, peanut butter, chopped parsley in creamed butter, and cheese may be used between the different layers if desired. Spread filling between each two slices and pile on top of each other. Wrap loaf in a damp towel and put into the refrigerator until just before serving, when it is cut in thin slices. If it is planned to serve the loaf whole and allow the guests to cut their own slices, as might be done at a buffet supper, the entire loaf may be frosted with tinted cream cheese to resemble a cake, then garnished with creamed cheese forced through a cake decorator, or with sliced stuffed olives, bits of pimiento, etc. This "frosting" should be applied shortly before serving.

NOISETTE SANDWICHES

Cut either graham or nut bread in thin slices. Spread lightly with butter and then lightly with orange marmalade. Put two slices together, remove crusts and cut in triangles. Garnish each sandwich with a half pecan or walnut meat placed in the center of the top slice.

BLACK AND WHITE SANDWICHES

Spread a slice of white bread lightly with creamed butter to which chopped parsley or watercress, and a few drops of lemon juice have been added. On top of this place a piece of whole wheat or nut bread and press lightly together. Remove crusts and cut in finger-shaped pieces.

BRIDGE PARTY SANDWICHES

Slice bread thin. Spread with any desired sandwich filling and place a second slice on top of the first. Press lightly together, then cut out with cooky cutters in the form of hearts, diamonds, clubs, and spades. Garnish top with tiny pieces of pimiento cut in heart or diamond shapes with garnish cutters, or pieces of ripe olives cut to form spades or clubs.

CLUB SANDWICHES

Toast 3 slices of bread for each sandwich. Spread with softened butter. Arrange lettuce and chicken slices on first slice; sprinkle with salt and pepper. Spread the second slice with mayonnaise. Add to first slice. Top with tomato slices and crisp bacon. Add third slice. Fasten together with toothpicks. Cut into triangles. Garnish with stuffed olives and pickle slices.

SALAD SANDWICHES

Slice a loaf of white bread lengthwise. Trim off crusts. Spread each slice with softened butter or margarine. Place a large spoonful of salad (minced vegetable, chicken, Waldorf, etc.) near one end of each slice. Roll the slices lengthwise, just enough to hold the salad in place. Cover sandwiches with damp cloth for 5 to 10 minutes. To serve, garnish with pickles, olives, and radishes.

TEA SANDWICHES

With a biscuit cutter cut circles from bread slices. Spread circles of bread with softened butter and top with cream cheese softened with honey. On this spread red raspberry jam. Place a dot of cream cheese mixture or whipped cream in the center.

TOASTED TEA SANDWICHES

Use circles cut from bread as in above recipe. Toast until brown on both sides. Spread with Honey Butter. Sprinkle with chopped nuts. Place under broiler until nuts are slightly browned and serve while hot.

TART SANDWICHES

Cut one piece of bread with a doughnut cutter and a second with the same cutter, but with the hole removed. Butter the one slice slightly, place the other on top, and fill the hole with jam or jelly.

CORNUCOPIAS

Trim crusts from thin bread slices, forming perfect squares. Spread with soft butter. Fold edges to form cornucopias. Fasten with toothpicks. Place in shallow pan and cover with damp cloth. Chill thoroughly. Fill with desired filling. Remove toothpicks to serve.

FROSTED SANDWICH LOAF

1 *large loaf of bread*	1 *cup grated raw carrots*
1 *small can salmon*	½ *cup chopped celery*
3 *tablespoons chopped pickle*	*Mayonnaise and butter*
2 *large tomatoes*	¾ *pound cream cheese*
½ *green pepper, chopped*	1½ *cups cream*

Remove crusts from bread. Cut into 4 slices, the long way of the loaf. Spread each slice with softened butter. Drain and flake salmon. Combine with chopped pickle, moisten with mayonnaise and spread on first slice. Cover second slice of bread with sliced tomatoes. Season. Combine green pepper with mayonnaise and spread over sliced tomatoes. Combine grated carrots and chopped celery. Season with salt and pepper, moisten with mayonnaise and spread on third slice of bread. Put the 4 slices together, press into loaf shape and wrap tightly in waxed paper. Chill. Spread top and sides with cream cheese softened with cream. Keep in refrigerator until ready to serve. Garnish with radish roses, parsley, carrot strips, stuffed olives, pimiento, etc. Cut into slices 1 inch thick.

INDIVIDUAL SANDWICH LOAVES

Day-old bread   *Tomatoes*
Olive-pimiento cheese spread   *Cream cheese*
Salad dressing or mayonnaise   *Milk*

Slice bread ¼-inch thick. Cut into rounds 2½ inches in diameter. Cover one round with olive-pimiento cheese spread, and place on it another round spread with salad dressing or mayonnaise. Add a slice of peeled tomato, and cover with a third round of bread spread with salad dressing or mayonnaise. Slightly soften cream cheese with milk, and frost each loaf with it. Garnish with watercress.

Individual Sandwich Loaves   *Frosted Sandwich Loaf*

SALMON SALAD SURPRISE LOAF

1 (20-ounce) loaf day-old white bread, unsliced
4 hard-cooked eggs, chopped
1 No. 1 can red salmon, flaked and boned
1 tablespoon grated lemon rind
1 tablespoon lemon juice
¾ cup finely chopped celery
1½ teaspoons salt
2/3 cup mayonnaise or salad dressing
1 tablespoon chopped green pepper
2 tablespoons sliced green olives

With a sharp knife, remove the crusts from a loaf of bread to make an even, box-shaped loaf. Cut a lengthwise slice from the top. Hollow out the center of the loaf, leaving side walls and bottom at least ½-inch thick. Place on cooky sheet. (Save center of loaf for bread-crumbs or stuffing.) Combine chopped eggs, flaked salmon, lemon rind, lemon juice, celery, salt, mayonnaise, pepper, and olives.

Loaf Topping:
1 tablespoon (1 envelope) unfla-vored gelatin
1 tablespoon dilute vinegar
1 cup mayonnaise or salad dress-ing
¼ teaspoon cayenne pepper
½ teaspoon Worcestershire sauce
1 hard-cooked egg, sliced
3 sliced olives

Mix gelatin with vinegar and dissolve over hot water. Slowly combine mayonnaise and dissolved gelatin. Add pepper and Worcestershire sauce.

To Complete Salmon Salad Surprise Loaf: Fill center of the loaf of bread with salmon salad. Cover with top slice of bread. Spread top and sides of loaf with topping mixture. Garnish with sliced egg and olives. Cover finished loaf with heavy waxed paper to prevent dis-coloration of mayonnaise from moisture. Place in refrigerator for 12 hours. To serve: Slice in 1-inch cuts. Serves 8.

Salmon Salad Surprise Loaf

1. Remove crusts from loaf of bread. Cut a lengthwise slice from top.
2. Hollow out center of the loaf, leaving side walls and bottom at least half an inch thick. Fill center of loaf.

3. Spread top and sides with topping mixture. Garnish and cover with waxed paper. Chill in refrigerator for 12 hours.

CARD PARTY
SANDWICHES

Cut an equal number of slices of white and whole wheat bread. Cut into desired shapes with fancy sandwich cutters. Cut fancy designs in half of the slices of white and whole wheat bread. Spread whole slices of bread with desired sandwich filling. Top spread slices with cut-out slices. The shapes cut out of the white bread in forming fancy designs may be fitted into the cuts made in the dark bread, and vice versa.

sandwich fillings

CHEESE SANDWICH FILLINGS

Cottage Cheese Filling: Combine 1 cup well-seasoned cottage cheese, 1 cup finely chopped peanuts, ½ teaspoon salt, and 1 tablespoon mayonnaise. Makes 8 to 10 sandwiches.

Cottage Cheese-Cucumber Filling: Peel 1 large cucumber and scrape the seeds out. Grate or grind, mix with 1 tablespoon grated onion and ½ teaspoon salt and put in a strainer. Let set over a bowl until just ready to make sandwiches. Mix well with 1 pint cottage cheese and dash of pepper. Additional salt to taste may be added. Makes 8 to 10 sandwiches.

Cottage Cheese and Green Pepper Filling: Cream well ½ pound dry cottage cheese with ⅓ cup evaporated milk. Add 1 teaspoon salt, ⅛ teaspoon pepper, 3 tablespoons chopped green pepper, and 1 tablespoon minced onion. Mix well. Makes 5 sandwiches.

Cream Cheese Filling: Blend 1 package (3 ounces) cream cheese and 1 tablespoon mayonnaise. Spread on thin slices of bread or spread one slice of bread with filling, the other with jelly.

Cream Cheese and Carrot Filling: Mix cream cheese with ⅓ as much grated raw carrot. Cover with watercress.

Savory Grated Cheese Filling: Mix grated cheese with onion juice, butter, and chopped parsley.

Cottage Cheese-Olive-Pimiento Filling: Mix creamed cottage cheese with chopped olives and chopped pimiento.

Cream Cheese and Dried Beef Filling: Cream 1 package (3 ounces) cream cheese with 2 tablespoons milk. Add ¼ cup shredded dried beef and 1 teaspoon grated onion. Blend well. Makes ½ cup.

EGG SANDWICH FILLINGS

Deviled Egg Filling: Mix well together 3 hard-cooked eggs chopped fine, 3 teaspoons chopped parsley, 3 teaspoons vinegar, ⅛ teaspoon dry mustard, ¼ teaspoon salt, and ⅛ teaspoon pepper.

Egg and Celery Filling: Moisten 3 finely chopped hard-cooked eggs and ½ cup finely chopped celery with mayonnaise or prepared sandwich spread. Makes about 1 cup.

Egg and Frankfurter Filling: Mix together and thoroughly chill 2 chopped hard-cooked eggs, 2 cooked ground frankfurters, 1 cup finely cut celery, 1 teaspoon salt, and ⅓ cup salad dressing. Makes 1½ cups.

Egg and Watercress Filling: Mix chopped hard-cooked egg, watercress, and mayonnaise.

Egg and Anchovy Filling: Cream yolks of hard-cooked eggs with butter and anchovy paste.

Egg and Spinach Filling: Mix ground hard-cooked eggs with half the amount of spinach.

Egg and Ketchup Filling: Moisten ground hard-cooked eggs with ketchup.

Egg and Liver Filling: Combine 4 chopped hard-cooked eggs with ½ cup minced cooked liver. Season with salt and pepper and prepared horseradish. Moisten with mayonnaise. Makes about 1½ cups.

Egg and Bacon Filling: Combine 4 chopped hard-cooked eggs, 6 slices chopped, crisp bacon, 3 tablespoons chopped olives and ¼ teaspoon salt. Moisten with mayonnaise. Makes about 1½ cups.

Egg and Ham Filling: Combine 4 chopped hard-cooked eggs, ¼ to ½ cup chopped boiled ham. Moisten with mayonnaise. Makes about 1½ cups.

FISH SANDWICH FILLINGS

Flaked Fish Filling #1: Place in a bowl 1 cup canned fish flakes, 1 tablespoon chopped celery, 1 tablespoon chopped pickle (sweet or sour), 3 tablespoons mayonnaise, ½ tablespoon horseradish, ¼ teaspoon salt, and ⅛ teaspoon pepper. Mix well.

Flaked Fish Filling #2: Mix flaked tuna with chopped celery and chopped nuts. Moisten with mayonnaise.

Flaked Fish Filling #3: Mix flaked tuna with chopped pickle and crushed pineapple. Moisten with French dressing.

Flaked Fish Filling #4: Combine 1 cup salmon, tuna or other canned seafood with ½ cup chopped celery. Moisten with mayonnaise.

Tuna and Egg Filling: Combine 1 cup flaked tuna, 2 chopped hard-cooked eggs and ¼ cup chopped stuffed olives. Moisten with mayonnaise.

Sardine Filling #1: Cream sardines with melted butter, flavored with salt, cayenne, and a generous amount of horseradish. Moisten with lemon juice.

Sardine Filling #2: Combine 1 can of mashed drained sardines, ½ cup finely chopped, peeled cucumber (seeds removed), and lemon juice to taste.

Sardine Filling #3: Mix sardines with chopped hard-cooked eggs, grated cheese, butter, and lemon juice. Season with curry powder.

Sardine and Egg Filling: Combine 1 can drained, mashed sardines and 2 hard-cooked eggs. Moisten with lemon juice to taste.

Shrimp Filling: Combine 1 cup chopped, cooked or canned shrimp, 3 tablespoons chopped celery, ¼ teaspoon salt, 1 teaspoon lemon juice, and mayonnaise to moisten.

Avocado-Shrimp Filling: Combine 1 cup minced avocado, ½ cup chopped cooked shrimp, 1 tablespoon lemon juice, and ¼ cup mayonnaise or salad dressing.

FRUIT AND VEGETABLE SANDWICH FILLINGS

Carrots and Peanut Filling: Grind together finely ½ cup salted peanuts and 1 cup raw carrots. Combine with 3 tablespoons mayonnaise and ¼ teaspoon salt. Makes 4 sandwiches.

Carrot, Raisin and Peanut Filling: Grind together coarsely 1 cup raw carrots, 1 cup salted peanuts, and 1 cup seedless raisins. Add ½ teaspoon salt, 2 teaspoons lemon juice, and 2 tablespoons mayonnaise Mix well and store in refrigerator. Makes 10 sandwiches.

Raw Vegetable Filling: Mix together thoroughly 1 cup chopped raisins, ½ cup shredded cabbage, ½ cup shredded carrots, ½ cup chopped apple, 1 tablespoon lemon juice, and 4 tablespoons salad dressing. Makes 4 sandwiches.

Combination Filling: Combine ½ cup seedless raisins, ½ cup shredded carrots, ½ cup cottage cheese, ⅛ teaspoon salt, and 1 tablespoon mayonnaise. Makes 12 sandwiches.

Dried Fruit and Nut Filling: Combine ½ cup finely chopped raisins, figs and dates, ½ cup chopped nut meats, ⅛ teaspoon salt, 5 teaspoons mayonnaise, and few drops lemon juice. Store in covered jar in refrigerator. Makes 4 sandwiches.

Celery and Almond Filling: Mix chopped celery and chopped almonds. Moisten with mayonnaise.

Cucumber and Radish Filling: Slice cucumbers thin; top with thinly sliced radishes. Moisten with mayonnaise.

Date and Nut Filling: Mix ground dates and chopped nuts. Moisten with orange juice.

MEAT AND POULTRY SANDWICH FILLINGS

Bacon-Pickle Filling: Fry 6 slices of bacon crisp. Crumble and combine with ½ cup chopped dill pickle, and ¼ cup mayonnaise. Makes 4 sandwiches.

Bacon-Cheese Filling: Blend 1 package (3 ounces) cream cheese with ¼ cup chopped cooked bacon, ½ teaspoon horseradish, ½ teaspoon Worcestershire sauce, and 1 tablespoon milk. Makes 3 sandwiches.

Ground Ham Filling: Combine ½ cup vinegar, 1 teaspoon prepared mustard, ½ teaspoon salt, ¼ cup light brown sugar, and 1 well beaten egg. Cook, stirring constantly, until boiling. Boil 5 minutes. Cool, then add ½ cup ground, cooked, spiced ham and mix well. Makes 8 sandwiches.

Ham and Cucumber Filling: Combine 1 cup ground cooked ham, ¼ cup diced cucumber, 3 tablespoons mayonnaise, and salt to taste. Mix well.

Dried Beef and Horseradish Filling: Moisten shredded beef with mayonnaise. Season with prepared horseradish.

Bologna and Egg Filling: Grind ½ pound bologna. Mix with ¼ cup chopped pickle, ½ cup mayonnaise, ½ teaspoon minced onion, dash of Tabasco sauce, 2 tablespoons pickle juice, 3 hard-cooked eggs, and ½ teaspoon salt. Makes 7 sandwiches.

Salami and Egg Filling: Combine chopped salami and chopped hard-cooked egg. Top with sliced onion or tomato.

Ground Liver Filling: Combine 1 cup ground, cooked liver, 1 teaspoon chopped pickle, 1 tablespoon pickle juice, 4 tablespoons mayonnaise, dash of Tabasco sauce (optional), and salt and pepper to taste. Mix thoroughly. Makes about 5 sandwiches.

Mock Chicken Filling: Combine 1 cup coarsely ground veal, ½ cup chopped or shredded raw carrots, ½ cup chopped celery, 2 tablespoons Chow Chow, 3 tablespoons mayonnaise, and salt to taste. Mix thoroughly. Makes 5 sandwiches.

Chopped Meat Filling: Mix together 1 cup chopped leftover meat, 1 teaspoon dry mustard, 2 finely chopped hard-cooked eggs and chopped pickle. Moisten with mayonnaise. Makes 5 sandwiches.

Chicken or Turkey Filling: Moisten chopped, cooked chicken or turkey with mayonnaise or salad dressing. Season with salt and pepper. If desired, add finely chopped almonds.

Tongue and Olive Filling: Combine 1 cup chopped cooked or canned tongue with ¼ cup chopped stuffed olives. Moisten with mayonnaise or salad dressing.

Chicken and Ripe Olive Filling #1: Combine 1 cup chopped chicken with ½ cup chopped celery, and ¼ cup chopped ripe olives. Moisten with mayonnaise.

Chicken and Ripe Olive Filling #2: Mix chopped cooked chicken and chopped ripe olives. Moisten with mayonnaise.

Corned Beef Filling: Combine 1 cup chopped corned beef, ½ cup chopped celery, 1 tablespoon prepared mustard, and ¼ cup mayonnaise. Mix well.

Meat Loaf Filling: Mix chopped cooked meat loaf with chili sauce.

*For an easy cheeseburger, place a spoonful of soft cheese spread
on each hot hamburger just before serving.*

hot sandwich suggestions

Broiled Cheese and Bacon Sandwiches: Prepare 1 cup shredded cheese
and 2 slices bacon, diced. Spread 6 slices of bread with cheese. Sprinkle
bacon over the top. Broil very slowly. Makes 3 sandwiches.

Broiled Tomato and Bacon Sandwiches: Toast slices of bread on one
side. Spread untoasted side with butter. Top with a slice of cheese.
Top cheese with a slice of tomato. Place bacon strips over tomato
slice. Broil in preheated broiler oven 3 inches below flame until bacon
is brown and cheese begins to melt.

Broiled Cottage Cheese Sandwiches: Season cottage cheese with salt
and paprika. Spread on buttered toast. Top with bacon strips and
broil slowly until bacon is crisp.

Baked Bean and Salami Sandwiches: Cut ¼ pound salami into tiny bits. Combine with 1½ cups canned baked beans with tomato sauce. Add 2 tablespoons each of chili sauce and prepared mustard, and ½ teaspoon minced onion. Mash with a fork. Spread between slices of bread. Broil the sandwiches, turning to brown on both sides.

Western Sandwich: For each sandwich fry 1 tablespoon minced onion in butter until slightly browned. Add 1 tablespoon minced cooked ham and stir in 1 slightly beaten egg. Cook slowly until firm. Season with salt and pepper. Serve hot.

Cheeseburger: Shape ground beef into patties about ¼ inch thick. Fry in butter on one side until brown. Turn and place a slice of American cheese on top of each patty. Cover pan and fry slowly until cheese is melted and underside of patties are browned. Serve hot.

Cheese Sauce over Meat Sandwiches: Melt 1 cup grated American cheese in 1 cup medium white sauce. Pour over any meat sandwich.

Grilled Cheese Sandwich: Toast bread on both sides under broiler. Butter one side of the toast. Cover with thin slices of sharp cheese. Place cheese under broiler so that it is about 5 inches from heat. Broil slowly until cheese is soft and melted. Serve hot.

Hot Roast Beef Sandwiches: Make sandwiches with toasted bread and slices of roast beef. Serve on hot plates with hot gravy poured over the sandwiches. Garnish with a sprig of parsley and a pickle.

Cranberry Meat Sandwich: Toast bread. Lay a slice of broiled meat or sliced roast meat browned in gravy on each. Top with generous spoonful of hot cranberry sauce.

Sauteed Meat Sandwiches: Moisten ground leftover meat with thick white sauce or gravy. Put between slices of bread. Brown on each side in hot fat.

Sauteed Tomato and Cheese: Spread bread slices with nippy mayonnaise. Put a slice of tomato and a slice of American cheese between each 2 slices. Dip in an egg-milk mixture and fry like French toast.

Cheeseburgers

BAKED STUFFED FRANKFURTERS

2½ cups breadcrumbs	⅓ cup melted butter
⅛ teaspoon pepper	1 teaspoon each sage and thyme
¼ teaspoon salt	10 frankfurters
1 small onion, minced	10 strips bacon

Combine crumbs, seasonings, onion, and butter; blend well. Split frankfurters lengthwise and fill with stuffing. Wrap each with strip of bacon and fasten with toothpicks. Broil 10 minutes or bake in moderate oven (350° F.) 30 minutes.

Apple-Stuffed Frankfurters: Use chopped apple instead of stuffing.

Cheese-Stuffed Frankfurters: Use slice of cheese instead of stuffing. Broil or bake until cheese melts and bacon is browned.

Relish-Stuffed Frankfurters: Combine 1 cup sweet pickle relish and 2 tablespoons prepared mustard. Use instead of stuffing.

Barbecued Frankfurters: Prick skins of frankfurters well. Arrange in shallow pan and pour over barbecue sauce. Bake, uncovered, in moderate oven (350° F.) 30 minutes.

CHEESE BARBECUE SANDWICHES

1½ cups grated processed cheese	½ teaspoon Worcestershire sauce
3 tablespoons chopped green pepper	3 tablespoons ketchup
½ cup chopped onion	1 tablespoon melted butter
2 chopped hard-cooked eggs	6 buns, split open
3 tablespoons chopped stuffed olives	

Combine all ingredients and place ¼ cup in each bun. Toast under preheated broiler 5 minutes. Yield: 6 sandwiches.

HOT SPANISH SANDWICHES

2 tablespoons chopped onion	1 tablespoon flour
2 tablespoons melted butter	Salt and pepper to taste
3 cups canned tomatoes	½ pound sliced bacon
1 green pepper, chopped	10 slices bread
½ cup chopped celery	Soft American cheese, sliced

Cook onion for a few minutes in 1 tablespoon fat. Add tomatoes, green pepper, and celery. Simmer, uncovered, 25 to 30 minutes. Blend remaining fat with flour and add to sauce with salt and pepper to taste. Stir until it thickens slightly. Fry bacon until crisp. Toast bread on both sides until golden brown. Make sandwiches of bread and bacon. Lay thin slices of cheese on top. Put on hot plates. Pour the hot tomato sauce over the sandwiches.

SAUCY HAMBURGERS

1 *pound ground beef*
1 *egg, slightly beaten*
1 *teaspoon salt*
Dash of pepper

6 *slices bread*
6 *tablespoons ketchup*
1 *medium onion, sliced*
2 *tablespoons fat*

Mix beef, egg, salt, and pepper. Toast bread on one side under broiler. Spread untoasted side with meat mixture, about ½ inch thick. Pour a tablespoon of ketchup on each slice on top of meat. Top with onion slice and brush with fat. Cook under broiler, turned low, until meat is done, about 20 minutes. Serves 6.

BARBECUE BURGERS

2 *tablespoons cooking fat*
1 *pound ground beef*
2 *large onions, chopped*
½ *cup diced celery*

1 *cup sliced mushrooms*
¼ *cup ketchup*
1 *cup canned tomatoes*
1 *cup water*

Fry meat, onions, celery, and mushrooms in hot fat until lightly browned. Add ketchup, tomatoes, and water. Season to taste with salt and pepper. If desired, 1 teaspoon chili powder may be added. Cover and simmer 15 to 20 minutes. Add more water if necessary. Serve on hot toasted buns. Serves 6.

BROWN BEAN SANDWICH

6 *slices bread*
Butter or margarine
1 *can brown beans*

1 *cup grated cheese*
6 *slices bacon*

Butter bread. Top each slice with beans and sprinkle with grated cheese. Cut bacon slices in half. Top each sandwich with two strips of bacon crisscross fashion. Bake or broil until the cheese melts and bacon is crisp. Yield: 6 sandwiches.

Brown Bean Sandwiches

HOT DEVILED HAM SANDWICHES

8 *slices toast*
½ *cup deviled ham*

¾ *cup medium white sauce*
2 *tablespoons diced sweet pickles*

Spread 4 of the hot slices of toast with deviled ham. Add diced pickles to white sauce and pour over toast slices. Top with another slice of toast and more sauce. Garnish each serving with a slice of pickle. Serves 4.

SOUFFLEED CHEESE SANDWICH

4 *to 6 slices bread*
3 *eggs, separated*
½ *teaspoon salt*

Dash of pepper
Dash of paprika
½ *cup grated sharp cheese*

Toast bread (crust removed, if desired) on one side. Add salt to egg whites and beat until stiff, but not dry. Add pepper and paprika to yolks and beat yolks until light. Fold yolks and cheese into egg whites. Heap on untoasted side of bread. Place on greased baking sheet. Bake in moderate oven (350° F.) until puffy and brown (about 15 minutes). Serve at once. Yield: 4 to 6 sandwiches depending upon size of slice and thickness of egg mixture desired.

BROILED FRENCH TOASTWICHES

6 *thin slices cooked meat*
12 *slices bread*

2 *eggs*
½ *cup milk*
12 *slices bacon*

Use leftover meat or ready-to-eat meats. Make into sandwiches. Beat eggs and add milk. Dip sandwiches into egg mixture. Place on hot broiler pan to broil until sandwiches are brown, about 5 minutes. Turn with a wide spatula to brown on second side. Arrange bacon slices on broiler when sandwiches are turned and finish all at the same time, about 5 minutes. Serve bacon and broiled sandwiches immediately. Serves 6.

SALMON TOASTWICHES

Spread softened butter on 10 slices white bread. Place 3 tablespoons salmon salad spread between each 2 slices. Combine 2 beaten eggs and ¼ cup milk. Dip each sandwich into egg-milk mixture, turning to coat both sides. Brown sandwich in hot fat in a skillet. Yield: 5 sandwiches.

CHILI CLUB SANDWICHES

4 *hamburger buns*
1 *can chili con carne, heated*
4 *thin slices American cheese*

4 *slices bacon*
4 *thin slices Bermuda onion*

Split and butter buns. Spread bottom halves with hot chili con carne. Arrange a slice of cheese and a slice of bacon on top of each. Broil under moderate heat until bacon is crisp and cheese bubbling. Add onion slices and remaining halves of buns. Serve very hot. Serves 4.

SLOPPY JOES

¼ *cup sliced onions*
½ *cup chopped green pepper*
2 *tablespoons cooking fat*
2 *peeled medium-sized tomatoes*
¾ *cup sliced mushrooms*

½ *pound ground beef*
1 *cup tomato juice*
¾ *teaspoon salt*
¼ *teaspoon pepper*
¼ *teaspoon paprika*

Cook onions and green pepper in hot fat until lightly browned. Cut tomatoes in small wedges and add with remaining ingredients. Cover and cook over very low heat 15 to 20 minutes. If desired, thicken sauce by sprinkling in a little flour and cooking until well blended. Serve over split toasted hamburger buns. Serves 4 to 6.

Sloppy Joes

APPETIZER FILLING ON FINGER ROLLS

Put 1 small onion, half of a medium-sized green pepper, and 6 slices of broiled bacon through a food chopper. Cut ½ pound of process cheese food into quarters lengthwise. Put the process cheese food through the food chopper and add it to the chopped onion, pepper, and bacon. Add ½ cup condensed tomato soup, ½ teaspoon salt, a dash of cayenne, and a dash of Worcestershire sauce. Split 2½-inch finger rolls and spread half of each with 1 tablespoon of the filling; cover with the other halves. Bake in a moderate oven (350° F.) until the rolls are hot and the filling is melted. Serve hot as an appetizer. This filling also may be used in frankfurter buns and cut into inch pieces before baking.

Appetizer Filling on Finger Rolls

*Bacon, Cheese,
and Tomato Sandwiches*

BACON, CHEESE, AND TOMATO SANDWICHES

Trim the crusts from slices of bread and toast bread on one side. Spread the untoasted side with mayonnaise. Place a slice of peeled tomato on each slice of toast. Place a slice of pasteurized process American cheese on each slice of tomato. Arrange two slices of partially broiled bacon on each slice of cheese. Place under moderate broiler heat until the cheese melts. Serve piping hot, and see why it's called America's favorite sandwich.

Cheese Strata

CHEESE STRATA

Arrange 6 slices of bread (crusts trimmed) in bottom of rectangular dish. Place a slice of pasteurized process American cheese on each slice of bread. Cover with 6 slices of bread (crusts trimmed). Beat 4 eggs. Add 2½ cups of milk and salt and pepper. Pour eggs and milk mixture over bread and cheese sandwiches. Let stand an hour. Bake in slow oven (325° F.) about 40 minutes. Serve plain or with your favorite jelly.

WAFFLE-GRILLED CHEESE SANDWICHES

For each sandwich, place 1 slice of process American cheese between 2 slices of bread. Brush top and bottom of sandwich with melted butter or margarine. Put sandwiches in waffle iron until bread is golden brown, and cheese is melted.

Waffle-Grilled Cheese Sandwiches

Frankfurters in Tomato Yeast Rolls

FRANKFURTERS IN TOMATO YEAST ROLLS

1 package roll mix
Tomato juice
½ cup grated Parmesan cheese
1 tablespoon chopped parsley

12 frankfurters
2 tablespoons melted butter or
margarine

Prepare roll mix according to directions on package, substituting tomato juice for liquid required. Roll into 12-inch circle and sprinkle with grated cheese and chopped parsley. Cut into 12 pie-shaped pieces and roll a frankfurter in each piece, rolling from wide edge of dough. Brush with melted butter or margarine and bake in hot oven (400° F.) for 15 to 20 minutes. Serves 12.

SALMON SANDWICH FONDUE

1 *8-ounce can salmon*
1 *cup minced celery*
¼ *cup mayonnaise*
1 *tablespoon prepared mustard*
¼ *teaspoon salt*
12 *thin slices whole wheat bread*
½ *teaspoon Ac'cent*

6 *slices American Cheddar cheese*
3 *beaten eggs*
2½ *cups milk*
2 *teaspoons Worcestershire sauce*

Drain salmon; flake, removing bones; add celery. Blend mayonnaise, mustard, and salt; add to salmon mixture; mix well. Spread between bread slices to make 6 sandwiches. Arrange sandwiches in shallow baking dish; top each with slice of cheese. Combine eggs, milk, Worcestershire sauce, and Ac'cent. Pour over sandwiches. Bake in slow oven (325° F.) 45 minutes. Makes 6 sandwiches.

COCKTAIL INDEX

SNACK INDEX